creative
cardmaking
a complete guide

NORTH LIGHT BOOKS

Cincinnati, Ohio

www.artistsnetwork.com

table of
contents

Creative Correspondence

Stenciling & Embossing Greeting Cards

introduction

There is no other communication so dear as a sincere greeting card. And a handmade card is even more special! In this day and age, knowing you took the time to create something just for that special someone is heart-warming. And this book proves that you can make and send spectacular decorative cards, even when you're pressed for time!

In *Creative Cardmaking: A Complete Guide* you'll find basic techniques, tips and guidance for crafting personalized greeting cards for your family and friends. Each project features clear, step-by-step instruction using easy-to-find decorative materials.

You'll learn to use rubber stamps; the basics of stenciling and embossing; how to make decorative cutouts and 3D layered effects; how to utilize vintage photographs and materials; even how to use non-traditional materials such as polymer clay and shrink plastic! This book has everything you need to know to become an expert card-maker. Make a few of the projects, then start creating your own original cards. You'll never run out of ideas!

GREETING CARDS
for EVERY OCCASION

MaryJo McGraw

NORTH LIGHT BOOKS

contents

THE PROJECTS, 22

iNTRODUCTiON

there is no other communication so dear as a sincere greeting card. Whether it is for a holiday, a special event or even just a thoughtful note, a greeting card is like a virtual hug. And a handmade card is even more special! In this day and age, knowing you took the time to create something just for that special someone is heartwarming.

Creating your own greeting cards can be very rewarding. And since the price of an especially nice printed greeting has skyrocketed, it certainly makes sense to create your own. Many cards can be made simply with a few products and papers that can be used over and over. That said, my advice is to buy the best products you can afford. After all, handmade items reflect the person who has created them. Quality shows, and in the long run, it saves time, money and effort when used effectively.

In this book, I have included a variety of creative techniques. You'll find a three-dimensional box card perfect for holding small treats, a Thanksgiving card made with a hand-carved turkey stamp, a pop-up card with a surprise inside and many more. The projects require some common craft supplies like cardstock and craft scissors, and also some supplies that may be new to you, like pewter stickers and acrylic tiles. That's part of the fun! All you need is a little time, a lot of imagination and a quick trip to your favorite stamping supply store. Soon, you'll be on your way to creating greeting cards for every occasion. Enjoy!

GETTING STARTED

everyone, I think, starts with the belief that they are saving money when they begin to create their own cards. While this is definitely true in the long run, an initial investment must be made on tools and supplies. The real reason for making your own greeting cards is to fulfill your own need to create something wonderful for someone special. Knowing this makes the time and effort you put into a project more precious.

Before you begin, there are a few basic things you need to know for making your own greeting cards. I like to think of these simple techniques as the building blocks. Are they absolutely necessary? No. But doing things properly the first time will make the entire experience much more enjoyable.

Basic Tools & Materials

Tools

There are a few tools that always come in handy when I'm making greeting cards or working on another type of crafting project.

Bone folder

The bone folder is a great tool for scoring paper and smoothing down creases. Bookbinders use it for turning corners and scoring. Some bone folders are actually made from bone as the name suggests, while others are made from resin or wood. They come in a variety of lengths and are very helpful in all kinds of crafts.

Brayer

Brayers come in so many varieties, it's hard to choose which to buy. For my money, the best all-around brayer is the detachable 4" (10cm) soft rubber brayer. It will handle most jobs and is much easier to clean than other brayers. You will also find sponge, acrylic, hard rubber and wooden brayers. Each yields a different result. Try them all and see which one you like the best.

Craft knife

A craft knife is an invaluable tool when creating greeting cards and other stamp projects. X-acto is the most common brand. The blade should be very sharp and should be changed often to ensure clean cuts. You will learn more about the proper way to hold a craft knife on page 16.

Craft scissors

A good pair of stainless steel craft scissors are a must for most craft projects. They should be lightweight and have a comfortable grip for easy maneuverability when cutting out fine details.

Double-stick tape

Double-stick tape comes in a variety of forms and is available at art supply stores. In this book, I have used regular double-stick tape and dimensional double-stick dots.

Embellishments

Beautifying your cards with decorative embellishments is the best part about card-making. Browse the aisles of your local craft store and experiment with all the different kinds of paint, markers, crayons, powders, pens and more.

Embossing powder

Embossing powder is required for many of the cards in this book. To use it, stamp an image with pigment or embossing ink. Dust the powder over the wet ink and shake off the excess. Use an embossing tool (heat gun) to melt the powder and create a raised design. Embossing powder comes in metallic, solid and multicolor forms.

Water-soluble crayons

These are available in stamp and art supply stores. I prefer soy-based crayons because they have a creamy texture and are loaded with pigment.

Powdered pigments

These are raw pigments used for a variety of purposes, including making your own paints. You can also use these pigments as a surface coating on paper or collage projects. Powdered pigments do need what is known as a "binder" to keep them adhered to your project. In this book, we will be using Diamond Glaze as a binder. Other options include white glue, paint media, gum arabic or spray fixative. Mix any of these with the powdered pigments to create a colored medium you can apply to many surfaces.

Thread, beads and cords

Decorative accessories such as thread, beads, paper cord, tassels and gift tags can be found at most stamp stores. I also find these items in specialty stores for beads and needlecrafts. Office supply stores are great for unusual items, too. Keep your eyes peeled because you never know what you'll find in the most unlikely places.

Paper

Always buy the best paper you can afford. When I lay out paper for a class, inevitably people choose the most expensive pieces first. Can you guess why? Great paper looks and feels fabulous. Paper is where I spend the bulk of my money every year.

Cardstock

I have used cardstock—a heavy, textured paper—for most of the greeting cards in this book. Cardstock comes in all sorts of colors and textures and is durable enough to withstand a little wear and tear.

Vellum

Vellum is a translucent paper with a smooth finish. It comes in a variety of weights, colors and patterns. Lighter weight vellum is easier to cut and score, but heavier vellum works better for heat embossing and painting.

Acetate

Although acetate is considered a plastic rather than a paper product, it can be used in a similar way as vellum. The clear plastic can be found in most stamp stores. Be sure to get embossable acetate (also known as "window plastic") in case you want to heat the piece. The thicker the laminate, the better it will work for the projects in this book because of the beating the pieces will take.

Stamps

There are millions of stamp designs out there, and again this is the time to invest in quality. I prefer well-trimmed, thick red rubber mounted on wood, or deeply etched unmounted rubber. Foam stamps are great for kids and temporary projects, but as a collector and an artist, I want a stamp that will hold up to use, abuse and time. All of the companies listed in the Resource Guide (pages 126 - 127) make quality stamps.

Ink

When it comes to ink, things can be very confusing. There are so many inks that perform a multitude of tasks, and they are available in every color under the sun! Let me break it down for you.

Dye ink

Most of the time, dye inkpads come with solid lids over the tops. This is because the ink is translucent and you cannot tell what the true color is until it has been stamped. Dye inks work on all types of paper and many porous surfaces. They are best for beginners and produce the most vibrant colors. Most dye inks will fade to some extent, and they tend to dry quickly, making them a poor choice for embossing. This also means dye inkpads can dry out quickly if you live in a dry climate.

Pigment ink

Slower-drying pigment ink is opaque and resembles paint. This ink is used for embossing or foiling with dry pigments. It is best suited for porous, uncoated paper. There are several brands, such as Brilliance, that dry on shiny and slick paper, but it takes a long time. To speed up the process, dry pigment inks with an embossing tool (heat gun). Since pigment inks are opaque, many are metallic or pearlized.

Solvent ink

Solvent ink, also called permanent ink, is made specifically for nonporous surfaces, but it also works well on paper. When dry, solvent ink does not smear—even when water is applied—making it perfect for watercolor techniques and markers. Since solvent ink works on every surface, it is my personal favorite.

Here is my basic advice: If you have never bought a single inkpad, buy a dye inkpad, a pigment inkpad and a solvent inkpad—each one in black. Then, buy your favorite metallic (gold, silver, copper or bronze) color in pigment ink and ten good colors of dye ink. These supplies should see you through most projects. After that, you are on your own in this addiction to color! I still buy almost every color of most of the brands out there.

Basic Techniques

There are a few basic techniques you'll need to know before you begin. These little tricks, which I've picked up over the years, will make every project easier and more enjoyable.

How to Hold a Craft Knife

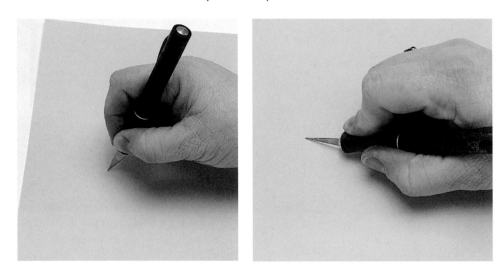

The best way to make precise cuts with a craft knife is to control your blade. A sharp blade is also important, so be sure to replace it often.

1. Position the Knife
Hold the craft knife like a pencil and point the blade straight down toward the paper.

2. Make the Cut
Push the point of the blade into the surface, and then pull it down as far as you can, holding the blade parallel to the surface as you cut.

How to Hold a Ruler

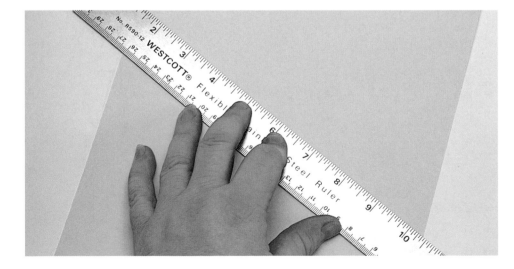

Holding your ruler correctly will make all the difference between a good card and a great card. Follow this technique and see for yourself!

Position the Ruler
Hold the ruler with your ring finger and thumb firmly positioned on the outside edge. This will prevent the ruler from slipping. Place your index and middle fingers directly on the ruler.

How to Ink a Large Stamp

Nothing is more frustrating than lifting the stamp from your paper, only to find half the image didn't transfer. You must be sure to ink your stamp properly, especially when using large stamps like some of the ones in this book. Keep trying. In the stamping world, you get plenty of chances to make a good impression.

1. Ink Stamp
For the best coverage, rub the surface of the stamp with a pad of ink.

2. Transfer Image
Keeping the stamp facing up, position the cardstock on the stamp and roll a soft rubber brayer over the back of the cardstock to transfer the image.

How to Clean Your Stamps

When cleaning your stamps, use a cleaner with conditioner in it. I prefer a solvent-type cleaner, which removes any ink or paint I might be using. I personally do not like to overclean my stamps. This can damage the cushion under the die and loosen the adhesive.

1. Apply Cleaner
Apply a generous amount of stamp cleaner to the rubber stamp.

2. Blot Stamp
Blot the stamp on a clean, dry paper towel and reuse as necessary or store.

How to Score Paper

Scoring is especially important on heavy cardstock. Many tools can be used, such as a bone folder, paper clip, ballpoint pen, stylus or the back of a craft knife. Using your ruler as a guide, press down hard to get a nice, crisp crease.

Score with Craft Knife
For a sharp crease, score with the back of a craft knife.

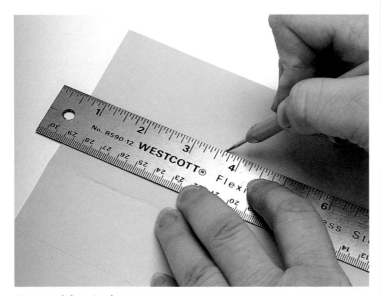

Score with a Stylus
For a soft crease, score with a stylus.

Always Use Tools
Never crease the paper by hand to score it.

TIP

For the most impressive pop-up and tri-fold cards, crisp scoring is a must!

How to Carve a Stamp

Carving your own designs into rubber is fun and addictive! Stamp carving tools are available in a variety of tip sizes, ranging from extremely thin to extremely wide. Soft white or pink rubber erasers work best for carving. You can even order large carving blocks up to 4' x 6' (123cm x 183cm) if you really get into it!

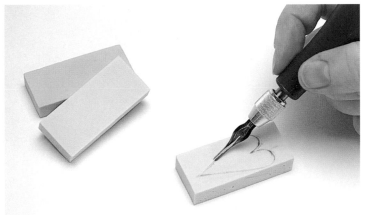

1. Draw and Trace Design
Draw your design in pencil on a soft rubber eraser. Trace the outline of the design with a thin carving tool.

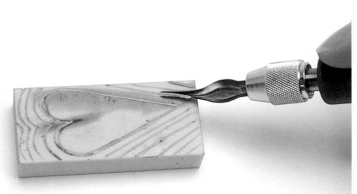

3. Carve Stamp
Carve around the stamped image with carving tools. Remove large chunks with a wide tip, and carve fine details with a thin tip.

2. Ink Stamp
Ink the stamp and stamp it onto paper. This will indicate the areas that still need to be carved and cleaned up.

4. Ink Stamp
Ink the stamp and stamp it onto paper again.

How to Carve a Stamp (cont.)

5. Cut Away Excess
Cut away the unwanted portions of the eraser with the craft knife.

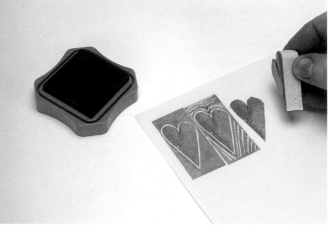

6. Stamp onto Paper
Stamp the inked image onto paper again to test it out.

How to Remove Smudges

We all make mistakes from time to time. It's part of the learning process. Accidental smudge marks can be easily fixed with a regular craft knife and a white eraser.

1. Scrape Paper
Using your craft knife, gently scrape the surface of the paper over the error. Be careful not to tear the paper.

2. Erase Rest
Rub the area with a white eraser to remove the rest of the smudge.

How to Make a Mask

Masking is an important technique to master, and practice makes perfect! In regular masking, the mask covers up the object, and the images are stamped around it. For an example of regular masking, see "In the Mail" on page 76. In mortise masking, the area around the object is masked, and the object itself is stamped. For an example of mortise masking, see "Comfy and Cozy" on page 114. Try both and see which technique you like best.

Many crafters use Post-it notes for masking because they are lightly adhesive and available in many sizes. I prefer Eclipse tape by JudiKins, and have used it for the projects in this book. This product is sold by the roll and is lightly adhesive on one side.

1. Stamp on Eclipse Tape
Ink a stamp and roll Eclipse tape over it.

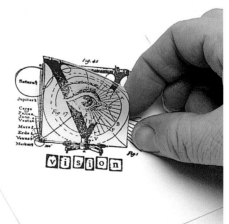

2. Cut Out Eclipse Tape
Cut out the portion of the stamped Eclipse tape you want to mask off. For a regular mask, use the object itself. For a mortise mask, use the area around the object.

3. Stamp Paper
Stamp the paper with colored inkpads.

4. Ink and Stamp
Ink a stamp with colored ink and stamp over the colors on the paper. Remove the mask to reveal a stamped card.

THE PROJECTS

now that you know the basics of card-making, you're ready to begin. The cards in this book are broken into five categories: Winter, Spring, Summer, Fall and Timeless Occasions. As you follow my step-by-step instructions, feel free to use your own stamps, colors and materials, and try not to limit yourself by the season. By swapping out a few stamps and a piece of cardstock, the Christmas Box card can easily become a tiny box to hold wedding favors. I hope you use the techniques shown in each project as a springboard for more fun and creative ideas. Remember, there is no right or wrong way to make a handmade greeting card. The more personalized it is, the better!

CARDS FOR WINTER

Winter is the time of year when families and friends get together to celebrate holidays and special occasions. What a perfect opportunity to create greetings that will make them glow with delight. I can think of nothing better than curling up by the fire on a cold winter's night with only my card-making supplies and my creativity. A simple, handmade greeting card may be the small gift that warms the heart of someone you love this season.

CHRISTMAS BOX

this is a simple and fun card to make for many holidays. The three-dimensional box can be filled with candy, small toys, gift certificates or money, which makes it perfect for Christmas or Hanukkah! There are many template stamps like this one available at your local stamp store.

TIP

This is an easy card to replicate over and over if taken in steps. I make holiday cards in bulk, completing one step each night. That way, I stay focused and get several cards done at once!

What you'll Need

Stamps*

- Box template stamp
- Present stamp
- Christmas tree stamp

Materials

- 3 pieces of green cardstock
- White cardstock
- Clear acetate square
- Black dye ink
- Red dye ink
- Green dye ink
- Clear-drying glue
- Glitter
- Double-stick tape
- Craft scissors
- Craft knife
- Ruler

See Resource Guide for stamp credits.

❶
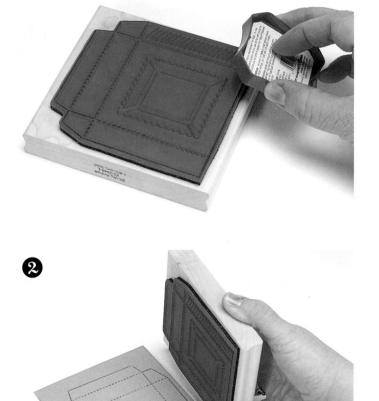

❷

❸
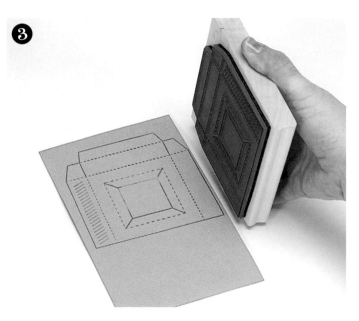

1. Ink Outside of Box Template Stamp
Ink the outside edge of the box template stamp with black dye ink.

2. Stamp on Cardstock
Stamp it onto two separate pieces of green cardstock. One will be the back of the box (panel A) and the other will be the door panel (panel B) that covers the card.

3. Ink and Stamp Inside of Box Template
Ink the entire box template stamp and stamp it onto another piece of green cardstock. This becomes the front of the box that has the picture frame (panel C).

4. Stamp Gift Image

Ink the present stamp and randomly stamp it on the blank side of the panel A with red dye ink. Repeat with panels B and C.

5. Cut Out Box Outline

Cut out the box shapes with craft scissors.

6. Remove Extra Panel

On panel B, cut off the two extra flaps, leaving a single flap to glue on the box.

7. Cut Out Box Center

Cut out the center of panel C with a craft knife.

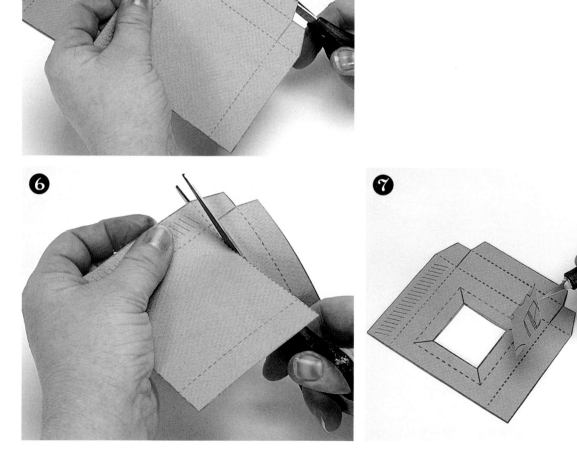

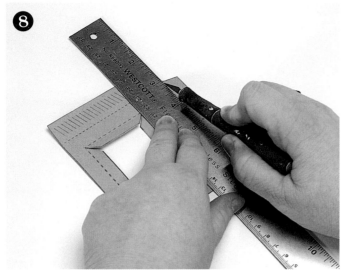

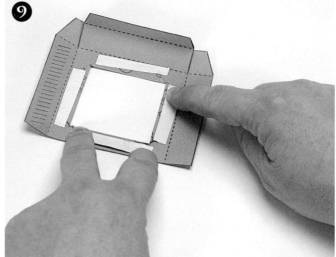

8. Score Along Dotted Lines
Using the back of a craft knife, score along the dotted lines on each panel.

9. Tape Down Frame
Tape down the inside window frame of panel C This gives a much more finished edge to the inside rim of the frame.

10. Add Acetate Square
Cut out a square of clear acetate and adhere it to the inside of panel C with clear-drying glue. Set aside.

11. Ink and Stamp Christmas Tree Image
Ink the Christmas tree stamp with green dye ink and stamp it on white cardstock.

TIP

For a stained glass effect,
try using colored acetate!

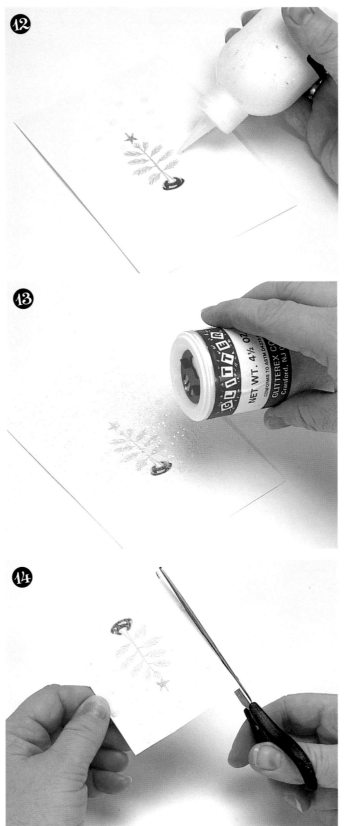

12. Add Glue
Add dots of clear-drying glue around the tree.

13. Add Glitter "Snow"
Sprinkle the wet glue with a generous amount of glitter to create the look of snow. Wipe away the excess.

14. Trim Cardstock
Trim the white cardstock to fit inside the frame.

15. Assemble Box
Attach panel A to panel C with double-stick tape.

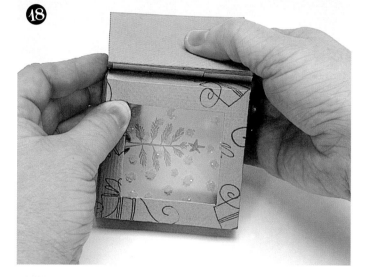

16. Arrange Flaps
Be sure the side flaps on panel C are positioned on the outside of the box.

17. Tape Box Shut
Adhere a strip of double-stick tape to the flap that will be tucked into the box to hold it closed.

NOTE: If you plan to put candy in the box, skip step 17.

18. Attach Door
Adhere a strip of double-stick tape to the small flap on panel B and attach it to the side of the box.

19. Bend Door to Open and Close
Bend panel B back and forth a few times to make sure it opens and closes properly. What a nice Christmas surprise!

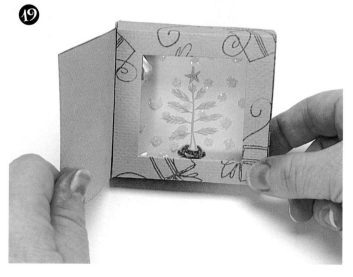

LIGHT THE MENORAH

acrylic paints are great for card-making because they layer well, are lightweight and clean up with water. These pearlized acrylic paints are gorgeous when applied to richly colored paper. For a softer, smoother finish, try using a cosmetic sponge instead of a stiff brush to apply the paint. Be sure the paint is completely dry before embossing so the powder sticks only to the image.

TIP

Edging this card with the same silver color as the embossing powder will really light up this Menorah!

What you'll Need

Stamps*

- Decorative stamp
- Menorah stamp

Materials

- 2 pieces of white cardstock
- Folded silver greeting card
- Dark blue acrylic paint
- Light blue acrylic paint
- Navy blue pigment ink
- Silver pigment ink
- Silver paint pen
- Stiff brush or cosmetic sponge
- Double-stick tape

See Resource Guide for stamp credits.

1. Apply Dark Blue Acrylic Paint

Generously apply dark blue acrylic paint to a piece of white cardstock with a stiff brush or cosmetic sponge.

2. Apply Light Blue Pigment Paint

Apply light blue acrylic paint to a separate piece of white cardstock.

3. Ink and Stamp Decorative Image

Ink the decorative image with navy blue pigment ink. Stamp along the bottom of the dark blue cardstock.

4. Ink and Stamp Menorah Image

Ink the Menorah stamp with silver pigment ink and stamp it onto the light blue cardstock.

5. Tear Card

Tear the top and bottom of the light blue cardstock to create jagged edges.

6. Outline Cards

Outline the edges of both cards with a silver paint pen.

7. Adhere to Greeting Card

Using double-stick tape, adhere the dark blue layer to the front of a folded silver greeting card. Next, adhere the light blue layer over the dark blue layer.

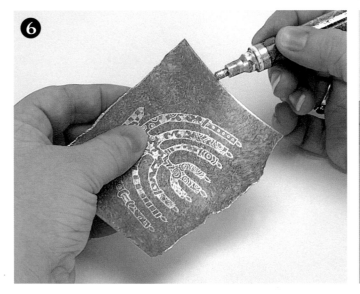

MORE BRIGHT IDEAS

Butterfly in the Sky

I wanted this majestic butterfly to look like it was emerging from the foliage, so I stamped the butterfly first and used paints and powders to decorate it. Then, I stamped the leaves, with metallic paint, over parts of the butterfly to set it back, behind the leaves.

Leaving an Impression

For this card, I stamped the leaves with dark acrylic paint on the card. Then, I layered a piece of cardstock stamped with lighter acrylic paints over it. The cord and ribbon hide the seam where the two pieces meet.

JOSEPH'S COAT

his festive card is great for ringing in the New Year—or any time of year! If you think back to kindergarten, you might remember using this resist method with crayons and black poster paint. While the end result might look a little more sophisticated, the technique is just as simple.

TIP

The closer and thinner you make the lines, the better this technique looks!

What you'll Need

Stamp*

◦ Nile flowers stained glass stamp

Materials

◦ White cardstock
◦ Silver paper
◦ Folded white greeting card
◦ Black solvent ink
◦ Black dye ink
◦ Black permanent marker
◦ Colored pencils
◦ Craft knife
◦ Craft scissors
◦ Craft glue
◦ Paper towels

See Resource Guide for stamp credits.

1. Sharpen Colored Pencil
Using a craft knife, sharpen several colored pencils.

2. Ink and Stamp Decorative Image
Ink the Nile flowers stained glass stamp with black solvent ink and stamp onto white cardstock.

3. Color in the Design
Fill in the white spaces of the image with colored pencils. You may color areas solidly or use loose lines to fill in portions of the design like I've done here.

4. Finish Adding Color
Finalize the colored pencil work, adding as much or as little color as you desire.

5. Cover with Dye Ink
Stamp black dye ink over the entire image.

6. Wipe Away Ink
Before the black ink dries, quickly wipe it away with a paper towel. The ink will adhere to all the areas not covered with colored pencil.

7. Trim Cardstock
Trim the sides of the cardstock with craft scissors.

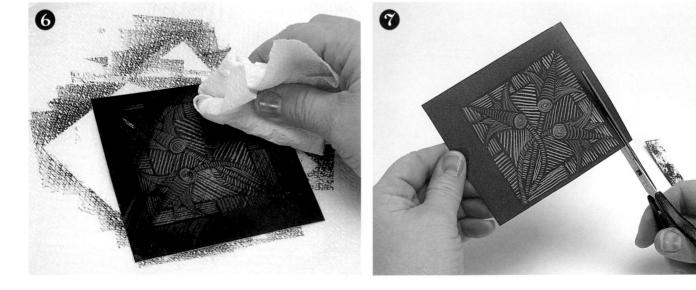

8. Outline Edges
Outline the edges of the cardstock with a black permanent marker.

9. Adhere Cardstock to Paper
Attach the cardstock to a slightly larger piece of silver paper with craft glue, leaving space at the bottom for a message if desired.

10. Attach to Greeting Card
Attach the stamped cardstock and silver paper to a folded white greeting card with craft glue.

GLAZED METALLICS

i have used this technique for many years to achieve a soft metallic finish on paper. It is great to try over an image that did not emboss well or one that is splotchy. High-quality pigment inks and paper make all the difference when crafting your own cards. For best results, I recommend using Encore brand pigment ink.

TIP

The pewter sticker on this card adds a fancy touch. To learn more about pewter stickers, see the Celebration of Summer card on page 78.

What you'll Need

Stamp*

- Swirl stamp

Materials

- White cardstock
- Folded blue greeting card
- Pewter sticker
- Silver pigment ink (Encore)
- Silver embossing powder
- Red, green and blue dye re-inkers
- Embossing tool (heat gun)
- Craft scissors
- Double-stick tape
- Paper towels

See Resource Guide for stamp credits.

1. Ink and Stamp Decorative Image
Ink the swirl stamp with silver pigment ink (Encore) and stamp onto white cardstock.

2. Add Embossing Powder
Sprinkle silver embossing powder over the ink, then tap the edge of the card to remove the excess powder.

3. Heat-Set Powder
Heat-set the powder with an embossing tool to melt it.

4. Cover Image

Use the same silver stamp pad to stamp all over the cardstock, completely covering the image.

5. Spread Ink with Finger

Rub the silver pigment ink into the surface of the card with your finger.

6. Add Dye

Squeeze a few drops of blue dye from a dye re-inker into a small dish. With your finger, smooth out the ink so it is fairly thin.

7. Buff Image

Buff the image with your inky finger so the dye sticks to the recessed areas. Continue buffing with red and green dye or the colors of your choice.

8. Heat-Set Dye
Heat-set the ink and dye with an embossing tool.

9. Buff Cardstock and Adhere to Greeting Card
Buff the cardstock with a paper towel to remove excess ink and dye. Trim the cardstock with craft scissors and adhere to a folded blue greeting card with double-stick tape. Add a pewter sticker for a finishing touch.

Try this!

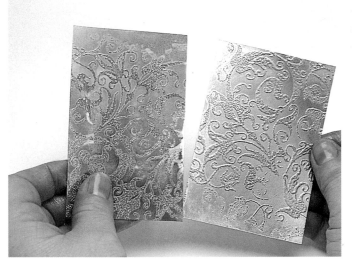

For a rougher look, shown on the left, rub vigorously with a paper towel and/or scrape with a craft knife to remove dye. For a softer look, shown on the right, simply use the buffing technique explained above.

CROSS MY HEART

in February, after the rush of the winter holidays, I am ready to create a few fun valentines with this tricky old pop-up inside. Be sure to add lots of confetti to the cards and send them in brightly colored envelopes. (Sealed with a kiss, of course.)

TIP

Be careful not to go overboard on your colors. For a simple and visually appealing look, I recommend choosing no more than three colors.

What you'll Need

Stamps*

- Hand-carved heart stamp (template on page 46)
- "Happy Valentine's Day" stamp

Materials

- Heart pocket template (page 47)
- Translucent white vellum
- Folded white greeting card
- Bright construction paper
- Dye ink, various colors
- Pencil
- Eraser
- Carving tools
- Double-stick tape
- Decorative paper punch
- Stylus
- Craft scissors or craft knife

*See Resource Guide for stamp credits.

1. Cut and Trace Heart Pocket
Cut out and enlarge the heart pocket template provided on page 47. Trace the outline and score marks of the template onto a piece of translucent vellum with a pencil.

2. Score Template
Score inside the slits with a stylus. Cut out the template with craft scissors or a craft knife.

3. Clean Up Vellum
Erase any pencil marks remaining on the vellum.

4. Crease Vellum

Crease the vellum along the score marks to make the heart pocket. The creases down the center of each heart should fold to the inside.

5. Stamp Images on Vellum

Carve a heart stamp using the template provided below (For carving instructions, see page 19). Randomly stamp the heart and "Happy Valentine's Day" stamps onto the inside of the heart pocket in various colors of dye ink.

6. Stamp Heart Image on Greeting Card

Stamp more hearts onto the outside of a folded white greeting card in various colors.

7. Position Heart Pocket in Greeting Card

Fold the heart pocket back into shape and place it inside the greeting card. Try closing the card to make sure it is in the correct position.

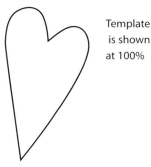

Template
is shown
at 100%

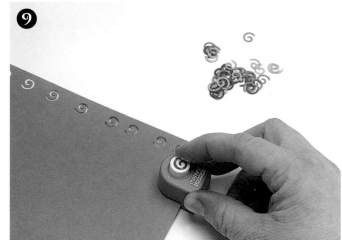

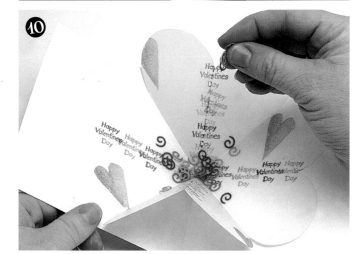

8. Adhere Heart Pocket

Adhere the heart pocket to the inside of the white greeting card with double-stick tape.

9. Punch Out Confetti

Use a decorative paper punch on bright construction paper to make colorful confetti.

10. Add Confetti

Open the card slightly, pour in the confetti, and carefully re-close the card.

Enlarge heart pocket template by 200%, then by 125%.

TIP

Add glitter to the inside of the heart for a shiny (and messy) touch.

HEARTS OF GOLD

this is a creative method of making vivid backgrounds for simple stamps. With a few dye inkpads and a stiff brush for applying color, you can count on getting brilliant results every time! The torn-edge background adds a modern flair and works exceptionally well for underwater or sunset themes.

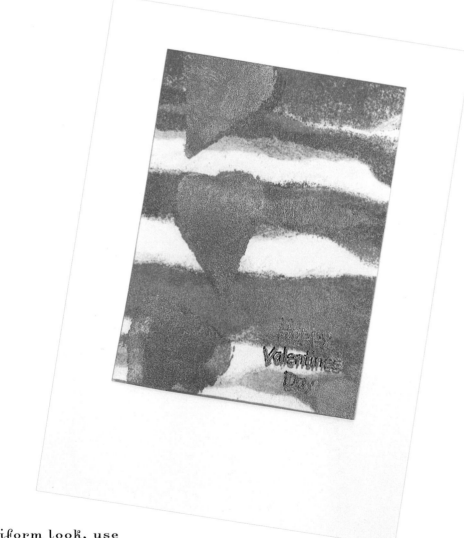

TIP

For a more uniform look, use decorative or regular scissors to cut the Eclipse tape.

What you'll Need

Stamps*

+ Heart stamp
+ "Happy Valentine's Day" stamp

Materials

+ White cardstock
+ Folded white greeting card
+ Dye ink, various colors
+ Gold pigment powder
+ Eclipse tape
+ Stiff brush
+ Craft scissors

See Resource Guide for stamp credits.

1. Mask Background
Tear off thin strips of Eclipse tape and adhere them to a piece of white cardstock to mask portions of the background.

2. Apply Dye Ink
Brush colored dye ink onto the cardstock and over the masks with a stiff brush. Remove and reposition the masks until the desired look is achieved.

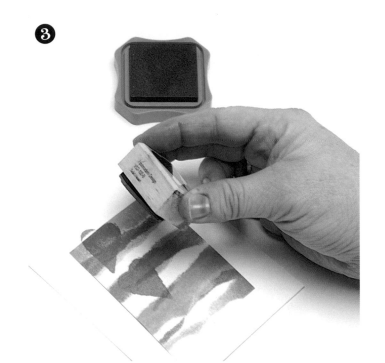

3. Ink and Stamp Heart Image
Ink the heart stamp with pink dye ink and stamp randomly onto the cardstock.

4. Ink and Stamp "Happy Valentine's Day"
Ink the "Happy Valentine's Day" stamp with black dye ink and stamp it onto the bottom right corner.

5. Add Pigment Powder and Adhere to Greeting Card
Dust with gold pigment powder and wipe away the excess. The powder will stick to the wet ink on the hearts and text. Trim the edges and adhere to a white greeting card.

MORE BRIGHT IDEAS

Tie-Dyed Flowers

Torn edges add dimension to cards such as this colorful creation. Hold a piece of paper (cardstock works best) against a flat surface with one hand and slowly tear the paper with the other. Voila!

Midas' Golden Touch

The shimmer of gold cardstock shines through on this card. Don't worry about tearing the edges in a straight line. The more jagged the tear, the better.

CARDS FOR SPRING

a fter a long winter, the bright colors of spring are like a breath of fresh air! These spring cards are filled with the vibrant colors of a season in bloom. Flowers and nature themes always make great cards for Easter and Mother's Day, but don't forget to keep your eyes open for fun and festive Mardi Gras imagery as well.

PARTY GRAS!

these days, you don't have to go to New Orleans to celebrate Mardi Gras. This extravaganza of crazy costumes and
delectable delights is an excellent time to create a special card,
no matter where you happen to live. The mix of creative patterns and vivid colors will whisk you away to The Big Easy,
where you'll toss your troubles aside and just have fun!

TIP

To decorate your card in
true Mardi Gras fashion,
use the official colors of
the festival: purple rep-
resents justice; green
represents faith; and
gold represents power.

What you'll Need

Stamps*

- Box template stamp
- Minstrel stamp

Materials

- 2 sheets of decorative paper
- White paper
- Acetate square
- Folded dark blue greeting card
- Black solvent ink
- Silver paint pen
- Colored pencils
- Glitter
- Double-stick tape
- Scoring tool
- Craft scissors or craft knife
- Ruler

*See Resource Guide for stamp credits.

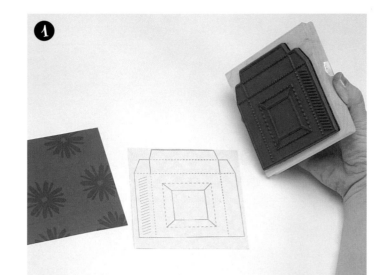

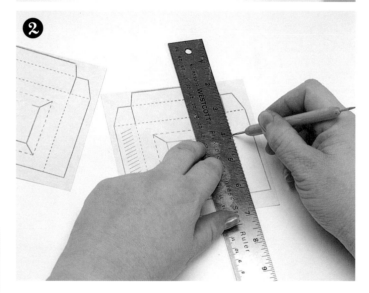

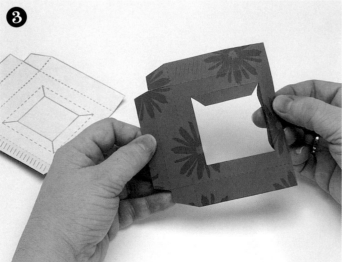

1. Cut and Stamp Decorative Paper
Cut two thin pieces of decorative paper to approximately 3" (7.6cm) square. Stamp the plain sides of each piece of paper with the box template stamp.

2. Score Paper
On one of the pieces of paper, score the outside lines and the window of the box with a stylus. This will be the frame. On the other piece of paper, score only the outside of the box. This will be the back panel for the frame. Cut out both shapes with scissors or a craft knife.

3. Fold Box
Fold the frame along the score marks.

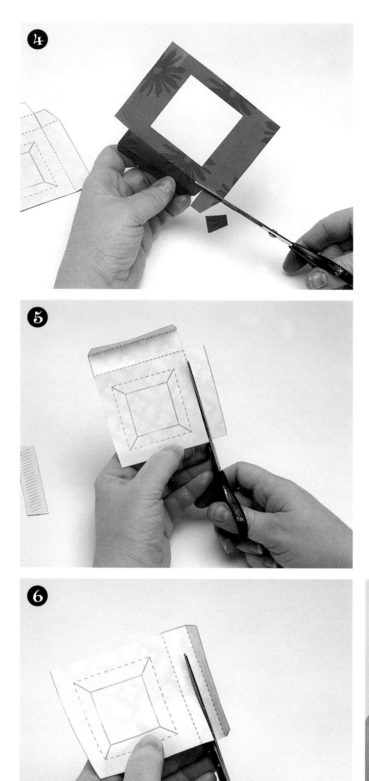

4. Remove Top Flaps
Cut off the little box flaps and bottom flap of the frame with craft scissors.

5. Remove Back Flaps
Trim off all flaps but one from the back panel piece.

6. Remove Top of Flap
Cut the top portion off of the remaining flap on the back panel piece, leaving a single tab.

7. Add Acetate Window
Cut a small square of acetate approximately 2½" x 2½" (6.4cm x 6.4cm) for the frame's window. Adhere the acetate with double-stick tape on the inside of the frame. Attach the remaining back panel flap to the inside of the frame as shown. Be sure the decorative paper is showing through the frame.

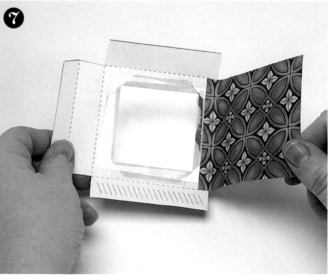

8. Add Minstrel Image

Stamp the minstrel image onto white paper using black solvent ink. Cut it out and decorate it with colored pencils. Place the image in the center of the back panel and add glitter to the window. Fold the frame over the back panel.

9. Fold Flaps

Fold the remaining flaps from the frame in and secure with double-stick tape. Edge the frame with a silver paint pen.

10. Adhere Box to Greeting Card

Use double-stick tape to fasten the decorative framed piece a folded dark blue greeting card.

PEEKABOO BUNNY

Whimsy meets whiskers in this Easter card, made just for a special little girl or boy. Tuck it into an Easter basket along with some colored eggs. To take this card a step further, glue Easter grass to the bottom of the card and add a small pink button for the bunny's nose.

TIP

This tri-fold method can also be used for other cards, so don't limit yourself to this design alone.

What you'll Need

Stamps*

- Swirl stamp
- Hand-carved Easter egg stamp (template on page 63)
- Hand-carved bunny face stamps (template on page 63)

Materials

- Bunny body template (page 63)
- Light yellow cardstock
- Vellum or tracing paper
- Blue solvent ink
- Dye ink, various colors
- Pencil
- Eraser
- Carving tools
- Craft knife
- Craft scissors
- Ruler

*See Resource Guide for stamp credits.

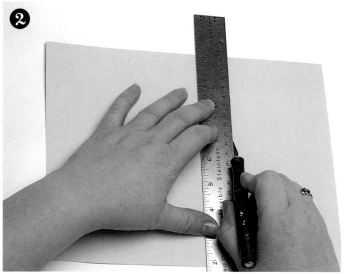

1. Mark Cardstock

Measure 3" (7.6cm), 7" (18cm) and 10" (25cm) and mark with a pencil on light yellow cardstock.

2. Score Cardstock

Score along the 3" (7.6cm) and 7" (18cm) marks with the back of a craft knife or a scoring tool. Erase any remaining pencil marks.

3. Tri-Fold Card

Fold the left panel to the back and the right panel to the front. This is called a tri-fold.

4. Ink and Stamp Swirls

Ink a swirl stamp with blue solvent ink. Flatten out the card and begin stamping the front about one-third of the way up on the left edge. Work your way upward and diagonally to the right edge of the page.

5. Fill Open Spaces

Re-ink the stamp and randomly stamp in between the open spaces of the yellow cardstock to fill in any gaps.

6. Trim Card

Use your craft knife to trim off the top of the card along the stamped edge.

7. Stamp Back of Card

Flip the card over and stamp randomly along the top edges with the swirl stamp.

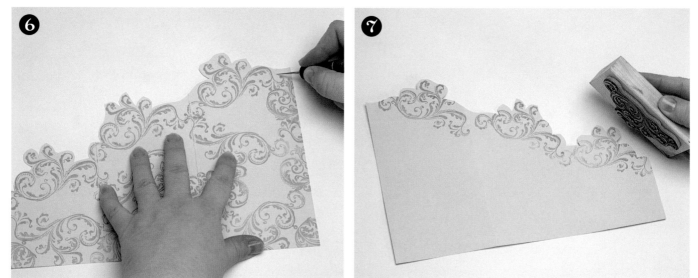

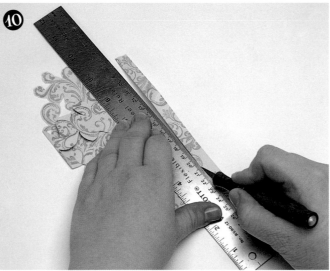

8. Fill Open Spaces
Fill the open spaces on the edges with more stamping.

9. Cut Out Random Pieces
Use your craft knife to cut out random bits and pieces from the inside of the card.

10. Trim Card
Using your ruler as a guide, trim the edges of the card with a craft knife.

11. Ink and Stamp Easter Egg Image
Carve an Easter egg stamp using the template on page 61. (For carving instructions, see page 19). Ink the stamp with colorful dye ink and stamp a border along the bottom of both sides.

TIP

Many Easter egg stamps can be found in your local stamping supply store if you don't wish to carve your own.

12. Cut Out Bunny Template

Cut out the bunny template provided on page 63.
Position the straight side of the template against a
folded piece of vellum or tracing paper and trace with
a pencil. Cut out the bunny shape.

13. Add Bunny Eyes and Nose

Dip a pencil eraser in pink dye ink and use it to dot the
bunny's eyes. Use a small triangular piece of eraser to
make a nose, and stamp it with pink dye ink.

14. Add Bunny Ears

Use the template on page 63 to carve the ear shape
from an eraser. Stamp it inside each of the bunny's ears
with pink dye ink. Poke the bunny's head through
holes in the back of the card.

TEMPLATES

Bunny template

Enlarge by 133%

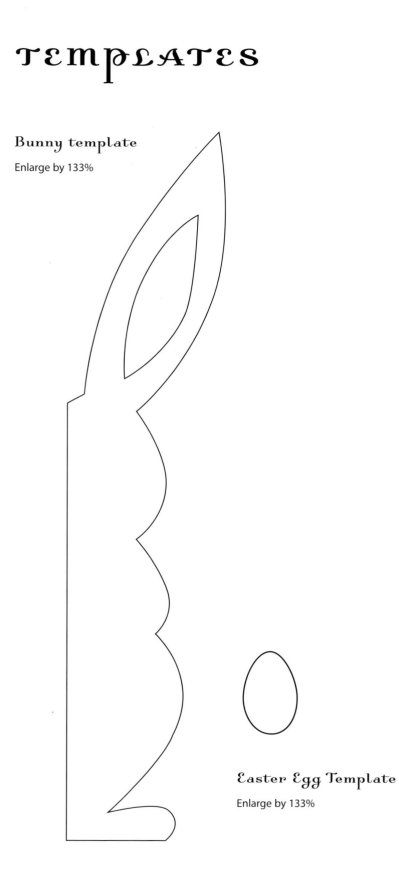

Easter Egg Template

Enlarge by 133%

sunbonnets in spring

here is a favorite trick of mine! The lamp stamps I used here don't have anything to do with spring, but with a little imagination and clever masking, they're transformed into bonnets! Take a good look at your stamps and try to imagine what else they could be. Who knows what you'll dream up!

TIP

This process works better when using different kinds of ink, or at least drastically different colors.

What you'll Need

Stamps*

- Dress stamp
- Chinese lantern stamp
- Lamps stamp

Materials

- White paper
- White cardstock
- Folded white greeting card
- Dye ink, various colors
- Silver dye ink
- Turquoise paint pen
- Eclipse tape
- Double-stick tape
- Craft scissors

*See Resource Guide for stamp credits.

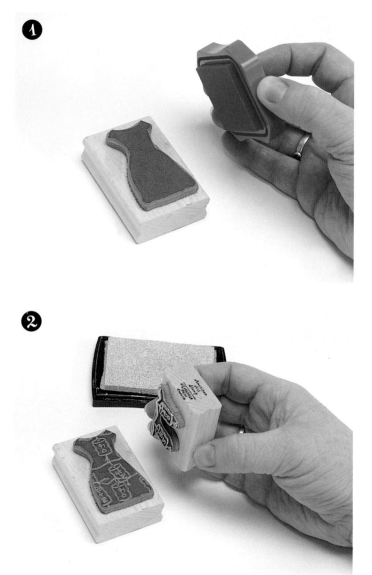

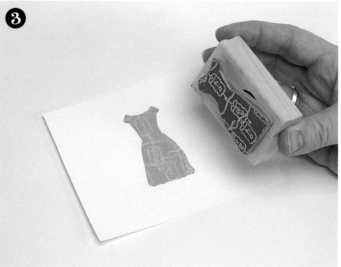

1. Ink Dress Image
Ink the surface of the dress stamp generously with orange dye ink.

2. Ink and Stamp Lantern Image
Ink the Chinese lantern stamp with silver dye ink and stamp the image onto the solid dress stamp to create designs on the dress.

3. Stamp Inked Dress Image
Stamp the dress image onto white paper.

4. Cut Out Dresses

Cut out the dress image with craft scissors. Repeat this process two more times using different colors.

5. Ink and Stamp Lamp Image

Ink the lamp stamp with various brightly colored dye inks and stamp the top of a piece of white cardstock.

6. Mask and Stamp Lamp Bases

Mask off the center of the white cardstock with Eclipse tape and stamp the cardstock again with the lamp image. Only the lamp bases should show up on the cardstock.

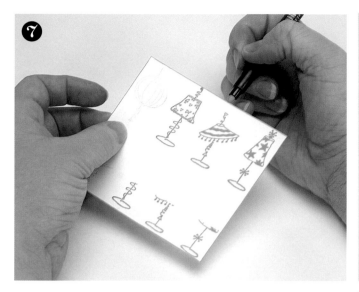

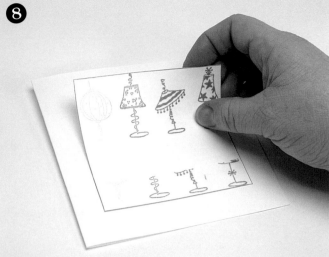

7. Trim Cardstock and Outline Edges

Trim the sides of the cardstock to make it square.
Outline the edges with a turquoise paint pen.

8. Adhere Cardstock to Greeting Card

Fasten the square cardstock onto a folded white greeting card with double-stick tape.

9. Adhere Dresses Over Lamp Bases

Adhere the cut-out dresses over the lamp bottoms
with double-stick tape.

A MOTHER'S LOVE

mom always appreciates a beautiful card—particularly one made by you! Creating a special card just for her will give you the chance to express your love in a way a store-bought card never could. Use her favorite colors and themes. Add a personal embellishment or an old photograph she will recognize. This is your opportunity to show your mom how much you have appreciated her all these years.

TIP

Galaxy markers are great for coloring in stamped images on light or dark paper. They are available in bright and pastel colors, metallics and glitters, and with fine, medium and broad tips.

What you'll Need

Stamp*

- Triple heart stamp

Materials

- Black solvent ink
- Pink dye ink
- Markers (Galaxy)
- Folded white greeting card

*See Resource Guide for stamp credits.

1. Ink and Stamp Heart Image
Ink the triple heart stamp with black solvent ink and stamp it onto the front of a folded white greeting card.

2. Decorate Hearts
Color in the hearts with markers (I use Galaxy brand) and allow the ink to dry.

3. Stamp Over Hearts
Use a pink dye inkpad to stamp over the triple heart image in the opposite direction.

CARDS FOR SUMMER

Summer cards are the forgotten greetings. Between vacations, soccer practice and swimming lessons, who has time for another project? But that doesn't mean there aren't many special events to celebrate, like Graduation, Father's Day and Summer Solstice. Card-making can be done virtually anywhere! A blanket, a cool glass of lemonade and your card supplies are all you need.

MAKE A SPLASH WITH THESE SUMMER CARDS:

FACING THE FUTURE

graduation is one of life's most cherished moments. Show your favorite grad how much he means to you with a special handmade greeting card. This one can be customized with the grad's school colors. Be sure to leave space for a personalized message (and perhaps a little spending money!).

TIP

Fill in the blank spaces of stamped images to give your cards a more polished look. I use thicker Galaxy markers to color in larger areas and gel pens for smaller, more detailed areas.

What you'll Need

Stamps*

- Large frame stamp
- Small frame stamp
- David stamp

Materials

- Blue cardstock
- Folded blue greeting card
- Black solvent ink
- White marker
- White gel pen
- Double-stick dots
- Craft scissors
- Craft knife

*See Resource Guide for stamp credits.

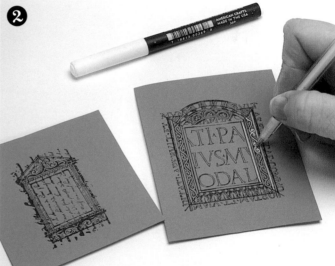

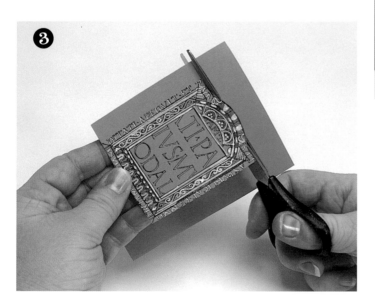

1. Stamp Frame Images

Cut the blue cardstock into two pieces, a larger one measuring about 4" x 6" (10.2cm x 15.2cm) and a smaller one measuring about 3" x 3½" (7.6cm x 8.9cm). Using black solvent ink, stamp the larger card with the large frame stamp and the smaller card with the small frame stamp.

2. Color in Open Spaces

Fill in all open spaces of the stamped frames with a white marker (I used Galaxy brand) and gel pen.

3. Trim Card Edges

Trim around the edges of both frames with craft scissors.

4. Cut Out Window
Cut out the inside window of the small frame with a craft knife.

5. Stamp and Color David Image
Stamp the David image onto a separate piece of blue cardstock and color in larger areas with a white marker.

6. Fill in Open Spaces
Fill in smaller areas with a white gel pen. For added detail, make tiny dots of gel pen on the face.

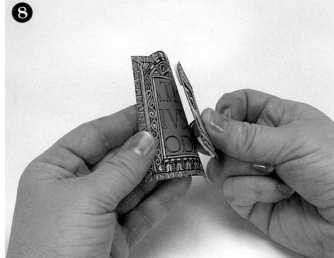

7. Adhere Small Frame to Face
Position the small frame over the David image so most of it can be seen through the window, and adhere with double-stick dots. Trim away all of the excess around the face.

8. Adhere Small Frame to Large Frame
Adhere the David image and small frame to the front of the large frame with double-stick dots.

9. Add Dots
Place more double-stick dots on the back of the frame.

NOTE: To adhere small areas, try cutting double-stick dots into smaller pieces with craft scissors.

10. Adhere to Greeting Card
Fasten the framed face to the front of a folded blue greeting card, leaving room at the bottom for a special message if desired.

IN THE MAIL

blank postage paper is available at many stamp and scrapbook stores. Or, try making your own by using a sewing machine without thread to perforate the paper. I love this little big head stamp. I think it's perfect for Father's Day!

What you'll Need

Stamp*

- Little big head stamp

Materials

- Perforated stamp paper
- Folded dark blue greeting card
- Black dye ink
- Dye ink, various bright colors
- Markers
- Gel pens
- Eclipse tape
- Stiff brush
- Double-stick tape
- Craft knife

See Resource Guide for stamp credits.

TIP

With simple masking, create a thin white border around the image for a professional postage look.

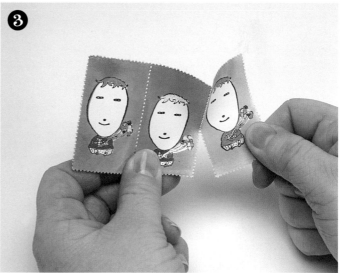

1. Ink and Stamp Image

Ink the stamp with black dye ink and stamp several times onto perforated stamp paper. Stamp the image onto Eclipse tape, and use a craft knife to cut out the outline of the image to make a mask. Apply the mask over three of the stamped images on the postal stamp.

2. Apply Dye

Apply various colors of dye ink with a stiff brush. Next, remove the mask and color in the stamped images with markers (I used Galaxy brand) and gel pens.

3. Separate Stamps

Tear the stamp paper apart at the perforations.

4. Adhere to Greeting Card

Cut pieces of double-stick tape to fit the back of each stamp and adhere diagonally from top-left to bottom-right onto the folded dark blue greeting card.

CELEBRATION OF SUMMER

i love these real pewter stickers, which are fairly new on the market. They come in a variety of shapes and designs. For this card, I uses inks to color in the fancy embellishments, but you may also prefer the pewter's natural finish. The 100% pewter stickers are soft and bendable, and they can be cut to size with craft scissors. Why not have a family reunion, summer solstice celebration or Independence day grill-out? The beauty of this card is that you can color coordinate it for any occasion.

TIP

This technique also works with foil stickers.

What you'll Need

Materials

- 6 pieces of decorative cardstock
- Folded tan greeting card
- Red and green solvent ink
- 2" (5cm) square pewter sticker
- Cosmetic sponge
- Craft scissors
- Double-stick tape
- Paper towels

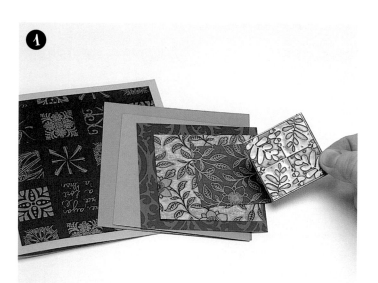

1. Cut Out Decorative Cardstock

Cut six pieces of decorative cardstock into squares of descending size. The sizes in this project are as follows: 5" x 5" (13cm x 13cm), 4½" x 4½" (11cm x 11cm), 4" x 4" (10cm x 10cm), 3½" x 3½" (9cm x 9cm), 3" x 3" (8cm x 8cm), 2⅛" x 2⅛" (7cm x 7cm). The pewter sticker should measure 2" x 2" (5cm x 5cm), and the greeting card should measure 5½" x 5½" (14cm x14cm). Layer the decorative cardstock in descending order with the smallest square on top. Adhere all the layers together with double-stick tape.

2. Ink Pewter Sticker

Apply two colors of solvent ink to the pewter sticker. For this project, I used red and green.

3. Spread Ink

Spread the ink around with a cosmetic sponge, completely covering the sticker.

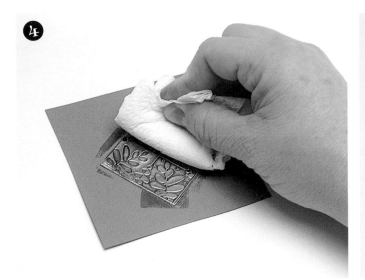

4. Remove Excess Ink

Blot the excess ink from the pewter stamp with a paper towel. Allow the ink to dry.

5. Adhere to Greeting Card

Using double-stick tape, adhere the layered cardstock to the greeting card. Next, adhere the pewter sticker to the cardstock.

MORE BRIGHT IDEAS

All the Leaves are Brown

Overlapping leaf stickers create the background on the pewter sticker in this card. Then, I used individual stickers in the center and along the edge as an accent. The pieces of the card are layered using double-stick dots to give it even more impact.

Toilettes

I applied a generous amount of dark green and blue solvent ink to the pewter sticker on this card. As a further embellishment, I also added a black satin ribbon trimmed in gold.

Daisies and Checks

Pewter stickers come in all shapes and sizes, as you can see in this card. Scrapbook stores have all sorts of coordinated papers where you can get pieces like these checks and stripes.

CARDS FOR FALL

fall is my favorite time of year. I love when the temperature drops and leaves turn beautiful shades of orange, brown and gold. It's the perfect time to roll up the sleeves of your favorite sweatshirt and get crafting! With a little ink, some colorful paper and a few stamps, you'll be amazed at how time flies. You may even get a jump on your winter holiday cards.

WARM UP THE SEASON WITH THESE FALL CARDS:

spooky sentiments

halloween is my all-time favorite holiday! It is such a fun time, purely for tricks and treats (my friends know I'm a real joker). It's thrilling to create cards for this spooky holiday because they can be scary, humorous, cute or a mixture of all three!

TIP

To prevent your embossing powder from settling and sticking to the bottom of the jar, give it a shake before and after every use.

What you'll Need

Stamps*

- Shrine stamp
- Pumpkin head stamp

Materials

- Orange cardstock
- Black cardstock
- Black pigment ink
- Black permanent marker
- Silver pigment ink
- Embossing powder
- Embossing tool (heat gun)
- Markers
- Gel pens
- Double-stick dots
- Craft knife

*See Resource Guide for stamp credits.

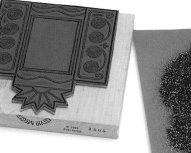

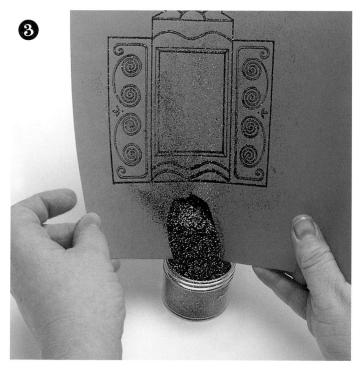

1. Ink and Stamp Frame Image

Ink the shrine stamp with black pigment ink and stamp onto orange cardstock. Quickly touch up the stamped image with a black permanent marker.

2. Apply Embossing Powder

Pour a generous amount of embossing powder over the stamped image. The powder will stick to the wet ink.

3. Save Excess Powder

Return the excess powder to the container.

4. Heat-Set Powder

Heat the stamped image with an embossing tool to set the powder in place.

5. Cut Out Center of Frame

Cut out the center of the shrine image with a craft knife. This becomes the frame for the card.

6. Color Frame

Color in portions of the frame with markers (I used Galaxy markers) and gel pens.

7. Ink and Stamp Halloween Image

Ink the pumpkin head stamp with silver pigment ink and stamp it onto black cardstock.

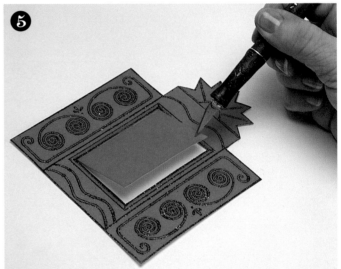

8. Adhere Image

Place the frame over the pumpkin head image and adhere with double-stick dots.

9. Make Stand

To make a stand for the frame, cut a triangle out of a scrap piece of black cardstock. Affix it to the back of the frame with double-stick dots.

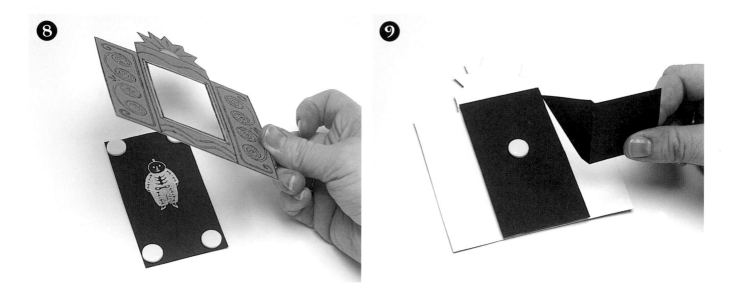

MORE BRIGHT IDEAS

Pumpkin Patch

This is another variation on the Halloween theme. I used double-stick dots to adhere the layers and to make the card three-dimensional.

GOBBLER GREETINGS

In this project, you get to carve your own turkey—turkey stamp, that is. Use the template provided to cut out the cute little gobbler. But beware! Carving can be addictive, and creating simple shapes from erasers can broaden your stamp collection. You'll quickly find that extra storage space in your craft room is something to be thankful for!

TIP

To deepen the warm fall tones in this card, I used an all-over vivid yellow paint as an overlay. This technique can be used with other colors as well. For instance, pink can be applied over blue and purple to brighten the look.

What you'll Need

Stamps*

- Hand-card turkey stamp (template on page 91)
- Leaf stamp

Materials

- Cream-colored cardstock
- Burgundy cardstock
- Folded tan greeting card
- Dye ink, various bright colors
- Black permanent marker
- Cosmetic sponge or stiff brush
- Pencil
- Eraser
- Carving tools
- Double-stick tape
- Craft scissors

See Resource Guide for stamp credits.

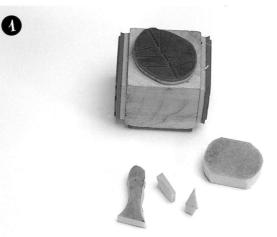

1. Carve Turkey Stamp

Carve the individual pieces of the turkey stamp using the templates provided on page 91. (For instructions on how to carve your our own stamps, see page 19).

2. Ink and Stamp Turkey Feathers

Ink a leaf stamp with several colors of dye ink and stamp onto cream-colored cardstock to form the turkey's feathers.

3. Stamp Turkey Body

Ink the body stamp with brown dye ink and stamp over the feathers.

4. Stamp Turkey Head

Ink the turkey's head stamp with brown dye ink and stamp above the body.

5. Stamp Turkey Beak and Feet

Ink the turkey's beak and feet stamps with orange dye ink and stamp below the body.

6. Stamp Turkey Legs

Repeat the process with the turkey's legs.

7. Dot Turkey Eye

Dot the turkey's eye with a black permanent marker.

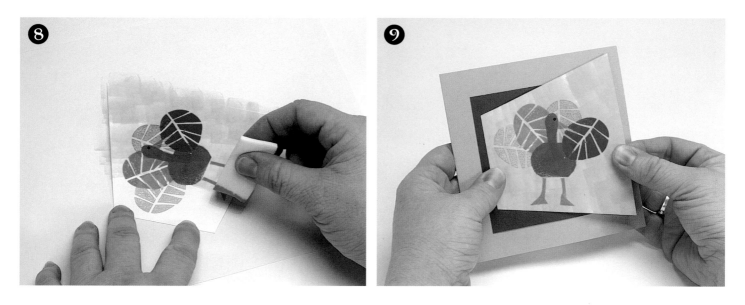

Templates are shown at 100%.

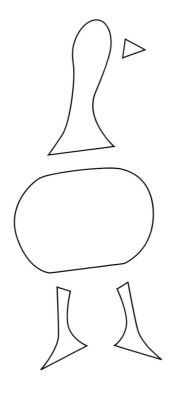

8. Cover with Yellow Ink
Cut the cardstock into an interesting geometric shape with craft scissors. Spread yellow dye ink over the entire turkey image with a cosmetic sponge.

9. Adhere Turkey Cardstock
Cut a piece of burgundy cardstock to the desired size and adhere to a folded greeting card with double-stick tape. Adhere the turkey card over the burgundy cardstock.

FALL FOLIAGE

acrylic tiles come in a myriad of shapes and sizes and can be found in most stamp supply stores. The clear tiles are lightweight enough to be used on cards. The ink selection is important on these tiles. Be sure to use a solvent ink or a pigment that can be dried with a heat gun. You may also want to try embossing the tiles for a metallic look.

What you'll Need

Stamp*

◆ Leaf stamp

Materials

◆ Thin decorative paper
◆ Folded light green greeting card
◆ Acrylic tile
◆ Metallic paint
◆ Copper paint pen
◆ Black solvent ink
◆ Stiff brush
◆ Double-stick tape
◆ Craft scissors

*See Resource Guide for stamp credits.

1. Paint Acrylic Tile
Use a stiff brush to cover an acrylic tile completely with metallic paint. (I used Halo Pink Gold paint by Lumiere.)

2. Apply Paint Pen
Fill in the unpainted areas with a copper paint pen. Allow to dry.

3. Remove Backing
Turn the acrylic tile onto the unpainted side and remove backing.

4. Ink and Stamp Leaf Image
Ink the leaf stamp with black solvent ink and randomly stamp it onto the unpainted side of the acrylic tile.

5. Reveal the Image
Continue stamping the leaves as desired. Allow to dry. The metallic paint shows through the stamped, unpainted side of the tile brilliantly.

6. Affix Decorative Paper
Using double-stick tape, adhere a piece of thin, decorative paper to the front of a light green greeting card at the fold. Trim off the excess.

7. Adhere Acrylic Tile
Adhere the acrylic tile to the front of the greeting card over the decorative paper.

Option: Acrylic Tile Experiment

There are so many creative ways to use acrylic tiles for craft projects. Here's a quick and easy idea I think you'll enjoy. The frog-shaped acrylic tile is covered with delicate gold leaf, giving it a faux metallic finish. Once the tile is dry, add it to any greeting card for instant shine.

1. Remove Tile Backing
Remove the backing from the frog-shaped acrylic tile.

2. Add Glaze
Using your finger, spread adhesive glaze on the frog piece.

3. Adhere Tile to Gold Leaf
Stick the adhesive side of the frog piece to gold leaf and allow to dry. (I used foil in this project, but tissue paper works just as well.)

4. Remove Excess Gold Leaf
Peel away the gold leaf and brush off any excess with a soft brush.

5. Fill with Paint Pen
Fill in any spaces with a gold paint pen.

TIP

Use a full, soft brush to dust off the excess foil. A brush that is too stiff may remove too much foil and leave a scratchy appearance.

CARDS FOR TIMELESS OCCASIONS

many special occasions celebrated throughout the year are not marked by a particular season. Birthdays, anniversaries and housewarming parties are just a few of the many events that will keep you busy making cards all year long. Add a personal touch by decorating an animal-lover's card with a paw-print stamp, or embellish a history buff's card with vintage images. If you can dream it, you can make it. That, to me, is by far the best part about card-making.

TINY DANCER

this is a great card for a girly-girl party, be it a birthday, shower or other special occasion. Pink and white are the ultimate feminine color combination, although any pastel colors will work just as well.

TIP

Use Eclipse tape to mask off the right side of the card in an uneven line. This will give the illusion of torn paper. This technique is also used in the "A Mother's Love" card on page 68.

What you'll Need

Stamps*

- Harlequin pattern stamp
- Ballerina stamp

Materials

- Folded white greeting card
- Light pink and dark pink pigment ink
- Black solvent ink
- Eclipse tape
- Light pink ribbon
- Stiff brush
- Craft scissors

See Resource Guide for stamp credits.

1. Mask Greeting Card

Use torn Eclipse tape to mask the outer edges of a folded white greeting card. Apply a generous amount of light pink pigment ink to the card.

2. Texturize Ink

While the ink is still wet, rub a stiff brush over the ink to texturize it. Allow the card to dry completely.

3. Add More Color

Repeat the process, applying dark pink pigment ink over the light pink layer.

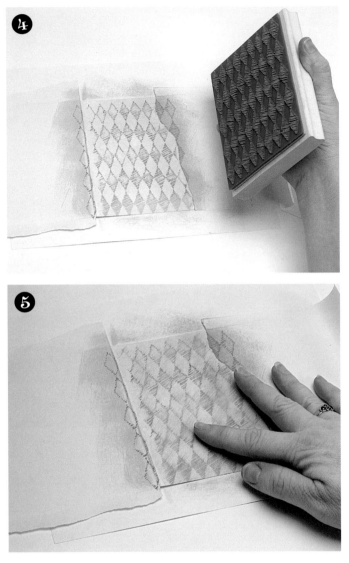

4. Ink and Stamp Harlequin Image
Ink a large harlequin patterned stamp with dark pink pigment ink and stamp over the greeting card.

5. Soften Image
To create a soft look, smear the image with your finger.

6. Ink and Stamp Ballerina Image
Ink a ballerina stamp with black solvent ink and stamp over the harlequin pattern.

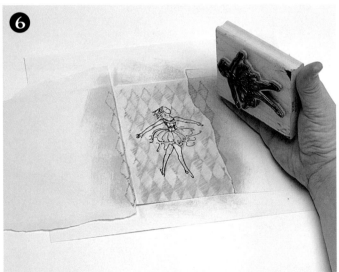

7. Remove Mask

Remove the mask of Eclipse tape and allow to dry.

8. Add Ribbon

Fasten a light pink ribbon to the front of the card and tie it in a bow. Cut the ribbon edges at an angle for a decorative look.

MORE BRIGHT IDEAS

Marshmallow Bunny

Before the decorative images were stamped onto the background, masks were applied to the marshmallow bunny image and the right side of the card. When the masks were removed, these areas remained unstamped. This creates a layered appearance.

I DO

When we think of wedding cards, we typically visualize the traditional white-on-white color scheme. But what about the nontraditional couple? Colorful weddings are becoming more and more popular today, and a splash of color will make an ordinary card bright and beautiful—just like the happy couple!

TIP

To make a fancy greeting card like this one, paint a piece of white cardstock with a sandy paint. Then, add an iridescent interference paint over the sandy paint to pearlize it. Add more interference paint to pearlize again. Score the card down the middle with a stylus or the back of a craft knife and apply the stamped image as desired.

What you'll Need

Stamps*

* Bride and groom stamp

Materials

* White cardstock
* Folded iridescent greeting card (see tip on page 102)
* Black dye ink
* Pearlized paint
* Silver paint pen
* Glitter
* Decorative ribbon
* Pewter sticker
* Double-stick tape
* Craft scissors
* Cosmetic sponge
* Paintbrush
* Brayer (optional)

See Resource Guide for stamp credits.

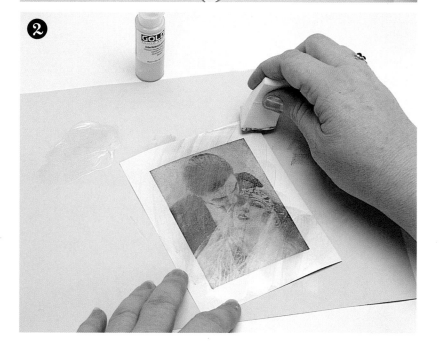

1. Ink and Stamp Bride and Groom Image

Ink the bride and groom image with black dye ink. Stamp onto a piece of white cardstock.

> NOTE: When inking a large stamp such as this, use a brayer to distribute the ink more evenly.

2. Apply Paint

Spread pearlized paint over the stamped image with a cosmetic sponge.

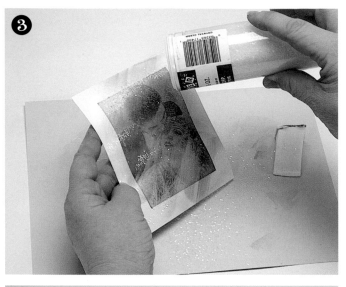

3. Apply Glitter
Add glitter to the wet paint and dust off the excess. Allow to dry.

4. Outline Edges
Trim the edges of the cardstock right up to the edge of the stamped image. Outline the edges with a silver paint pen.

5. Add Ribbon and Adhere to Greeting Card
With double-stick tape, adhere the cardstock and a decorative ribbon to a folded silver greeting card. Finally, adhere a pewter sticker over the ribbon.

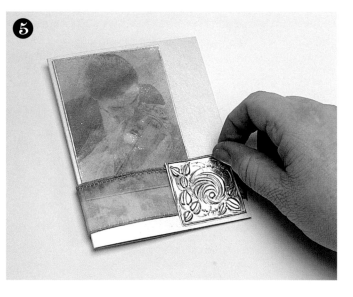

MORE BRIGHT IDEAS

Family Matters

This card is an example of how glitter can be a subtle embellishment. Adhere the image to a glossy greeting card in a soft shade of turquoise, and attach a decorative ribbon for a charming touch.

Stars in Your Eyes

A simple, white greeting becomes a sparkling masterpiece just by adding glitter to a simple face stamp. Black ribbon and decorative paper also add visual appeal.

BUNDLE OF JOY

Pastel pink or baby blue, a handmade baby shower invitation will surely make mommy and her guests smile. With the help of a box template, this quick and easy card looks like it took all day to make. I used a simple envelope template to make an all-in-one look. It can be used for other occasions, too. Make several of these at a time to keep ahead of your card-making for every occasion.

TIP

Use yellow cardstock and green ink for a gender-neutral invitation.

What you'll Need

Stamps*

• Baby bottle stamp
• "You're Invited" stamp
• Little gift stamp

Materials

• Box template (page 109)
• Pink or blue cardstock
• White cardstock
• Dye inks, various colors
• Pink or blue paint pen
• Pencil
• Stylus
• Double-stick tape
• Craft scissors

*See Resource Guide for stamp credits.

1. Cut Out Template
Enlarge and cut out the box template on page 109. Trace the template with a pencil on the pink or blue cardstock.

2. Score and Cut Box
Score with a stylus where the folds will be, and cut out the box with craft scissors.

3. Ink and Stamp Bottle Image
Ink the baby bottle stamp with colored dye ink and stamp randomly onto the box. Set aside.

4. Decorate Inside of Card
Cut out a piece of white cardstock to the size of the inside of the box, about 5½" x 4¼" (14cm x 10.8cm). Ink the "You're Invited," baby bottle and little gift stamps with various colored dye inks and stamp onto the white cardstock. Outline the edges with a pink or blue paint pen.

5. Adhere Cardstock to Inside of Box
Adhere the white cardstock to the inside back panel of the box with double-stick tape.

6. Close Box
To close the box, fold the flaps inward beginning with the top and bottom, then the left and right. Tuck the flaps under to secure.

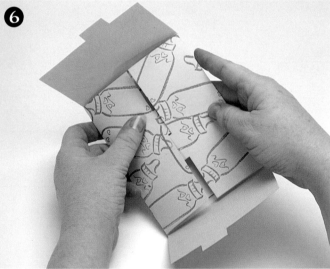

Enlarge template to 167%.

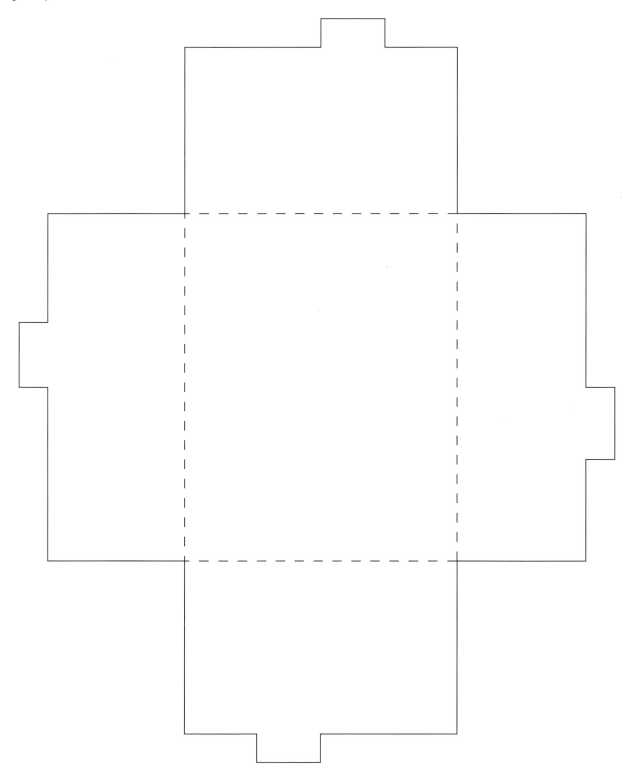

SWEET CELEBRATION

translucent vellum is still the easiest way to add elegance to any card. The variety of colors and patterns available in most craft stores makes it easy to create the ultimate individual look. Choose colors and prints that remind you of the birthday girl or boy and find wrapping paper to coordinate!

What you'll Need

Stamps*

- "Happy Birthday" stamp
- Birthday cake stamp

Materials

- 2 pieces of decorative paper
- Turquoise vellum
- Folded white greeting card
- Silver dye ink
- Purple dye ink
- Double-stick tape
- Craft scissors

See Resource Guide for stamp credits.

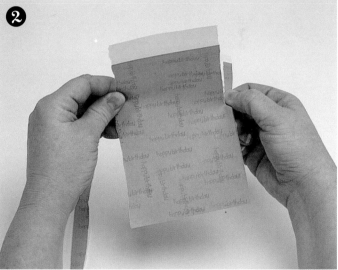

1. Ink and Stamp "Happy Birthday"
Ink the "Happy Birthday" stamp with purple dye ink and stamp randomly onto turquoise Xyroned vellum. (Running vellum through a Xyron machine will add a sticky coating to one side.)

2. Tear Vellum
Tear the edges of the stamped vellum on both sides.

3. Adhere Decorative Paper
Using double-stick tape, adhere a 3" (7.6cm) square piece of decorative paper diagonally onto the front of a folded white greeting card.

4. Adhere Vellum to Greeting Card
Cover the entire front of the greeting card with the stamped vellum.

5. Ink Cake Image
Ink a birthday cake stamp with silver dye ink.

NOTE: When using a triple stamp pad as shown, ink only one cake image.

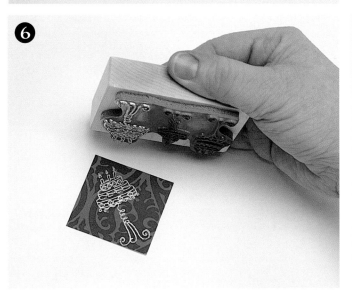

6. Stamp Cake Image onto Decorative Paper
Cut out another square of decorative paper measuring 2" (5cm) square. Stamp the cake image in the center of the square.

7. Adhere Decorative Paper to Card
Using double-stick tape, adhere the small square over the vellum on the greeting card, positioning it diagonally over the larger square. Trim the bottom of the card as necessary.

MORE BRIGHT IDEAS

Beautiful Greenery

The layered squares of paper in this card add such elegance, your loved ones will never know how easy it is to make. Choose decorative paper in matching shades, or use the scrap paper you have saved from other projects.

Colors of Fall

Using paper with different patterns and textures will make your cards more interesting and fun. Vary the shapes of the paper as well. Here, the circle among all the squares really sets off the simple leaf.

COMFY AND COZY

masking can be so impressive when done well—and Eclipse tape makes it super simple. Look for stamps with open areas, like this overstuffed couch, so you can use all your favorite small designs to decorate the fabric.

TIP

Creating a plaid pattern with a word stamp is easy. Stamp the words so they run both horizontally and vertically and use varying amounts of ink on the stamp to create light and dark lines.

What you'll Need

Stamps*

- Comfy chair stamp
- "Thank You" stamp

Materials

- Folded white greeting card
- Dye ink, various bright colors
- Black solvent ink
- Orange paint pen
- Eclipse tape
- Craft knife

*See Resource Guide for stamp credits.

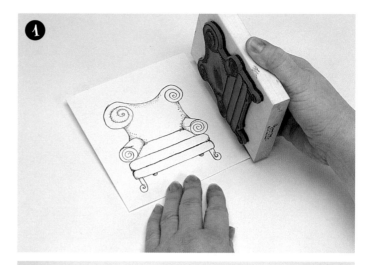

1. Ink and Stamp Chair Image

Ink the comfy chair stamp with black solvent ink and stamp onto a folded white greeting card.

2. Roll Eclipse Tape Over Stamp

Ink the stamp again and roll Eclipse tape over it to transfer the image.

3. Cut Out Chair Image

Cut out the chair image from the Eclipse tape with a craft knife. You will be left with an outline of the chair, which will be your mortise mask. (For more information on masking, see page 21.)

NOTE: Save the chair cut-out to use as a regular mask on another card.

4. Cut Mask in Two Pieces
Cut the mortise mask into two pieces. This will make it easier to work with.

5. Apply Mask and Stamp "Thank You"
Apply the mask around the chair image on the greeting card. Ink the "Thank You" stamp with various colors of dye ink and stamp it horizontally and vertically onto the greeting card. Remove the mask.

6. Mask Inside of Greeting Card
Cut out another piece of Eclipse tape and stick it to the inside of the greeting card, masking all but the far right edge.

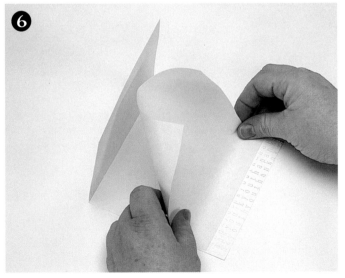

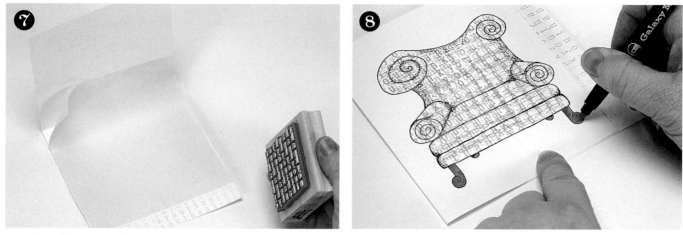

7. Ink and Stamp "Thank You"

Ink the "Thank You" stamp with various colors of dye ink and stamp the inside edge of the greeting card. Remove the mask and trim the front of the greeting card along the right-hand side so that the inside edge is visable.

8. Color Chair Feet

Color the feet of the chair with an orange paint pen.

MORE BRIGHT IDEAS

Have a Seat

Use the regular and mortise chair masks to create cards with different patterns and colors on the chair and walls. If you plan to apply the masks over and over, I suggest using a heavier paper, as it will hold up to more wear and tear.

COCKTAILS, ANYONE?

dusting metal pigments over wet pigment ink can give a card an elegant, matte metal look. When combined with an array of whimsical stamps, this card is the perfect mix of sophistication and fun. Metal pigments are a bit more difficult to find, but well worth the effort. They truly look like foil leaf and are usable with any type of pigment ink.

TIP

Keep the metal dust under control with a lint roller. Simply roll over the metallic area of the finished card to pick up any remaining dust. I use lint rollers for cleaning up glitter and other dry pigments as well.

What you'll Need

Stamps*

• Cocktails stamp
• Filler drink stamp

Materials

• Green cardstock
• Silver cardstock
• Folded silver greeting card
• Black pigment ink
• Gold pigment powder
• Spray fixative
• Paper cord
• Soft brush
• Pencil
• Double-stick tape
• Craft scissors

*See Resource Guide for stamp credits.

1. Ink and Stamp Cocktails

Ink the cocktails stamp with black pigment ink and stamp it onto green cardstock.

2. Fill in Blank Spaces

Use a filler drink stamp to stamp in the blank spaces.

3. Apply Pigment Powder

Use a soft brush to dust the card with gold pigment powder. The powder will adhere to the wet ink.

[119]

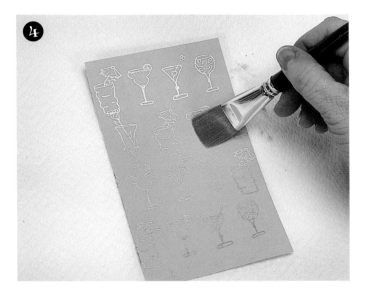

4. Remove Excess Powder
Wipe away the excess powder.

5. Apply Fixative
Spray the entire card with fixative (I used Krylon Spray Workable Fixative) to prevent smudging and protect the card from the elements.

6. Adhere Cardstock to Greeting Card
Trim the green cardstock and adhere to the front of a folded silver greeting card with double-stick tape.

7. Stamp and Adhere Image
Stamp one of the images from the cocktails stamp onto a small scrap of green cardstock. Trim around the edges of the image and adhere it to a slightly larger square of silver cardstock with double-stick tape. Trim again as needed.

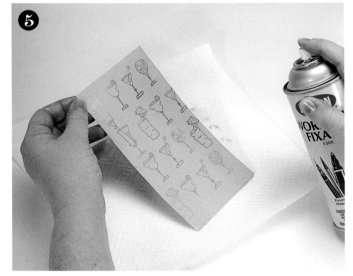

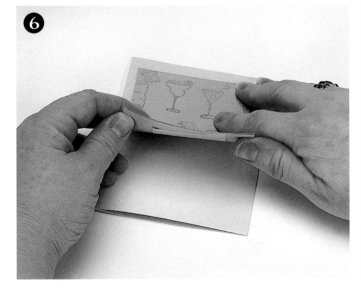

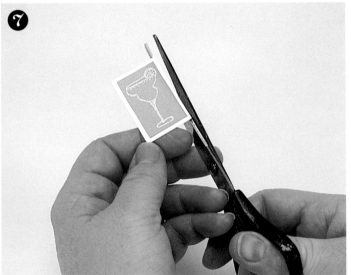

8. Adhere Silver Cardstock

Adhere the small square of silver cardstock to the center of the green cardstock.

9. Add Cord

Add a paper cord to the card and knot at the top.

10. Curl Cord Ends

Curl the ends of the cord with a pencil.

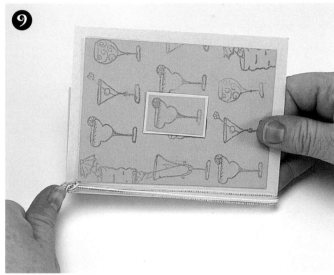

HOME SWEET HOME

When you need to whip up a quick housewarming or hostess card, this is the design for you. Choose stamps with crisp geometric edges to keep this card simple. These house stamps are just the ticket! With a little creative cutting, the colors seem to shine right through the windows.

TIP

To prevent light colors from getting muddy, use the dye stamp pads in order from lightest to darkest.

What you'll Need

Stamps*

* House stamp
* "Party" stamp

Materials

* Folded white greeting card
* Black solvent ink
* Dye ink, various bright colors
* Black permanent marker
* Eclipse tape
* Craft knife
* Ruler

See Resource Guide for stamp credits.

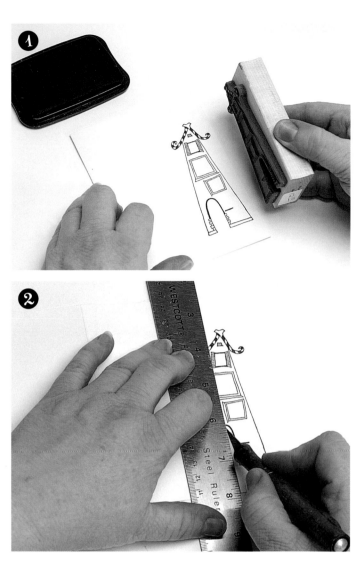

1. Ink and Stamp House Image
Ink the house stamp with black solvent ink and stamp the image onto the right-hand edge of a folded white greeting card.

2. Cut Through House
Open the card and lay it out flat. Using the straight edge of the ruler and a craft knife, cut a border through the house, taking care not to detatch the house from the front of the card.

3. Cut Out Windows and Door
Cut out the windows, door and around the right side of the house. The house becomes the right-hand border of the card.

4. Outline Edges

Outline the edges of the house image with black permanent marker.

5. Mask Inside of Card and Stamp with Inkpads

Mask off the inside of the card with Eclipse tape, exposing only the far right edge. Stamp the edge with dye inkpads in varying colors. Remove the mask and allow the ink to dry.

6. Ink and Stamp "Party"

Mask off the front of the card, exposing only the bottom edge. Ink the "Party" stamp with brightly colored dye inks and stamp along the bottom of the card.

7. Add Finishing Touch

To finish the card, use a ruler and black permanent marker to draw a line above the "Party" stamps.

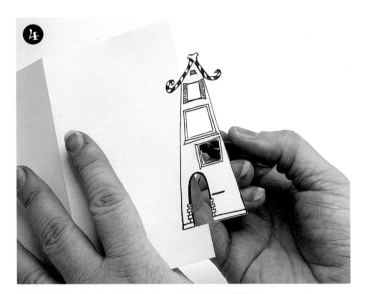

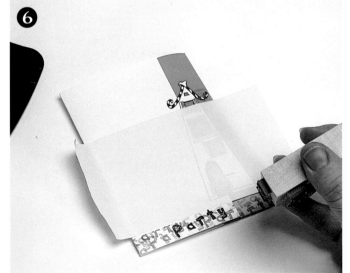

More Bright Ideas

Cut It Out

Stamping the gift image at playful angles makes for a terrific edge for the cut-out. I created the colored background first, then stamped the gift boxes and colored them to complement the background that shows through.

'Tis the Season

Making fancy edges along the side of a card is much easier than it looks. Here, I stamped red and green inkpads and silver stars on the inside edge and colored in the house stamp with markers.

Resources

Stamp Suppliers

American Art Stamp
3870 Del Amo Blvd.
Suite 501
Torrance, CA 90503
Phone: (310) 371-6593
www.americanstamp.com
• Stamps used: Present; Little gift;
"You're Invited"; Triple hearts; Lamps;
Chinese lantern; Dress; "Happy
Valentine's Day"; Birthday cake; "Happy
Birthday"; Cocktails; "Party"

Art Gone Wild
3110 Payne Ave.
Cleveland, OH 44114
Phone: (800) 945-3980
www.agwstamps.com
• Stamps used: Box template

DeNami Design
P.O. Box 5617
Kent, WA 98064
Phone: (253) 437-1626
www.denamidesign.com
• Stamps used: Baby bottle

Earth Tone Images
56 E. Lancaster Ave.
Ardmore, PA 19003
Phone: (610) 645-6500
www.earthtoneimages.com
• Stamps used: Handprint

Judi-Kins
17803 S. Harvard Blve.
Gardena, CA 90248
Phone: (310) 515-1115
www.judikins.com
• Stamps used: Leaves and butterfly;
Swirl: Funky swirl; Fall leaves; Star;
Harlequin background; Ballerina; Nile
flowers stained glass; Primitive flower;
Minstrel; Retro circle; Mini squares; Polka
dots

paula best and co.
507 Trail Dr.
Moss Landing, CA 95039
Phone: (831) 632-0587
www.paulabest.com
• Stamps used: Menorah

Postmodern Design
P.O. Box 720416
Norman, OK 73070
• Stamps used: David; Boy and girl;
Molly's face

Post Script Studio/Carmen's Veranda
P.O. Box 1539
Placentia, CA 92871
www.postscriptstudio.com
• Stamps used: Shrine; Marshmallow
bunny

River City Rubber Works
5555 S. Meridian
Wichita, KS 67217
Phone: (877) 735-2276
www.rivercityrubberworks.com
• Stamps used: Leaf

Rubbermoon
P.O. Box 3258
Hayden Lake, ID 83835
(208) 772-9772
www.rubbermoon.com
• Stamps used: Pumpkin head;
Pumpkins; House; Christmas house;
Little bird

Stamper's Anonymous
Williamsburg Square
25967 Detroit Rd.
Westlake, OH 44145
Phone: (888) 326-0012
www.stampersanonymous.com
• Stamps used: Large frame stamp;
Small frame stamp

Stampotique
9822 North 7th St.
Suite 7
Phoenix, AZ 85020
Phone: (602) 862-0237
www.stampotique.com
• Stamps used: Little big head; Comfy
chair; "Thank You"

Other Suppliers

American Crafts
165 N. 1330 W. B3
Orem, UT 84057
Phone: (800) 879-5185
www.americancrafts.com
• Galaxy markers and gel pens

Amy's Magic Leaf
173 Main St.
West Leechburg, PA 15656
Phone: (724) 845-1748
• Paper Foil Ephemera

Coffee Break Design
P.O. Box 34281
Indianapolis, IN 46234
Fax: (800) 229-1824
• Eyelets

Colorbox
P.O. Box 98
Anacortes, WA 98821
Phone: (888) 448-4862
www.clearsnap.com
• Inks

Envelopes Please
9685 Kenwood Rd
Cincinnati OH 45242
Phone: (513) 793-4558
www.stampawayusa.com
• Templates

Golden Paints
188 Bell Road
New Berlin, NY 13411
Phone: (607) 847-6154
www.goldenpaints.com
• Acrylic paints

Jacquard
540 Lake Cook Rd.
Suite 160
Deerfield, IL 60015-5604
Phone: (847) 945-8700
www.jacquard.com
• PearlEx powdered pigments

Magenta
• Pewter stickers, printed papers

Marvy Uchida
3535 Del Amo Blvd.
Torrance, CA 90503
Phone: (800) 541-5877
www.uchida.com
• Inks

On the Surface
P.O. Box 8026
Wilmette, IL 60091
Phone: (847) 675-2521
• Threads and fibers

Really Reasonable Ribbon
P.O. Box 199
Sugar Loaf, NY 10981
www.reasonableribbon.com
• Ribbons

Speedball Art Products Company
2226 Speedball Rd.
Statesville, NC 28677
Phone: (800) 898-7224
www.speedballart.com
• Carving supplies

Suzi Finer Artworks & Artware
238 S. Robertson Blvd
Beverly Hills, CA 90211
Phone: (310) 360-1800
www.suzifiner.com
• Pewter stickers

Tsukineko, Inc
17640 N.E. 65th St.
Redmond, WA 98052
Phone: (800) 769-6633
www.tsukineko.com
• Inks

USArtquest
7800 Ann Arbor
Grass Lake, MI 49240
Phone: (517) 522-6225
www.usartquest.com
• Pinata inks

Bead and Button
page 245

Sisters
page 245

VINTAGE GREETING CARDS
WITH MARYJO MCGRAW

VINTAGE
GREETING CARDS
WITH MARYJO MCGRAW

NORTH LIGHT BOOKS
Cincinnati, Ohio

WWW.ARTISTSNETWORK.COM

table of contents

GETTING THE VINTAGE LOOK!

pg. 144

The look of heirloom papers, photos and

ephemera has always held a certain fascination for me.

There is no time better spent than a day rummaging through antique

stores or flea markets searching for the odd embellishment

or antique photograph.

After years of collecting, I have quite a nice stash. The problem is

I never want to use the actual vintage items unless I have a huge

collection of them. So I try to use tricks, techniques and a color

copier or scanner to fool the eye of the card's recipient into thinking

the items are the real thing.

In this book I have recreated the look I love, using items old and

new, including ribbons, rickrack, buttons and my family's old photos

(along with products that can alter their appearance).

I HOPE YOU'LL ENJOY MAKING A FEW OF THESE

CARDS YOURSELF.

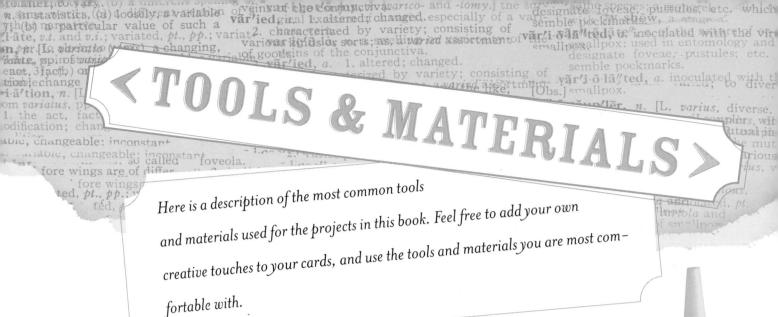

< TOOLS & MATERIALS >

Here is a description of the most common tools and materials used for the projects in this book. Feel free to add your own creative touches to your cards, and use the tools and materials you are most comfortable with.

PAPER

Always search out the best quality paper for your cards and projects. Paper is the first item that gets noticed on a greeting card, and if it is flimsy or feels cheap it reflects on you. For greeting cards in particular I prefer heavyweight cardstock.

In the paper world there are coated and uncoated stocks, and both have their place in card making. Coated stocks are generally smooth to the touch and can be glossy or smooth. There are even pearlized and shimmering coated cardstocks. Inks and paints tend to sit on the surface of these papers making it difficult to use pigment inks that need to dry by absorbing into the paper. Uncoated cardstock has a more toothy feel that inks and paints sink into. A beautiful watercolor paper is the perfect example of uncoated paper.

For a truly vintage-looking greeting, I like a heavy uncoated ivory cardstock. For cards that have a vintage flavor, I have used papers in heirloom colors that are both coated and uncoated.

TRANSLUCENT VELLUM

Translucent vellum is a sheer paper that is now available in many weights and colors. It has a matte feel and an elegant appearance. Translucent vellum also comes in ready-made envelopes, which are perfect for vintage greetings.

Another type of paper with a similar look to vellum is glassine, which is a waxy sheer paper. Glassine comes in several colors and is also available in many envelope sizes. There is also a variety of plastic papers that have a similar look but feel slick and are more modern looking.

ADHESIVES & MEDIUMS

Today there are many types of adhesives available, from old-fashioned pastes to new polymer mediums. In this book I have used several kinds.

DIAMOND GLAZE

Diamond Glaze is perhaps my favorite adhesive/medium. It can be used as a basic glue for paper when brushed on thin or as a heavy adhesive for three-dimensional embellishments. Since it is clear it is also excellent for shiny non-porous surfaces like mica tiles, acetate, beads and glitters. Diamond Glaze can also be used as a fixative over chalk and watercolor paint and crayons or it can create a vinyl look by simply brushing it evenly on paper or tissue. Finally it can be mixed with a huge array of inks, paints and dyes.

OMNI GEL

An excellent medium, Omni Gel is made specifically for photo transfers onto paper, fabric, metal, glass, leather and wood. It is also a great adhesive for heavy materials and is exceptionally good for non-porous items.

Diamond Glaze

MICROGLAZE

This super-fine wax is excellent as a fixative for many surfaces, including paper, polymer clays, leather and many mixed media projects. It can also be mixed with powdered pigments and buffed into surfaces such as paper. Since it leaves no oil ring on paper, it is a great resist wax to hold back paints and inks. The excess can be buffed away once the color has dried.

GEL MEDIUMS

Golden molding pastes, heavy or solid gels, and soft gels can be used on cards to change the textures and weight of paper, cardstock or chipboard. These mediums are created to be used with paints, inks and other colorants. They can often be used as an adhesive in collage projects and can be especially good at holding three-dimensional pieces on paper. Gel mediums can also be used to transfer color copies from paper to other surfaces as well.

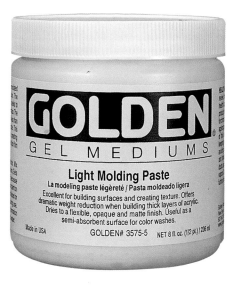

Molding Paste

DOUBLESTICK TAPES

Doublestick tapes are invaluable card-making accessories. A double-sided paper-lined tape is what I use on most projects since it can be torn and cut into usual shapes and sizes. There are several brands of clear doublestick tape that I keep on hand for projects that are sheer (like vellum). I also keep repositionable tape ready for those times when you could use an extra hand.

BEESWAX

Different types of wax have long been used as adhesives. You can brush melted beeswax over pictures and artwork to adhere and protect the surface. Once the wax has set, it can be scraped to any thickness and even buffed to a soft sheen. While the wax is warm, try stamping images into the surface to create decorative patterns. Embellishment items added to the hot wax create added texture. Remember to be very careful when using beeswax, so you don't burn yourself.

POLYMER CLAY

Polymer clays are great for paper projects since they are lightweight and can be rolled very thin. Polymer clays can be sanded and even trimmed with scissors when rolled thin. There are many types of polymer clays and all will work for these projects with slightly varied results. I prefer Premo for my projects because it remains slightly flexible and does not become brittle over time.

ANTIQUING & STAINING MEDIUMS

To achieve a vintage look, there are several mediums available.

WALNUT INK

This ink is especially good for antique coloring since it is a rich cocoa brown. Walnut ink comes in two varieties: liquid and crystals. I prefer the crystals since they allow a wider range of looks. The amount of hot water added to the crystals alters the depth of color from a deep dark stain to a pale watercolor-like effect. The crystals themselves can be sprinkled on wet paper for interesting effects as well.

There are imitation walnut inks on the market that are made from peat instead of walnut. This ink also has a unique look, but has a bit of a greenish tint rather than the true brown of the real walnut ink.

SHOE POLISH

A great antiquing medium for the vintage look is shoe polish. Shoe polish is still around in many forms. In this book I use the old-fashioned paste wax polishes that come in a few colors as well as neutral, which is excellent for resist techniques. Creme shoe polish can also be used, but the color is more intense, so start slowly on a test patch and use less.

GOLDEN FLUID ACRYLICS

These are the perfect acrylics to use on paper. They are quick drying and translucent, and do not warp the paper surface like heavier acrylic products. These paints can be dry-brushed onto paper to create beautiful backgrounds. They are also excellent for staining surfaces. Fluid acrylics come in a huge array of colors and can be mixed with any mediums.

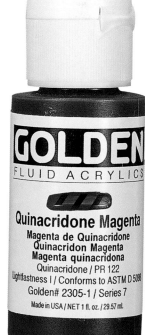

Fluid Acrylics

Japanese Screw Punch

TOOLS

There are several tools that will be helpful when making your vintage greeting cards.

BONE FOLDER

A bone folder is a book-binding tool used to score and crease papers. It is a smooth tool shaped like a letter opener and made out of bone (hence the name), wood or resin.

CRAFT KNIFE

A craft knife is one of the most important tools in a card maker's kit. I still refer to what is known as a No. 11 size knife with a soft grip handle, but there are many styles available today including retractable pen knives, which are very safe. Change the blades often to ensure clean and easy cutting.

JAPANESE SCREW PUNCH

This wonderful tool is technically a bookbinder's instrument that fits well in any paper fanatic's kit. With it you can punch various-size holes in any paper, leather, clay or even thin metal surface. This amazing tool will punch through many layers at a time, which is why bookbinders love it!

I use this on all projects where I need to punch through several layers at once. There are punches that can be hammered through several layers, and on some surfaces a regular handheld hole punch will work.

INKS & APPLICATORS

Vintage doesn't have to mean brown. There are a wide range of inks and applicators that make it easy to add color.

PIÑATA COLORS

Piñata Colors are very pigmented alcohol inks that leave brilliant color on non-porous surfaces. These inks come in a great range of color, are inexpensive and are perfect on three-dimensional embellishment items like buttons, mica, hardware and more. These inks can be used to color acetate as well.

Piñata Color

CLARO EXTENDER

This extender is specifically made for extending alcohol ink without diluting the color.

COLOR DUSTERS

Mini stippling brushes for paints, pastel chalks, inks and more, Color Dusters are a great inexpensive tool for applications of all kinds on paper.

LEAFING PENS

Leafing pens come in a variety of colors, including gold, copper and silver. These particular pens are an excellent way to edge, touch up and decorate paper, mica tiles, foil ephemera, beads, buttons and much more. Leafing pens work on paper, cardstock, cardboard and non-porous surfaces, and when several layers are applied, it truly looks like metal. Other types of paint pens will do an effective job but will not have the same rich look.

Color Dusters

Leafing Pen

CARD EMBELLISHMENTS

Be creative when embellishing your cards. Everyday items found in a junk drawer can make terrific add-ons to cards. Here are some of my favorite embellishments.

SMALL HARDWARE

Many small hardware items, such as eyelets, solid heads, brads and typewriter key frames, have become widely available in paper, scrapbook and stamp stores, as well as local chain craft stores. I especially like the very tiny brass brads. The notions department in sewing stores is also a good area to check for these and other small embellishment items.

Many of these metal items can be attached to paper with a small hammer and a setting tool. In the case of the typewriter key frames, a small hammer is all you will need.

Paper Foil Ephemera

MICA TILES, CHIPS AND GLITTER

Mica is an iridescent mineral that can be pulled apart into thin sheets. These sheets can be used for almost any application where acetate is used to add a vintage look to many surfaces. When cut down into chips or glitter, mica gives an antique look over paper, wax or other media that are preferred over standard mylar glitters.

PAPER FOIL EPHEMERA

Antique embossed foil papers can be difficult to come by. Luckily there are companies now that replicate the look for a decent price. Be careful when using foil ephemera, as the embossing laminates several pieces tightly together. Slowly pull apart the layers because this paper is easily torn.

Mica Tiles

Miscellaneous Embellishments

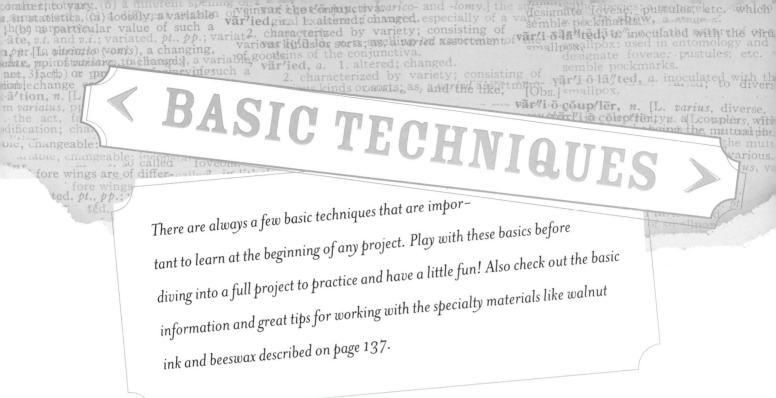

There are always a few basic techniques that are important to learn at the beginning of any project. Play with these basics before diving into a full project to practice and have a little fun! Also check out the basic information and great tips for working with the specialty materials like walnut ink and beeswax described on page 137.

STAMPING BASICS

There are three basic types of inks: pigment, dye and solvent. All three are used in this book. As a simple rule of thumb, here is how each works: Dye ink dries through evaporation on porous surfaces like paper. It fades over time in most cases.

Pigment dries by absorption and in some cases by heat. Pigment is a thicker, more opaque ink than the other types.

Solvents are made to dry on all surfaces, porous or non-porous. Solvents are transparent in appearance, much like dyes. In this book a particular ink is specified for each project.

The majority of ink pads in use today are the raised surface type. These are easiest to ink properly since the ink pad is applied to a rubber stamp. Old-fashioned pads are made of felt and covered in linen.

STEP ONE
Ink the stamp.

STEP TWO
Press the stamp to the paper using firm and even pressure, then lift.

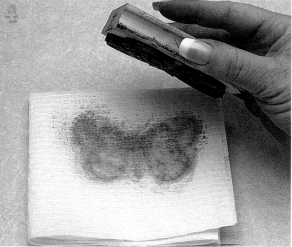

STEP THREE

Clean your stamp with a good strong cleaner. A good cleaner will have a conditioning agent in it to keep the stamp surface soft and pliable. You can also use products like baby wipes or window cleaners to clean the stamp, but they will not condition it. I prefer a solvent-type cleaner with a conditioner since it will remove all types of ink and paint.

STEP FOUR

After applying the cleaner, allow it to penetrate the surface. Wipe the surface of the stamp well with a paper towel or an old terry cloth towel.

SPECIALTY INKS

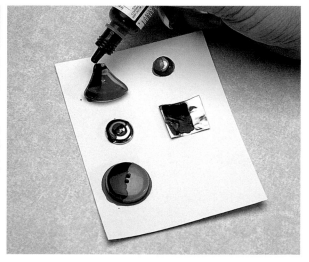

WALNUT INK

In this book, to achieve a vintage look on many of the projects, I have used walnut ink. This ink has a look that is not easily duplicated with other inks or paints. It is available in liquid or granular crystal form. The liquid is usually a medium-strength color, which can be diluted. The granular form is what I prefer since it can be adjusted to any strength with hot water, or used as a powder on wet surfaces.

PIÑATA COLOR

Piñata Color is an alcohol-based (solvent-based) ink that can be applied to a huge array of surfaces including glass, paper, polymer clay, plastics, mica and metals. Simply add a drop of this ink to a button or plastic bead. It can also be brushed like paint on larger surfaces.

SETTING EYELETS

Eyelets create a professional look to cards and paper projects if they are set correctly. The right setting tool is the key. Look for a setter with a nipple end rather than the widely used cone shape. Use as small a hammer as you can find. A heavier hammer can apply too much pressure and smash the eyelet.

STEP ONE

Using a screw punch, awl or tiny hole punch, punch a hole for the eyelet. Check for the correct size of punch for the eyelets chosen.

STEP TWO

Insert the eyelet into the hole.

STEP THREE

Turn over the piece and insert the setting tool into the eyelet.

STEP FOUR

With the setting tool in place, tap evenly and firmly a few times with a small hammer.

Remove the setting tool, and with the hammer, tighten and finish the back of the eyelet with a few light taps.

8 percent yellow screen

COLOR-COPYING PHOTOS

All of the vintage photos in this book have been color copied using carbon-based toner. In many cases your scanner will work for simple projects that are only to be cut out and glued on a surface. For the projects that require the photo to be transferred from paper to a different type of surface, carbon-based copies must be used. Most good office supply stores and many printers can do the job for you. I have all my photos copied onto large paper that I can store for later use.

Black-and-white photos tend to have a gray appearance when simply copied as is. I usually ask for an 8 to 10 percent yellow screen to be added over the photo to give it some warmth. A good professional can help with this. You can also scan the photos at home and adjust the color to your liking on the computer before taking them to be copied.

10 percent yellow screen

12 percent yellow screen

This is the how-to part of the book

containing 23 step-by-step cards, featuring

a vintage look or antique quality created with a

few simple techniques and plenty of fun embell-

ishments. I have used a variety of materials, and most

are available at your local art, craft, hardware,

stamp or scrapbook store. Many of the embellish-

ment items are from my own collection, and I am sure you have a

similar stash of your own in a shoe box somewhere.

If you are just starting out collecting, look in antique, thrift

and junk stores as well as online and at garage sales.

I am exceptionally lucky finding sewing notions! Always buy the

whole sewing, hat or shoe box full of goodies and keep an eye out for

the stuffed grab bag. You certainly do not need the exact

embellishment items to complete these projects. Substitute

anything of a similar size, shape or texture.

USE THOSE IDEAS THAT POP INTO YOUR HEAD
WHILE CREATING—AFTER ALL IT'S ONLY
PAPER!

MATERIALS LIST

- copy of black-and-white photograph
- stiff brush (stencil or stippling brush)
- brown shoe polish
- paper towels
- two bamboo paper clips (online or in many stamp stores)
- doublestick tape
- complementary paper
- word stamp
- black ink
- dark folded cardstock

POINT OF ORIGIN

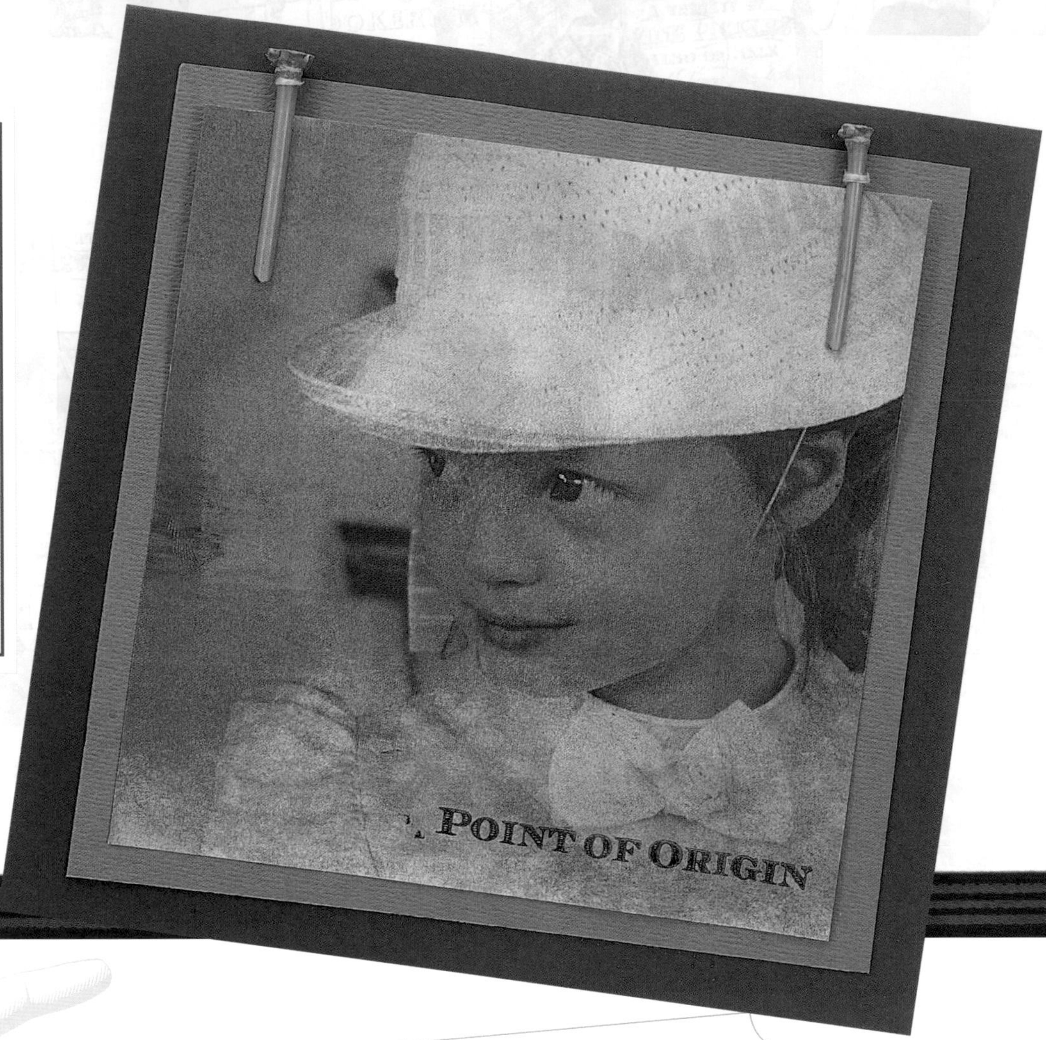

Aging and protecting color copies of favorite photos is simple using this shoe polish technique. Old-fashioned paste shoe polish is especially effective because it is a light buffing wax with a small amount of colored pigment. I apply it to black-and-white copies, yet it can also be used to age a wide array of paper products. Always test a small patch to see the effect on different weights and textures of papers.

TECHNIQUE:
Shoe Polish Overlay

CREATIVE MATERIAL:
bamboo clips

< POINT OF ORIGIN >

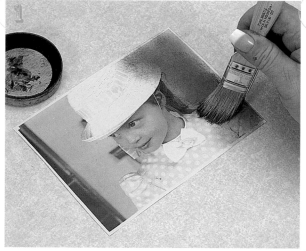

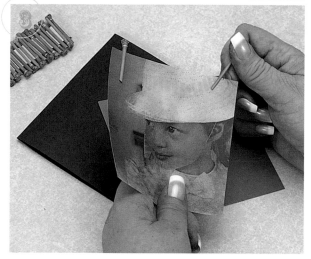

STEP ONE

This is a black-and-white photo that has been copied on the standard setting. Using a quick up-and-down motion with a stiff brush, apply a small amount of brown shoe polish to the photo. A stippling or stencil brush is perfect for this technique.

STEP TWO

Once the copy is completely covered with polish, buff and blend the polish with your fingers or a paper towel.

STEP THREE

For a bit of embellishment I added two bamboo paper clips to the top of the piece. Secure the clips with a piece of doublestick tape.

TIP

THE LONGER THE
SHOE POLISH IS LEFT
ON BEFORE BUFFING,
THE DARKER THE
ANTIQUING WILL BE.

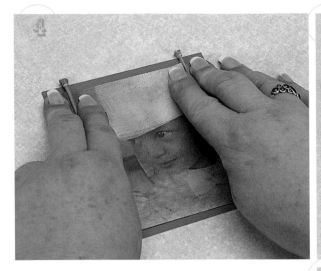

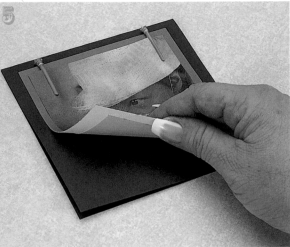

TIP

☞

USE WORDS CUT FROM

A THRIFT STORE

BOOK OR DICTIONARY

INSTEAD OF A STAMP.

STEP FOUR

Using a bit more doublestick tape, apply the copy to a layer of complementary paper.

STEP FIVE

Apply doublestick tape to the back of the piece, then center on dark folded cardstock.

STEP SIX

Stamp a word or two along the bottom of the copy in black ink.

Martini Time

The removable border band holds the card together. The band is easy to make using doublestick tape for an adhesive. The tape also makes it easy to remove the band and open the card.

To protect color copies apply a thin layer of neutral shoe polish then buff away the excess. This waterproofs as well.

< V I P >

Walnut ink is another easy way to antique paper and other porous surfaces. This ink has a very rich color quality that is hard to duplicate with other inks or paints. While it is not widely available, it is easily found through specialty stamp and calligraphy stores, the Internet and mail-order art supply houses. I prefer the granules to premixed liquid, since the granules can be mixed in different strengths or used by themselves on wet surfaces.

TECHNIQUE:
Walnut Ink

CREATIVE MATERIALS:
ticket stub, game pieces, rickrack

MATERIALS LIST
- walnut ink
- soft brush
- scrap paper
- spray water bottle
- watercolor paper
- yellow or gold folded cardstock
- rickrack
- paper towels
- color-copied photo (or scanned photo)
- photo corners
- doublestick tape
- old ticket stub
- game pieces
- Diamond Glaze (or epoxy or super glue)

ADMIT ONE
To The Hulman Terrace.

ADMIT ONE
To The Grounds

V I P

STEP ONE

Mix up three small dishes of walnut ink in varied strengths. (Steps 1–5 show how to vary the ink strength. You will need a very deep brown, a medium brown and a light brown for the card.) Place one teaspoon of the granules into a small glass dish.

STEP TWO

Add in two teaspoons of hot water and mix until dissolved.

STEP THREE

Using a piece of scrap paper, apply a very deep brown mixture of walnut ink to the paper.

TIP

IF YOU DON'T WANT TO CREATE OR STORE SEVERAL SHADES OF INK, START WITH A LIGHT MIXTURE AND LAYER THE INK, WAITING FOR EACH LAYER TO DRY BEFORE APPLYING THE NEXT.

TIP
☞

CONTINUE IN THIS FASHION
UNTIL YOU HAVE ACHIEVED THE
TONES OF INK THAT YOU LIKE.
ALL OF THE INK CAN BE SAVED
AND STORED IN AIRTIGHT
BOTTLES OR JARS. MARK EACH
WITH A LABEL COLORED WITH
THE INK INSIDE.

STEP FOUR

Spray the walnut ink with plain water while it is still wet to lighten it. Set aside to dry.

STEP FIVE

Add two teaspoons more of the hot water for a weaker solution.

STEP SIX

Once you have made the three strengths of ink, use a soft brush to spread a medium mixture of walnut ink onto a piece of watercolor paper. Let dry.

TIP

MUSLIN, RIBBON AND
MOST NATURAL FIBER
CAN BE DYED WITH
WALNUT INK.

STEP SEVEN

Apply a light brown mixture of walnut ink with a soft brush to both sides of a yellow or gold piece of cardstock. The cardstock here is pearlized, which adds interest. Set aside to dry.

STEP EIGHT

I have decided to use rickrack for the trim. It is easy to antique with walnut ink. Dip the trim into the strongest solution of ink.

STEP NINE

Place the trim onto several layers of paper towel. Spray sections of the trim with water to lighten. This will create a more natural aged look. Allow the trim to dry thoroughly.

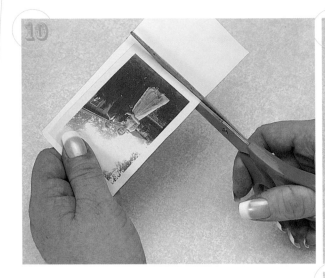

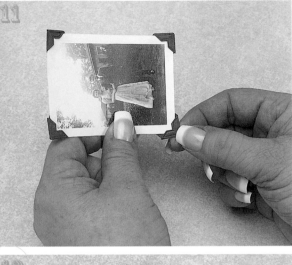

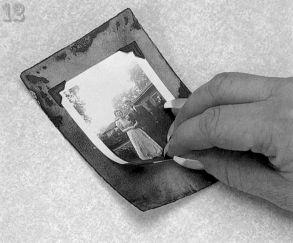

STEP TEN
Trim a color copy or scanned photo leaving a ¼" (6mm) border all the way around the photo.

STEP ELEVEN
Add photo corners to the trimmed photo. Moisten the photo corners with water before adding to the antiqued watercolor paper.

STEP TWELVE
Using doublestick tape, add the photo to the antiqued watercolor paper layer.

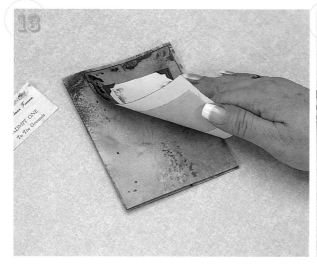

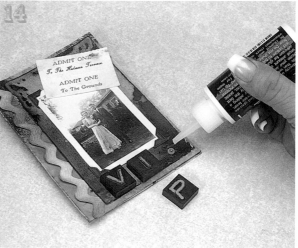

STEP THIRTEEN

*Layer the watercolor paper and photo onto the folded cardstock
(from step 7).*

STEP FOURTEEN

*Add all of the embellishments. Tie on the rickrack. Use double-
stick tape to add the ticket to the front.*

*Glue must be used for the game pieces. Diamond Glaze
takes a while to dry, but it holds heavy items on paper very well.
Epoxy and super glues also will work.*

< SEA GLASS MEMORIES >

Whether you find it on the beach or at the craft store, this is a great way to use a frosty piece of sea glass. Add the sea glass to a walnut ink colored card with an heirloom-looking ribbon and you have a quick and easy card full of memories. The quick addition of a foil embellishment sets off the edges of the sea glass.

TECHNIQUE:
Walnut Ink

CREATIVE MATERIALS:
sea glass, antique-style ribbon

MATERIALS LIST

- color-copied photo
- piece of sea glass
- clear glue
- silver leafing pen
- spray water bottle
- heavy cardstock
  (or watercolor paper)
- walnut ink granules
- stiff brush
- paper towel
- scoring tool
- antique-style ribbon
- gold foil flower

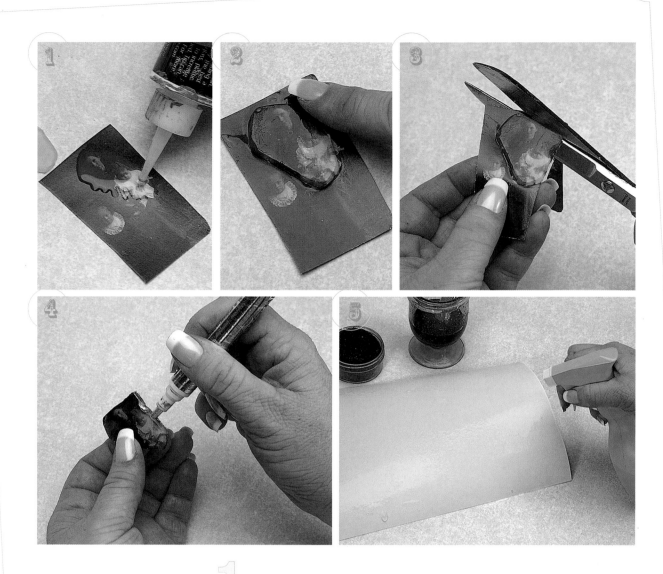

STEP ONE
Glue a color-copied photo to the back of a large piece of sea glass. A clear glue is best.

STEP TWO
To eliminate some of the frosted look so that the picture can be seen, add a drop or two of the same clear glue to the top of the sea glass. Let dry.

STEP THREE
Trim the excess paper from the sea glass.

STEP FOUR
Apply a silver leafing pen to the edges of the glass. Set aside to dry.

STEP FIVE
Spritz plain water on a piece of heavy cardstock or watercolor paper.

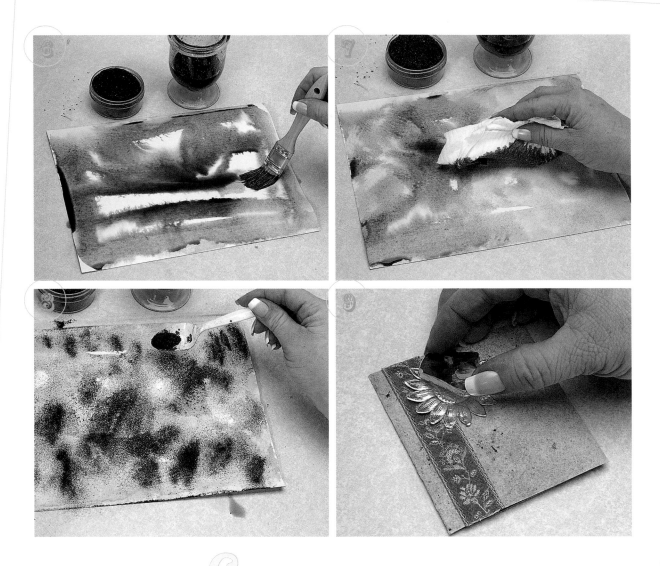

STEP SIX

Using a stiff brush, spread on a medium brown mixture of walnut ink (see pages 151–152 for information on mixing different ink strengths).

STEP SEVEN

Blot sections of the paper with a paper towel. You can also achieve some interesting looks using crunched up plastic instead of a paper towel.

STEP EIGHT

For a speckled look, apply some of the dry granules of walnut ink to any wet spots. Let dry, then brush away any excess granules.

STEP NINE

Cut the cardstock to the desired size. Score and fold. Since this ribbon is very heavy, I used a small amount of glue to adhere it to the cardstock. Use clear glue to position a gold foil flower onto the card, then add the sea glass.

Colored Sea Glass

Foil pieces are easy embellishments. This foil piece was cut in half lengthwise, with space left between the two pieces when glued to the card. The sea glass was placed in the middle of the embellishment.

Triple Threat

Use both light and dark photos to provide contrast. Notice the high contrast between the two lighter pieces with the darker piece in the middle. The white background adds to the intensity and helps show the vintage quality of the photos beneath the glass.

MATERIALS LIST

- rubber stamp and stamp pad (or a color-copied photo)
- cardstock
- MicroGlaze (or a light clear paste wax or a neutral shoe polish)
- walnut ink
- brush
- paper towels
- folded cardstock
- doublestick tape
- rusted metal corners
- clear glue

Using a light clear wax like MicroGlaze, or even a neutral shoe polish, is a great way to keep color in its place. When using the wax-resist technique, it is a good idea to do a test piece just to get the hang of where to apply the wax. Rusted metal accents are perfect embellishments for this monochromatic look.

TECHNIQUE:
Wax Resist

< ANCIENT EDGE >

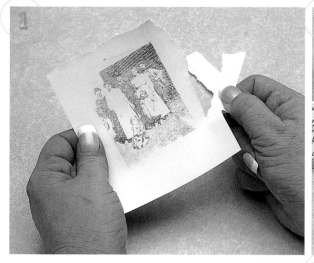

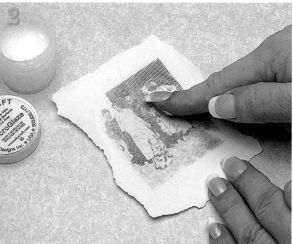

TIP

IF YOU TEAR THE
PAPER TOWARD YOU,
A VERY ROUGH EDGE
REMAINS. FOR A MORE
SMOOTH EDGE, TEAR
THE PAPER AWAY
FROM YOU.

STEP ONE

Photocopy or stamp an image onto cardstock. Tear away the excess paper.

STEP TWO

Apply MicroGlaze to the parts of the copy that are to remain light. Start with a small amount and work it into the surface of the paper.

STEP THREE

Brush on the walnut ink. The rough torn edges pick up more ink and will be much darker.

TIP

RUSTED METAL

EMBELLISHMENTS

ARE AVAILABLE AT

MANY CRAFT, PAPER

AND STAMP STORES.

STEP FOUR

Wipe off the excess ink and wax with a paper towel. Buff the piece again with a clean paper towel.

STEP FIVE

To waterproof, add another thin layer of wax to the whole piece.

STEP SIX

After adhering the piece to folded cardstock with doublestick tape, add rusted metal corners with a small amount of clear glue.

Hats Off

This background is created by using the wax–resist technique on uncoated cream–colored paper. I used thick watercolor paint instead of walnut ink to vary the color. The metal–rimmed tag was dipped in beeswax.

FLUID TIME

There are many types of solvents, including nail polish remover and many kinds of alcohol, that can transfer images from copier paper to cardstock. I like the way this stamp cleaner works. Many solvents and alcohols will not need heat—simply let them dry on their own. When working with solvents, alcohols or even smelly paints and inks, I prefer to be outside so that I do not have to be concerned with ventilation. If you must be indoors, keep the windows open and the fan running!

TECHNIQUE:
Liquid Photo Transfer

CREATIVE MATERIALS:
plastic watch crystal, mica flakes

MATERIALS LIST

- color-copied photos
- coated paper
- stamp cleaner (or nail polish remover or alcohol)
- heat gun (or hair dryer)
- bright-colored ink pad
- rubber stamp
- foil embellishments
- clear glue
- folded cardstock
- doublestick tape
- button
- plastic watch crystal
- assorted Piñata Colors (alcohol inks)
- brush (or sponge)
- Claro Extender
- mica flakes (or glitter)

164

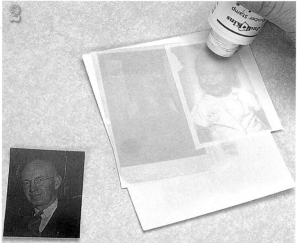

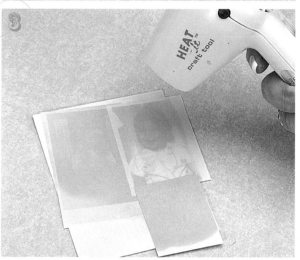

TIP

MANILA SHIPPING
TAGS WORK ESPECIALLY
WELL FOR TRANSFERS
SINCE MANILA IS A
COATED PAPER.

STEP ONE

Choose and trim the color-copied photos. I have found that coated papers tend to work best for transfers, so use a coated cardstock for the card. Float the stamp cleaner completely over the surface of the coated paper.

STEP TWO

Lay the color copies face down into the stamp cleaner on the coated paper, then coat the back of each copy with the stamp cleaner.

STEP THREE

To speed the drying process, use a heat gun or hair dryer.

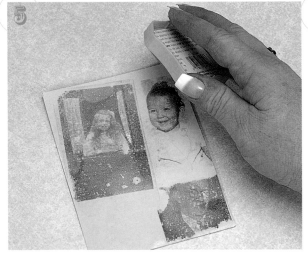

STEP FOUR

Remove the copies as soon as the pieces are dry. Do not let the paper cool or sit too long, as it will become difficult to remove. Afterward the image can be a bit sticky. Simply allow it to dry for a few minutes before moving on.

STEP FIVE

Now that everything has transferred, apply a little color to the paper using a brightly colored ink pad.

STEP SIX

A few stamped images are a nice addition to the open spaces.

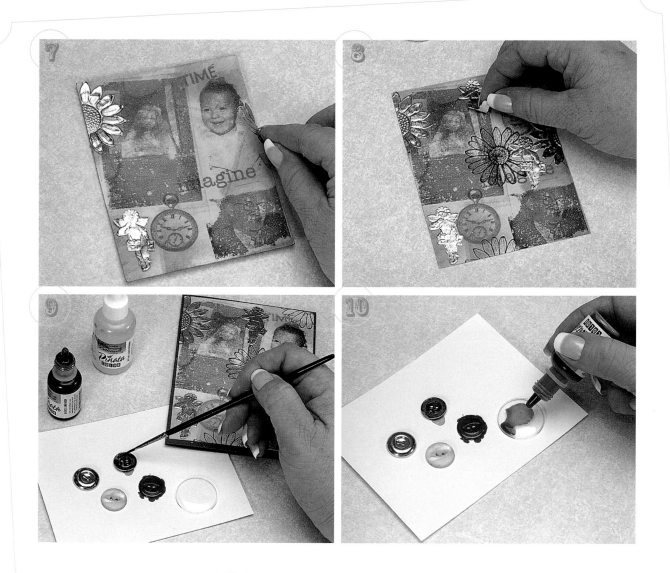

STEP SEVEN

Glue on a few foil embellishments.

STEP EIGHT

Trim the piece as necessary. Add a few more foil pieces, then apply the paper to folded cardstock with doublestick tape.

STEP NINE

There are a couple more embellishments to add: the button and a plastic watch crystal. These knick-knacks needed a color change, though, to fit the look of the card. Piñata Colors (alcohol inks) will color these items quite easily. Just apply a drop and then move it around with a brush or sponge. These inks are vividly colored and will stain your fingers, so always use a brush or sponge to apply.

STEP TEN

Add orange Piñata Color to the watch crystal.

STEP ELEVEN
To lighten the ink in the center of the crystal, add a drop or two of Claro Extender. This will enable the picture beneath to be seen more clearly.

STEP TWELVE
Add a small amount of glue to the rim of the crystal and to each of the buttons.

STEP THIRTEEN
Position all of the three-dimensional embellishments.

STEP FOURTEEN
If there is any glue peeking out, add a few mica flakes or glitter to cover it.

Destination

Monochromatic inks make transferred photos stand out better. A torn paper layer can soften the look of a heavily graphic card design.

Monochrome

Using the card recipient's initials is a nice, personal touch. Corner rounders and punches are excellent embellishment tricks for very large cards.

MATERIALS LIST

- family photos with small faces
- copper washer
- craft knife
- metal stamping alphabet set
- metallic copper-toned paper
- small, heavy hammer
- dark shoe polish
- paper towels
- Diamond Glaze
- ruler
- rust-colored folded cardstock
- Omni Gel (or thick multi-purpose glue that works with metal)
- antique-style ribbon
- old watch face
- tiny face plate

I found some copper washers and thought I would create jewelry with them. Instead one found its way onto this charming card. Copper is a soft metal and is very easy to impress with metal stamps. Copper is also a great metal to patina.

TECHNIQUE:
Stamped Metal

CREATIVE MATERIALS:
copper washer, old watch face, antique-style ribbon, tiny face plate

PRECIOUS

< MEMORY WINDOW >

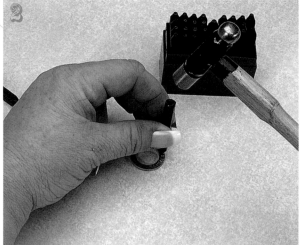

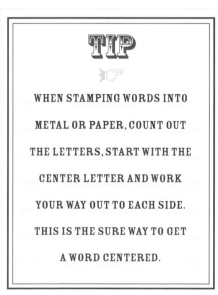

STEP ONE

Look for little heads in family photos, then have them copied onto one sheet. Select one that fits into the center of the washer. Using a craft knife, cut out the head leaving at least ⅛" (3mm) all the way around. Set aside.

STEP TWO

Metal stamping sets are available at many small hardware and stamp stores, and online. This particular one is very tiny. Copper is great to stamp into because it is so soft. Stamp out a word by positioning each letter perpendicular to the surface of the washer. Hit the top of the stamp with a small, heavy hammer. Two or three good strong taps should do the trick.

STEP THREE

Put a small amount of dark shoe polish onto the letters using a craft knife.

> **TIP**
>
> WHEN STAMPING WORDS INTO
> METAL OR PAPER, COUNT OUT
> THE LETTERS, START WITH THE
> CENTER LETTER AND WORK
> YOUR WAY OUT TO EACH SIDE.
> THIS IS THE SURE WAY TO GET
> A WORD CENTERED.

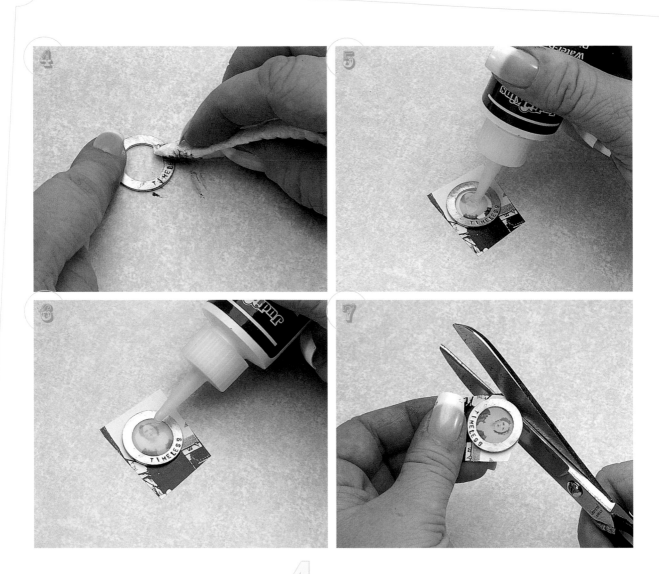

STEP FOUR

Rub the polish into the stamped letters with a paper towel. Buff off the excess.

STEP FIVE

Place the washer over the cut photo. Begin to fill the interior of the washer with Diamond Glaze.

STEP SIX

Completely fill the interior of the washer with Diamond Glaze and let dry thoroughly.

STEP SEVEN

Trim the excess paper using a craft knife or scissors.

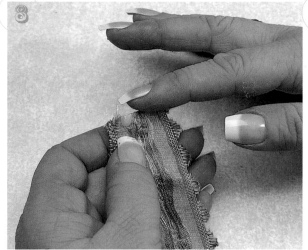

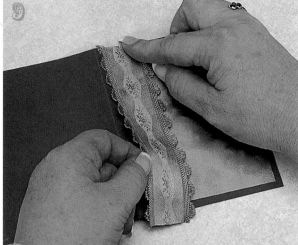

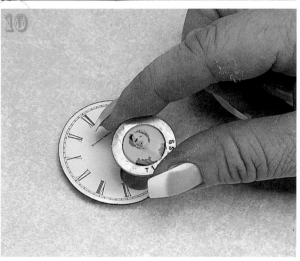

STEP EIGHT

Prepare the card by layering a metallic copper-toned paper piece on the front of rust-colored cardstock. Add glue to the back of the ribbon.

STEP NINE

Glue a heavy antique-looking ribbon to the front of the card.

STEP TEN

An old watch face is an excellent accompaniment to the washer. If you cannot find a real one, a paper one will do. Glue the washer to the watch. You will need a thick multipurpose glue that works with metal. Omni Gel is a good choice.

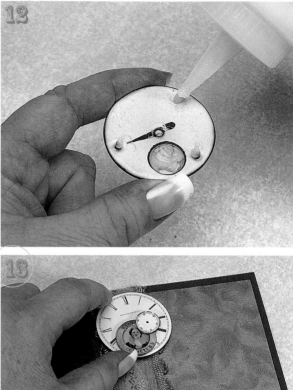

STEP ELEVEN
Add the tiny face plate on top of the washer.

STEP TWELVE
Add the Omni Gel to the back of the watch face.

STEP THIRTEEN
Lay the piece on the front of the card. Let dry.

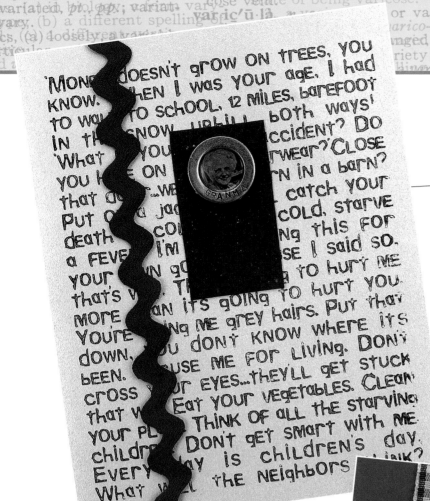

Granma Says

Some stamps say it all, and this is one of my favorites. Does this sound familiar? "When I was your age, I had to walk to school, twelve miles, barefoot, in the snow." Or how about, "Money doesn't grow on trees, you know." Funny sayings, phrases or descriptive words make great backgrounds and are an easy way to personalize your card.

Sweet Sunflower

The foil embellishment underneath the washer helps create the sunflower image. You can also place the ribbon underneath the flower to create a stem.

< **NAPKIN** >

Napkins these days are beautifully printed with artwork that is perfectly sized for greeting cards. I look for vintage-looking napkins or imagery that can be cut out easily. Also look for Japanese tea napkins. These napkins are great because the rice paper is thin and easy to collage. Choose a heavy cardstock for this card because the typewriter key frame spikes are easier to use on firmer paper. Typewriter key frames may be tricky to find, so check out the Resources on page 252.

CREATIVE MATERIALS:
*vintage-style napkin,
metal typewriter key frame,
an old playing card*

MATERIALS LIST
- vintage-looking napkin or imagery
- brush
- clear glue
- heavy cardstock
- bone folder (or ruler)
- gift wrap flower cutouts
- old playing card
- color-copied photo
- metal typewriter key frame
- black permanent marker
- gold leafing pen
- small hammer

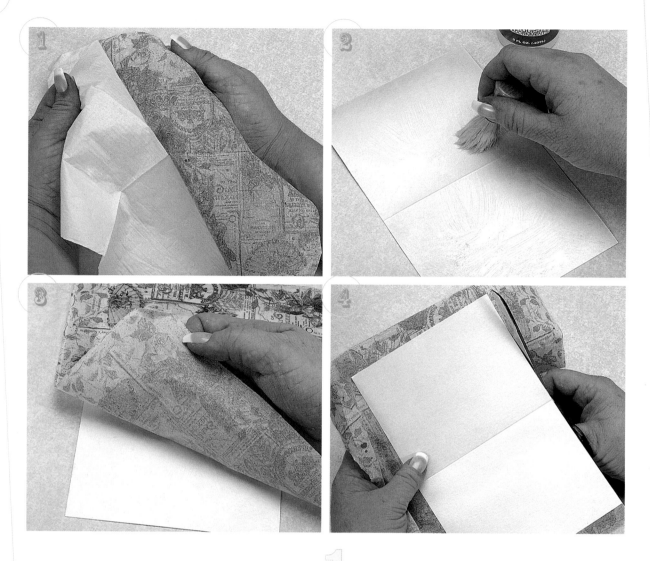

STEP ONE
Printed napkins are often two-ply. Carefully pull the printed layer from the plain backing.

STEP TWO
Brush an even layer of glue on the selected cardstock.

STEP THREE
Smooth the napkin onto the cardstock gently with a bone folder or ruler.

STEP FOUR
Trim away any excess napkin.

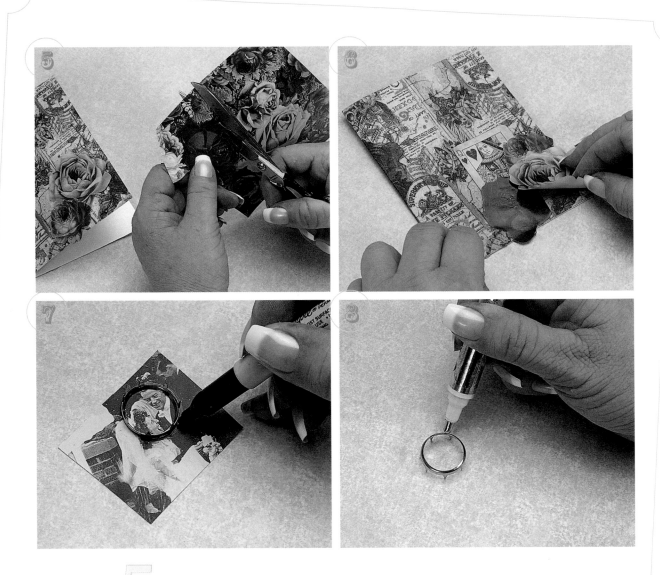

STEP FIVE
Fold the cardstock. Cut out flowers from old gift wrap and glue them on for extra decoration.

STEP SIX
Glue on an old playing card. Trim off any collage pieces hanging over the cardstock edges. Let dry.

STEP SEVEN
Choose the copy of the photo to be used inside the frame. Trace around the frame on the photo with a black permanent marker or pen.

STEP EIGHT
So that the color of the metal frame is better suited to the card, use a gold leafing pen over the metal rim. Set it aside to dry completely for about five minutes.

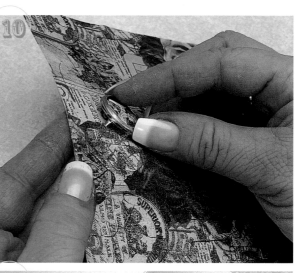

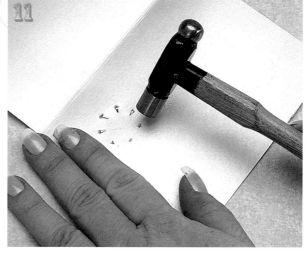

TIP
☞

FOR ADDED SHINE.
YOU CAN INSERT A
PIECE OF ACETATE OR
MICA BEFORE THE
PHOTO IS ADDED.

STEP NINE

Trim the photo on the inside of the marker or pen marking (from step 7) and insert the photo into the frame.

STEP TEN

Push the spikes through the cardstock.

STEP ELEVEN

Turn over the cardstock. With a small hammer, tack down the spikes. Tack them toward the center (inward) so that the frame will lay flat.

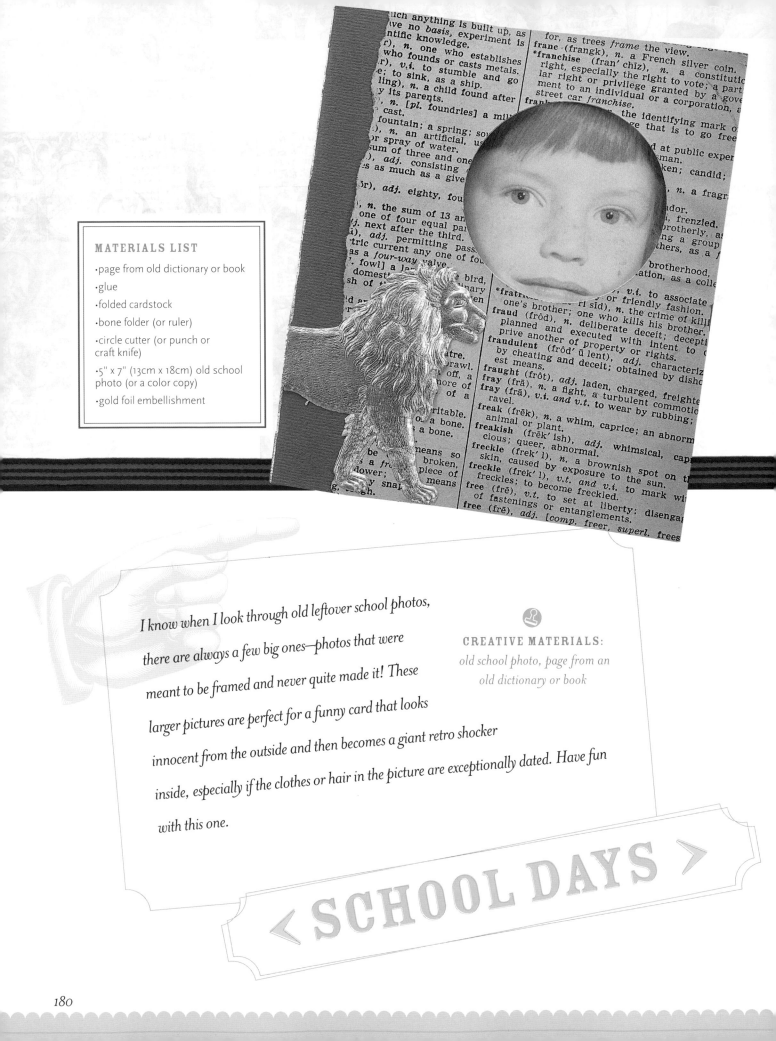

MATERIALS LIST

- page from old dictionary or book
- glue
- folded cardstock
- bone folder (or ruler)
- circle cutter (or punch or craft knife)
- 5" x 7" (13cm x 18cm) old school photo (or a color copy)
- gold foil embellishment

I know when I look through old leftover school photos, there are always a few big ones—photos that were meant to be framed and never quite made it! These larger pictures are perfect for a funny card that looks innocent from the outside and then becomes a giant retro shocker inside, especially if the clothes or hair in the picture are exceptionally dated. Have fun with this one.

CREATIVE MATERIALS:
old school photo, page from an old dictionary or book

< SCHOOL DAYS >

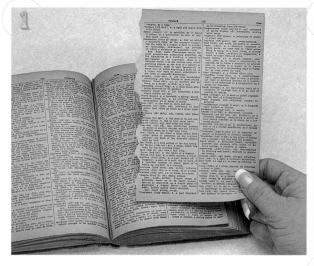

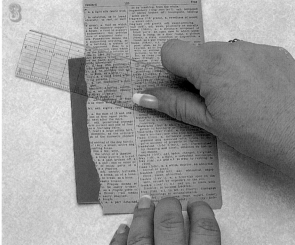

STEP ONE
Tear a page from an old dictionary or book.

STEP TWO
Spread glue over the front two-thirds of the cardstock.

STEP THREE
Attach the old page to the front of the cardstock, leaving the torn edge approximately ¾" (2cm) from the fold. Smooth the paper gently with a bone folder or a ruler.

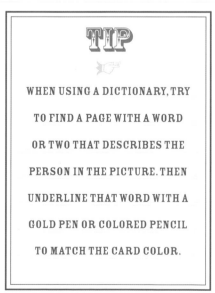

TIP

WHEN USING A DICTIONARY, TRY TO FIND A PAGE WITH A WORD OR TWO THAT DESCRIBES THE PERSON IN THE PICTURE. THEN UNDERLINE THAT WORD WITH A GOLD PEN OR COLORED PENCIL TO MATCH THE CARD COLOR.

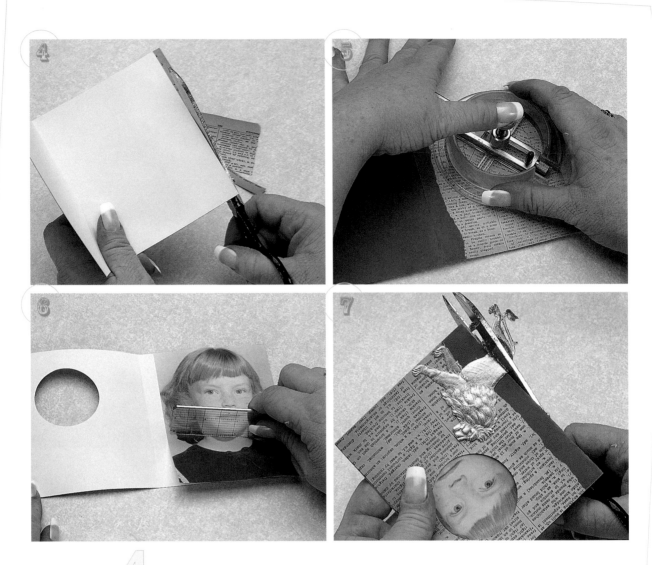

STEP FOUR

Trim away the excess.

STEP FIVE

Using a circle cutter, punch or craft knife, cut a circle (approximately 2¼" [6cm] in diameter) toward the top of the card .

STEP SIX

Choose a 5" x 7" (13cm x 18cm) color copy of an old school photo. Insert the copy into the card so that the face is positioned fully in the circular window. Glue the copy to the interior of the card, then smooth the card with the ruler.

STEP SEVEN

Add a few appropriate embellishments. Here I added a gold foil lion, since I am a Leo (yes, that's me, age six). Trim as needed.

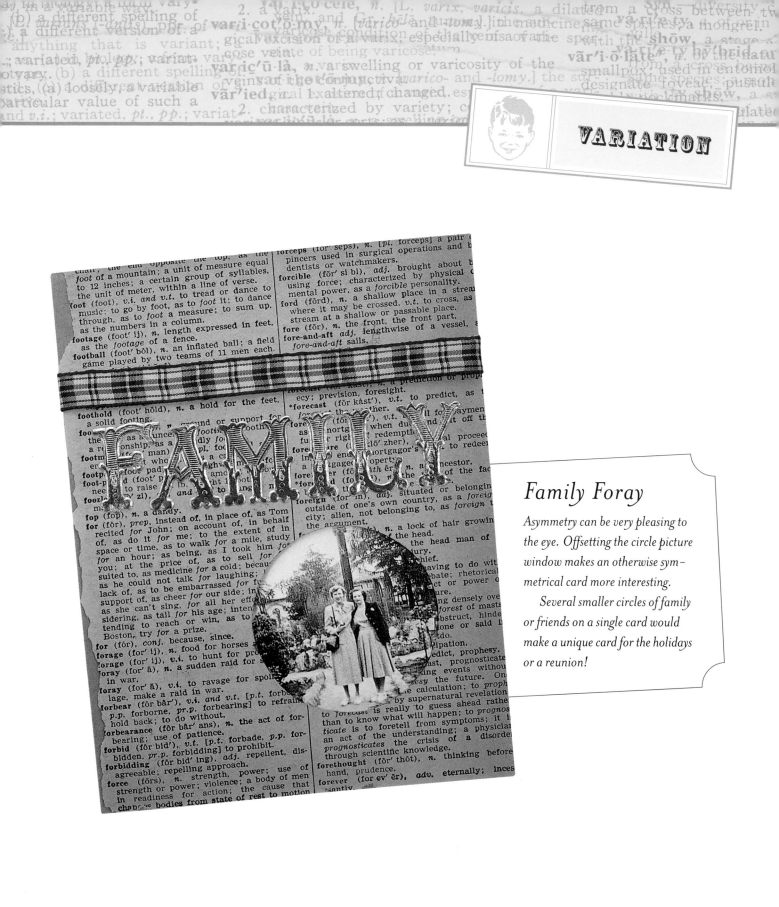

Family Foray

Asymmetry can be very pleasing to the eye. Offsetting the circle picture window makes an otherwise symmetrical card more interesting.

Several smaller circles of family or friends on a single card would make a unique card for the holidays or a reunion!

After creating several cards, my copies are generally in shreds. I usually have a few tiny faces left along with circle cutouts from other window cards. Here is a unique window card from those leftover scraps.

The cabochon is the perfect size for tiny faces and can be found at most craft and bead stores. I framed the cabochon with a rusty crown washer. I found the rusty crown washers at my local army surplus store! Needless to say I bought them all.

CREATIVE MATERIALS:
leftover scraps from other window cards, cabochon, crown washer

MATERIALS LIST

- Diamond Glaze
- color-copied photo
- clear acrylic cabochon
- leftover window card cutout
- folded cardstock
- doublestick tape
- crown washer
- copper tape

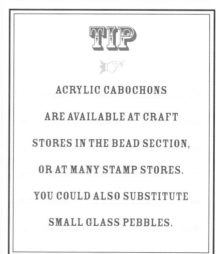

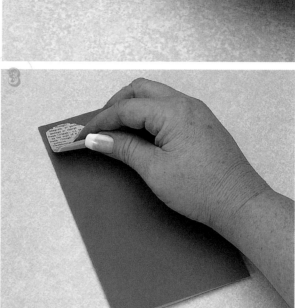

STEP ONE
Put a dab of Diamond Glaze on the picture.

STEP TWO
Drop the cabochon over the picture. Let the piece dry, then trim closely around the edge of the cabochon.

STEP THREE
Place the leftover cutout (this circle had a bit of a trim on one side) in the upper left corner of the cardstock with doublestick tape.

TIP

ACRYLIC CABOCHONS
ARE AVAILABLE AT CRAFT
STORES IN THE BEAD SECTION,
OR AT MANY STAMP STORES.
YOU COULD ALSO SUBSTITUTE
SMALL GLASS PEBBLES.

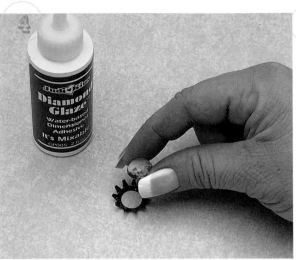

STEP FOUR

Apply a small amount of glue to the inside rim of the crown washer. Place the cabochon into the washer. Let dry.

STEP FIVE

Copper tape is a great accent on cards with metal embellishments. It is generally used for stained glass. The tape also comes in silver and brass. This tape has a release liner or backing piece that needs to be removed before applying it to the surface. To keep the tape from sticking to itself, attach just the top portion by pulling back the release liner. Then pull the liner slowly while positioning the tape onto the cardstock.

STEP SIX

Glue on the cabochon.

Family Jewel

With the ribbon and cabochon, you have the beginnings of a necklace. Simply add a jump ring to attach the cabochon to the ribbon, and you're ready to go.

Crown Jewel

A card that's a gift, too! This card's embellishment is a ready-made necklace. Remove the ribbon and attached cabochon, and use it as a choker necklace.

I use only real beeswax for these techniques because it gives an antique look and is still transparent. It also remains easy to work with once it has cooled. And the best part about beeswax is the honey scent!

Beeswax is usually found at large craft stores or good art supply houses in the fabric paint aisle, or with the candle-making supplies.

I cannot emphasize this statement enough: Be extremely careful with hot wax! Not only can it be difficult to remove from surfaces—it can burn you! Needless to say, these are not projects I recommend for children.

TECHNIQUE:
Beeswax as Adhesive

< IMPRESSIONS in WAX >

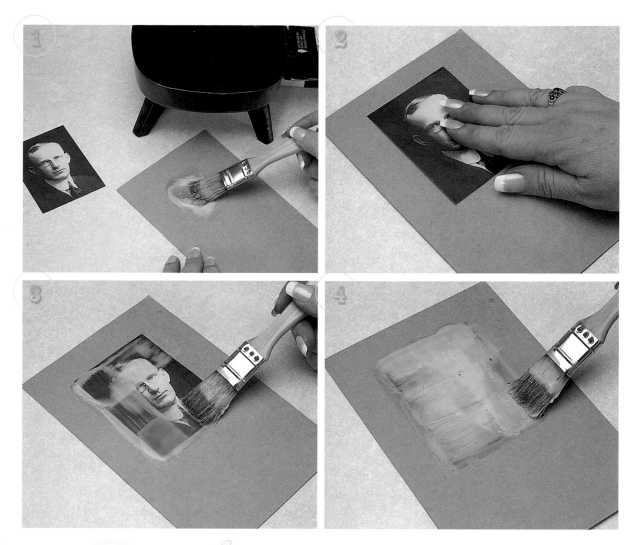

STEP ONE

Before you begin, find something to melt the wax in. The wax must remain hot while you are working on each piece, so you will want a heat source that has good temperature control. I prefer a small electric skillet. Heat the wax until it is clear but not boiling. Trim the copied photo. Use a cheap disposable paintbrush that does not shed too much to place a small amount of hot wax on the cardstock.

STEP TWO

Quickly place the picture on the wax to secure it in place.

STEP THREE

Evenly brush the wax over the photo.

STEP FOUR

Continue to brush layers of wax over the picture until you can barely see the image. Try to keep the edges as even as possible.

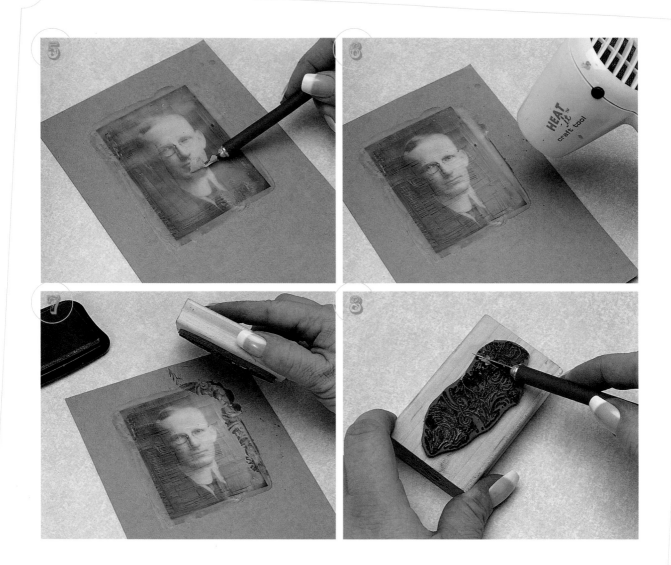

STEP FIVE

When the wax has set, carefully scrape through the wax to reveal the image, especially around the face. Leave the wax thicker on the edges of the piece. Add texture by scratching lines into the wax with a craft knife.

STEP SIX

On the thick edges, soften the wax with a heat gun. Just a little heat to soften—do not remelt the wax.

STEP SEVEN

Stamp old-fashioned designs into the edges of the wax. Pigment or solvent inks work best on wax. Gold, black or brown inks look nice on the yellowish wax.

STEP EIGHT

If wax becomes embedded in the stamp, scrape it off with a craft knife. Then apply a little heat with the heat gun and wipe quickly with a paper towel.

STEP NINE

Scrape and scratch the card surface again for texture.

STEP TEN

Trim the cardstock evenly around the waxed area. Repeat the same stamped image in soft brown around the edge of the cardstock.

STEP ELEVEN

Edge the cardstock with a gold leafing pen.

STEP TWELVE

Affix the finished piece to the deep purple cardstock using photo corners and a small piece of doublestick tape.

< KID STUFF >

This picture is of my Uncle Jack and his friends. On this card, instead of glitter, I used small mica chips. They have a much more antiqued look than other glitters available today and are easily adhered with wax or glue.

TECHNIQUE:
Beeswax as Adhesive

CREATIVE MATERIALS:
mica tile, mica chips, old buttons

MATERIALS LIST

- beeswax
- color-copied photo
- heavy cardstock
- brush
- large mica tile
- mica chips
- gold foil letters
- heat gun
- craft knife
- old buttons
- gold leafing pen
- folded cardstock
- doublestick tape
- ribbon

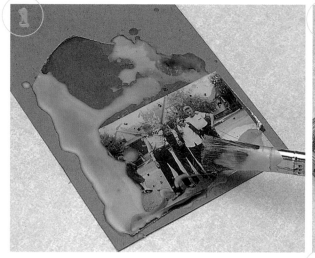

STEP ONE

Melt the wax as described on page 189. Trim the copy of a photo. Secure the picture to heavy cardstock by brushing on a small amount of wax. Layer a large mica tile over the picture, then add wax around the edges to hold it in place.

STEP TWO

Build up the wax around the edges by drizzling it from the brush. While the wax is still hot, add mica chips. Cover the chips with more wax.

STEP THREE

Add a layer of wax at the top of the picture, then quickly apply gold foil letters.

CAUTION

HOT WAX CAN CAUSE
BURNS. BE CAUTIOUS
WHEN USING.

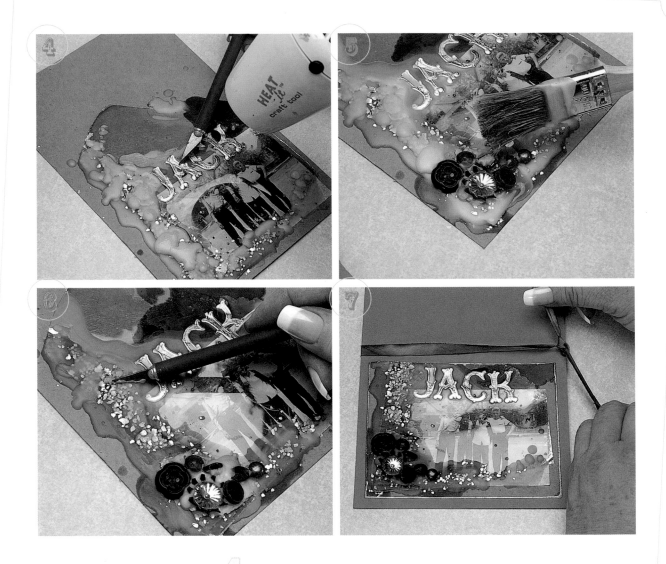

STEP FOUR
Warm the wax with a heat gun, then adjust the letters with the tip of a craft knife.

STEP FIVE
Reheat the wax and add old buttons. Drip wax over the buttons to secure them.

STEP SIX
Let the piece set up. Then scrape away selected areas to reveal more of the chips, buttons and foil letters.

STEP SEVEN
Trim the cardstock, then edge it with a gold leafing pen. Adhere to the folded cardstock with doublestick tape. Accent the card with a ribbon.

Party Time

The background piece is terra-cotta paper dipped in beeswax. The beeswax turned the paper a darker color. Test all papers beforehand, so you don't have any color surprises.

Snowy Day

The background paper was antiqued using repeated light washes of walnut ink. The entire band—background paper, foil frame and photo—was dipped in beeswax.

This great old photo shows my mother and her twin brother visiting the scariest Santa I have ever seen. The original photo is faint, so I have copied it in a darker tone and given it an eight percent color screen. Color copies for this technique must be carbon-based toner copies, not laser printed. Select a photo that has high contrast: all-light or all-dark photos will not transfer clearly. The perfect photo has very definite lights and darks in the same picture. Many glues or gel mediums and pigment powders will work for this technique.

TECHNIQUE:
Gel Photo Transfer

CREATIVE MATERIAL:
mica pieces

MATERIALS LIST

- Omni Gel
- color-copied photo (made with carbon-based toner)
- brush
- ceramic tile (or other slick surface)
- mica
- Diamond Glaze
- rusty brown Piñata Color (alcohol ink)
- hole punch
- white and dark cardstock
- small brads
- small flat beads
- doublestick tape
- folded cardstock

STEP ONE
Place a large dollop of Omni Gel on the copied photo.

STEP TWO
Brush the glue horizontally. Let the glue set for a minute.

STEP THREE
Add another dollop of Omni Gel and brush it vertically over the copy. Repeat the process several times, brushing diagonally, vertically and horizontally. Let the piece dry overnight.

STEP FOUR
Trim away the excess copy paper.

STEP FIVE
Submerge the piece in water. When paper is wet enough, it will look very mottled.

STEP SIX
To remove the paper, place the piece glue-side-down on a tile or other slick surface, to keep it from slipping and tearing the transfer.

STEP SEVEN
Rub the paper off of the transfer with your fingers, keeping the surface wet.

STEP EIGHT
Cut the mica to fit the photo transfer.

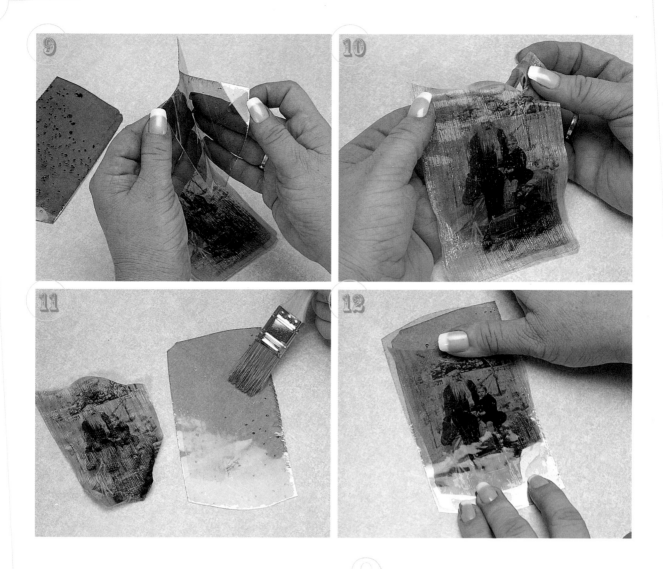

STEP NINE
Separate the mica piece into thin sheets.

STEP TEN
Carefully tear the gel transfer to give it a raw edge.

STEP ELEVEN
Apply Diamond Glaze to the mica.

STEP TWELVE
Position the gel transfer faceup on top of the mica. Add a little Diamond Glaze to the front corners of the transfer, then layer another piece of mica on top of the transfer.

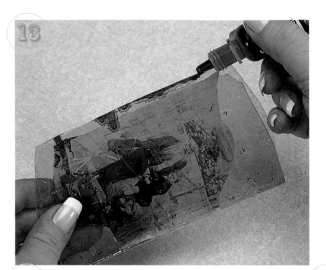

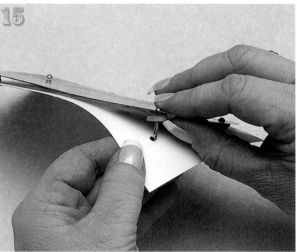

STEP THIRTEEN
Drip a little rusty brown Piñata Color onto the mica edges to give the mica an aged look.

STEP FOURTEEN
Punch holes through the mica and the white cardstock.

STEP FIFTEEN
Attach the mica to the white cardstock using small brads through the punched holes. Add small flat beads to act as separators. This little bit of spacing allows light in behind the mica. Attach the white cardstock to dark cardstock using doublestick tape. Then attach the dark cardstock layer to the front of folded cardstock using doublestick tape.

Treasures

Here I used the liquid transfer method, but did not remove all of the paper. For photos without good contrast, leave some of the paper so the image shows through better.

Happy Heart

After I transferred the image for this card, I dipped it and the mica into beeswax to give the image a leafy appearance. I embellished the card using common charms that can be found in most craft stores.

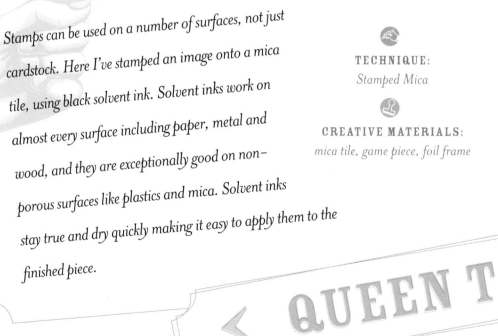

MATERIALS LIST

- rubber stamp
- mica tile
- black solvent ink
- red Piñata Color (alcohol ink)
- brush
- spray water bottle
- cardstock
- walnut ink
- Diamond Glaze
- game piece
- folded cardstock
- foil paper frame
- foil paper photo corners
- doublestick tape

Stamps can be used on a number of surfaces, not just cardstock. Here I've stamped an image onto a mica tile, using black solvent ink. Solvent inks work on almost every surface including paper, metal and wood, and they are exceptionally good on non-porous surfaces like plastics and mica. Solvent inks stay true and dry quickly making it easy to apply them to the finished piece.

TECHNIQUE:
Stamped Mica

CREATIVE MATERIALS:
mica tile, game piece, foil frame

< QUEEN T >

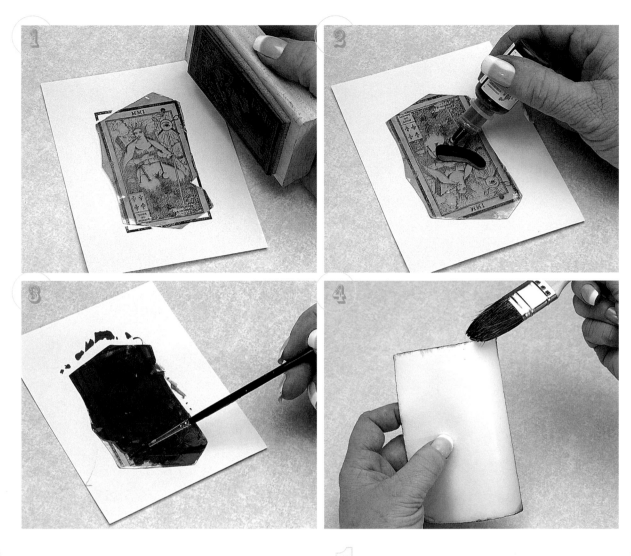

STEP ONE

Stamp an image directly onto the mica tile with a solvent black ink.

STEP TWO

Add four drops of red Piñata Color to the back of the tile.

STEP THREE

Use a brush to move the ink over the tile. Let dry.

STEP FOUR

Wet the edges of the cardstock, then apply walnut ink to the edges with a brush.

STEP FIVE

With a small amount of glue, attach the dry mica to the card-stock. Glue the game piece to the bottom right-hand corner. Using a brush, apply glue to the back of the foil paper frame.

STEP SIX

Attach the frame to the mica and press to secure.

STEP SEVEN

Trim the foil paper photo corners.

STEP EIGHT

Affix the cardstock piece to the folded cardstock using double-stick tape. Glue on the corners.

Solemn David

You don't need old photographs to make a vintage greeting card. This image was stamped onto mica using black solvent permanent ink. The background was stamped with a pigment pad and rubbed with shoe polish. The background was edged with a gold leafing pen.

Vision

These background leaves were stamped with dye and pigment inks and rubbed with brown shoe polish. I added a torn strip of vellum, before stamping the image onto mica.

< TICKET to the PAST >

Shipping tags are very versatile and can be used for more than just a tag. Here I've used the shipping tag as the main embellishment for the card.

I've made a variation of a transfer by changing the color and texture of the Omni Gel with pigment powder to create a tintype appearance. Any metallic color can be used to get this look.

TECHNIQUE:
Faux Tintype

CREATIVE MATERIALS:
shipping tag, mica chips, old ribbon

MATERIALS LIST

- walnut ink
- large shipping tag
- color-copied photo (made with carbon-based toner)
- scrap paper
- Omni Gel
- stiff brush
- metallic pigment powder
- paper towels
- mica chips
- glitter
- rubber stamp with word design
- black permanent ink
- old ribbon
- doublestick tape
- folded cardstock

STEP ONE

Apply a medium brown mixture of walnut ink to a large shipping tag (see pages 151–152 for information on mixing different ink strengths). Set aside to dry.

STEP TWO

Select a color copy to transfer. Trim the copy to the final size you want to apply to the tag. Lay the copy on scrap paper, picture side up. Apply a good dollop of Omni Gel to the copy. Dip a stiff brush into metallic pigment powder, then apply the powder to the wet glue.

STEP THREE

Brush on this mixture horizontally first. Wait a few seconds, then brush vertically. This mixture should be rather thick and even on the copy. Let it dry, then trim away the excess paper.

STEP FOUR

Soak the piece in water. Depending on the thickness of the copy and scrap paper, this could take a few minutes.

STEP FIVE

Peel the scrap paper away. Dip the piece back in the water. Gently begin rubbing the copy paper off of the metallic surface. Repeat this process until the paper has been removed. Blot dry with a paper towel.

STEP SIX

Adhere the tintype to the shipping tag by brushing a thin layer of glue onto the back of the tintype.

STEP SEVEN

Add a little glue around the edge of the tintype, then sprinkle on the mica chips and glitter.

STEP EIGHT

Ink your stamp with black permanent ink.

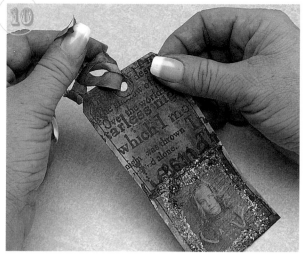

STEP NINE

Stamp the top of the tag with a large word pattern in black ink.

STEP TEN

Attach an old ribbon loop.

STEP ELEVEN

Using doublestick tape, apply the tag to folded cardstock.

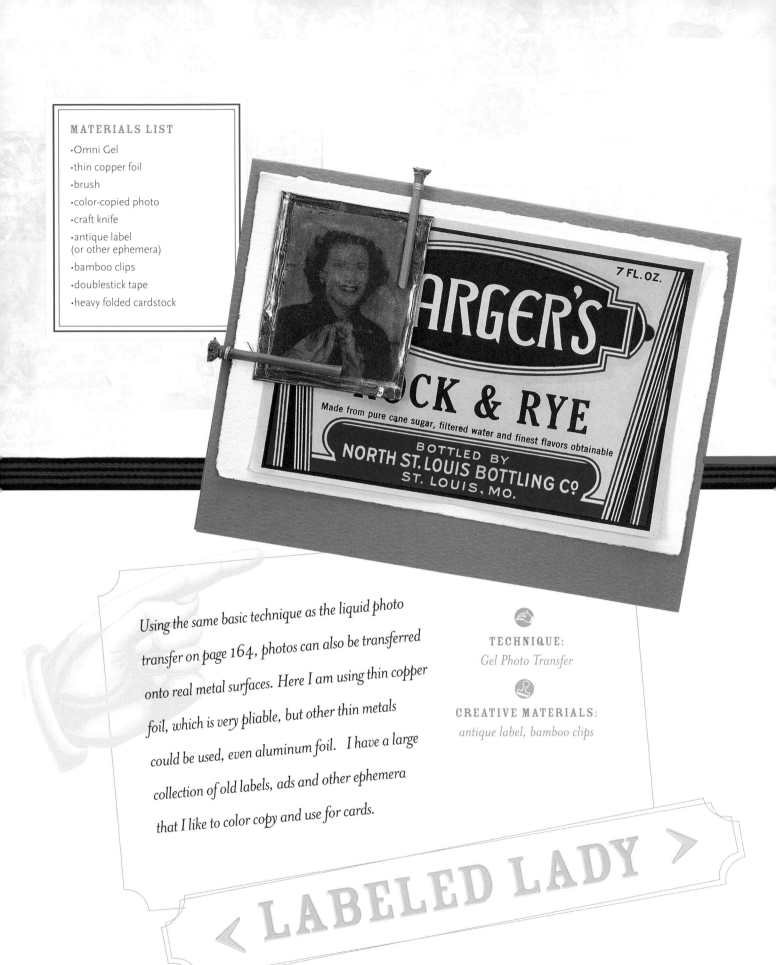

Using the same basic technique as the liquid photo transfer on page 164, photos can also be transferred onto real metal surfaces. Here I am using thin copper foil, which is very pliable, but other thin metals could be used, even aluminum foil. I have a large collection of old labels, ads and other ephemera that I like to color copy and use for cards.

MATERIALS LIST
- Omni Gel
- thin copper foil
- brush
- color-copied photo
- craft knife
- antique label (or other ephemera)
- bamboo clips
- doublestick tape
- heavy folded cardstock

TECHNIQUE:
Gel Photo Transfer

CREATIVE MATERIALS:
antique label, bamboo clips

‹ LABELED LADY ›

STEP ONE

Apply Omni Gel to a piece of foil (approximately a 2½" x 2⅛" [6cm x 5cm] piece), brushing horizontally. Cover the entire piece of foil. Then repeat the process with vertical strokes.

STEP TWO

Adhere the color copy face down to the gel.

STEP THREE

While the gel is still wet, remove the excess from the edges of the metal using a craft knife. Let dry.

STEP FOUR

Dip the piece in water to wet the paper. When the paper is wet through, it will have a mottled appearance. Begin rubbing the paper off of the metal. Repeat the process until the image can be seen and all of the paper has been removed.

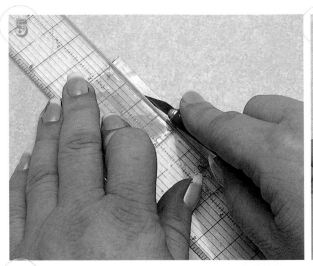

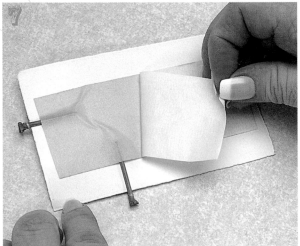

STEP FIVE

*To create a more finished edge on the metal, score ¼"
(6mm) inside all four sides with the back of a craft
knife. Turn under the edges.*

STEP SIX

*Attach the metal to an antique label or other ephemera
using bamboo clips.*

STEP SEVEN

*Secure the clips with a large piece of doublestick tape.
Add this piece to heavy folded cardstock.*

O' My Darling

To create a vintage look, use cotton, silk and wool ribbons rather than modern synthetic materials.

< RED RIDING HOOD >

The folds here are scored with the back of a craft knife. I like this type of scoring because it gives a very crisp crease. To achieve a more textured appearance, I like to crunch the metal then flatten it again, giving it an older look. The addition of the photo corners frames the metal and gives it a more finished appearance.

TECHNIQUE:
Stamped Metal

MATERIALS LIST
- metal piece
- scissors
- rubber stamp
- black solvent ink
- photo corners
- craft knife (or scoring tool)
- cardstock
- doublestick tape
- solid head eyelets
- hole punch
- eyelet setter
- hammer

STEP ONE
This metal has a few crinkles in it. If yours does, too, run it along the back of a pair of scissors to smooth it out.

STEP TWO
Cut the metal to size. This piece is approximately 2" x 2" (5cm x 5cm). Stamp an image on the metal using black solvent ink. Add photo corners to the piece.

STEP THREE
Using a craft knife, score the cardstock 4" (10cm) in from the edge. Fold it over, then score again at the open edge. This creates a flap that is folded over the front of the card.

STEP FOUR
Fold over the flap.

STEP FIVE
Attach the stamped metal piece to the cardstock with doublestick tape.

STEP SIX
To make a metal band for the flap using leftover metal strips, attach equal widths of strips together with solid head eyelets. These eyelets work in the same fashion as regular eyelets; they simply have a solid head on the top. Punch ⅛" (3mm) holes on each end of the strips.

STEP SEVEN
Insert the first solid head into a punched hole. Then turn over the piece and hammer the eyelet back down. Wrap the strip around the card flap to adjust the fit. Remove the strip from the card and insert the final eyelet. Set it with the hammer.

STEP EIGHT
The band should slide right on over the flap.

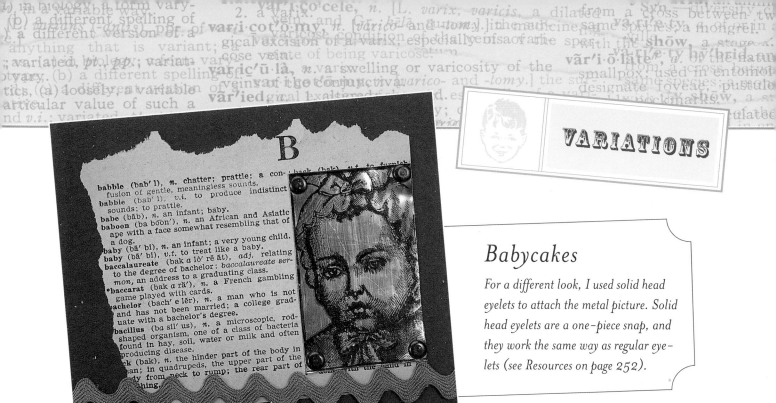

Babycakes

For a different look, I used solid head eyelets to attach the metal picture. Solid head eyelets are a one-piece snap, and they work the same way as regular eyelets (see Resources on page 252).

Baby Face

To achieve the multiple colors in the metal, I sporadically heated the metal sheet with a barbecue lighter. The heat transforms a copper-colored sheet of metal into a rainbow of colors.

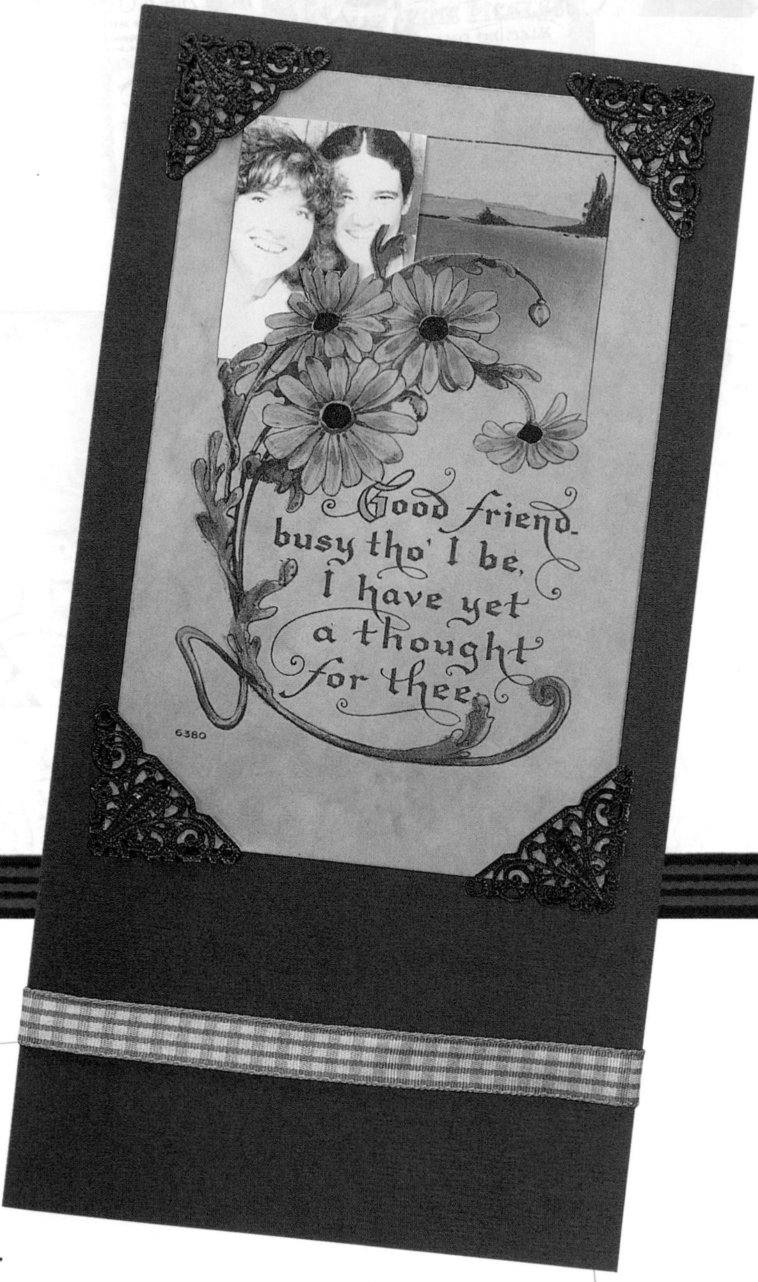
Good friend, busy tho' I be, I have yet a thought for thee.
6380

MATERIALS LIST

- rusted metal corners
- metal clippers
- sharp craft knife
- postcard with flower design
- color-copied photo booth photo
- scoring tool
- cardstock
- doublestick tape
- glue
- vintage ribbon

Pictures from photo booths are not so easy to find in antique stores anymore. Luckily I have a few of my own. Some of the expressions are priceless. They are beautifully paired with old postcards, which are still widely available and relatively inexpensive. Many of the old postcards have lovely sentiments, and the size of these photos are easily worked into the design of a card using a simple slot.

CREATIVE MATERIALS:
photo booth picture, old ribbon, vintage postcard

< FOREVER FRIENDS >

STEP ONE

I have chosen to use rusted metal corners, available at many craft stores, for this project. These corners are quite large, so I am using some small metal clippers to cut them in half.

STEP TWO

With a sharp new craft knife, cut around part of the postcard design. Even though this flower design is complicated to cut around, the size of the opening needed for the photo is fairly small.

STEP THREE

Cut out one photo booth copy. Insert the copy into the slot in the postcard.

STEP FOUR

Score and fold the cardstock.

STEP FIVE

Apply doublestick tape to the back of the postcard. Cover the corner of the copy with tape as well. Attach the piece to the greeting card.

STEP SIX

Add a dot of glue to the corners of the postcard. Spread the glue a bit with the craft knife. Lay the rusted metal corners on the glue.

STEP SEVEN

Toward the bottom of the card, create a band by tying on a vintage ribbon.

> **TIP**
>
> USING BANDS THAT NEED
> TO BE REMOVED ADD
> TO THE ANTICIPATION
> OF OPENING THE CARD!
> IT MAKES A SIMPLE
> CARD SEEM MORE LIKE
> A PRESENT.

Old Money

The circle punch fit perfectly into the circle on the colonial money to provide a picture window. Reproduction colonial money is available from many East Coast historical societies.

< TRIPLICATE >

By using a thick application of watercolor paint over stamped images then removing a small bit of the paint by adding water and blotting, you can create a wonderful faux fresco that has the feel of paint peeling away revealing hidden pictures. Use only inexpensive or student-grade watercolors for this project. Good water-colors are too expensive for this project.

TECHNIQUE:
Faux Fresco

CREATIVE MATERIAL:
vintage jewels

MATERIALS LIST
- rubber stamp
- black solvent ink
- watercolor paper
- tube watercolor paints
- stiff brush
- heat gun
- paintbrush (or watercolor brush)
- paper towel
- iridescent pigment ink
- folded cardstock
- doublestick tape
- vintage jewels
- clear glue

TIP

☞

THE BLOBS OF COLORS
WILL STAIN THE PAPER
DIRECTLY UNDERNEATH. FOR
INSTANCE, IF YOU WANT A
FACE TO BE A SPECIFIC TONE,
PLACE THAT COLOR BLOB
DIRECTLY ON THE IMAGE.

STEP ONE

Stamp an image three times with black solvent ink onto water-color paper.

STEP TWO

Place small blobs of watercolor paint over the stamped images.

STEP THREE

Using a stiff brush, dab the paint over the images, completely covering them. Try not to overmix the colors.

STEP FOUR

Let dry or use a heat gun to speed the drying.

STEP FIVE

With a paintbrush, apply a little puddle of water where the image was.

STEP SIX

Blot the water away by pressing with a paper towel for a few seconds. Do not pat the water off. Patting will blend the paint.

STEP SEVEN

Repeat the process until parts of the images can be seen.

STEP EIGHT

Trim away the excess paper. For further decoration, add a few designs on the edges with iridescent pigment ink.

STEP NINE

Mount the piece on cardstock using doublestick tape. Add a few vintage jewels with a tiny amount of glue.

Porcelain Fresco

Use a light touch when removing paint. You want to make sure you have a good light/dark contrast and a nice balance of the matte and watercolor finishes.

Triplets

Photo corners are a quick and easy way to attach a layer of paper. And these lick-and-stick photo corners are especially easy because you don't need glue or tape.

225

Using watercolor paint without added water can create a very textured look and feel to plain paper. The texture makes this card background look like antique wallpaper. If you like a more shimmery look, use a light metallic pigment ink instead of watercolor.

TECHNIQUE:
Faux Wallpaper

< PORTRAIT >

STEP ONE

Place globs of dark watercolor paint all over a piece of cardstock. Use a pouncing motion with your brush to move the paint.

STEP TWO

Let dry, or speed up the drying time with a heat gun.

STEP THREE

Apply light watercolor paint to the design stamp using a brush.

TIP

👉

THIS IS A GREAT
TECHNIQUE FOR GRUNGY
OR DISCOLORED PAPERS.
THE PAINT COVERS
EVERYTHING, EVEN
EMBOSSED SURFACES.

STEP FOUR

Stamp the image on the painted piece. Stamp the design off the edges, turning the paper as you go.

STEP FIVE

Trim down the cardstock to fit the front of the folded cardstock and mount it with doublestick tape. Trim a copied picture to fit and attach with photo corners.

TIP

WHEN CHOOSING THE COLORS OF PAINT,
REMEMBER THAT THE HIGHER THE CONTRAST,
THE MORE INTERESTING THE BACKGROUND
WILL BE. IF THE BACKGROUND NEEDS TO BE
MORE SUBTLE, A MONOCHROMATIC LOOK
WOULD BE A GREAT WAY TO GO.

Three Monkeys

Use decorative scissors to create an interesting border that sets off the different layers.

Family Ties

For different effects, try the faux wallpaper technique on various paper finishes. I used a shimmer, coated paper for the yellow layer.

229

< MIRROR IMAGE >

Flat surfaces don't have to look flat. Use layers of textures to achieve dimension. I colored a small mirror with alcohol inks, added a stamped design and finished it by applying a cutout photo collaged to the front. This piece can also be made into a fun necklace. Layer the mirror onto or place it inside of an old watch case or locket.

TECHNIQUE:
Stamped Mirror

CREATIVE MATERIALS:
small mirror, ribbon

MATERIALS LIST

- assorted Piñata Colors (alcohol inks)
- small round mirror
- paper towels
- Claro Extender
- rubber stamp
- watercolor paint
- color-copied photo
- Diamond Glaze
- paintbrush
- gold leafing pen
- folded cardstock
- ribbon
- clear glue

STEP ONE
Apply a few drops of yellow Piñata Color to the mirror. Allow the ink to spread.

STEP TWO
Add a couple drops of other colors until there is a nice mix of colors. Let dry.

STEP THREE
If the ink becomes too dark or muddy, blot gently with a paper towel, then add a drop or two of Claro Extender.

STEP FOUR
Stamp a design with watercolor paint on the mirror.

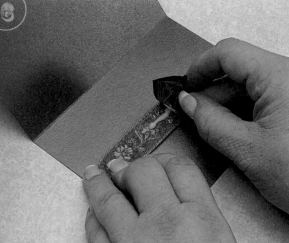

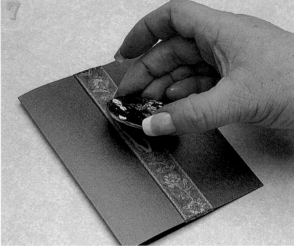

STEP FIVE

Cut out a copied image. Trim the image so it fits right along the mirror edge. Spread a thin layer of Diamond Glaze over the mirror. Lay the cutout on the mirror. If you want the cutout to be glossy, spread a small amount of Diamond Glaze over the image. Let dry. Edge the mirror with a gold leafing pen.

STEP SIX

Attach ribbon around the front of the card vertically. Glue the ribbon ends together inside the card.

STEP SEVEN

On the front of the card, glue the mirror to the center of the ribbon.

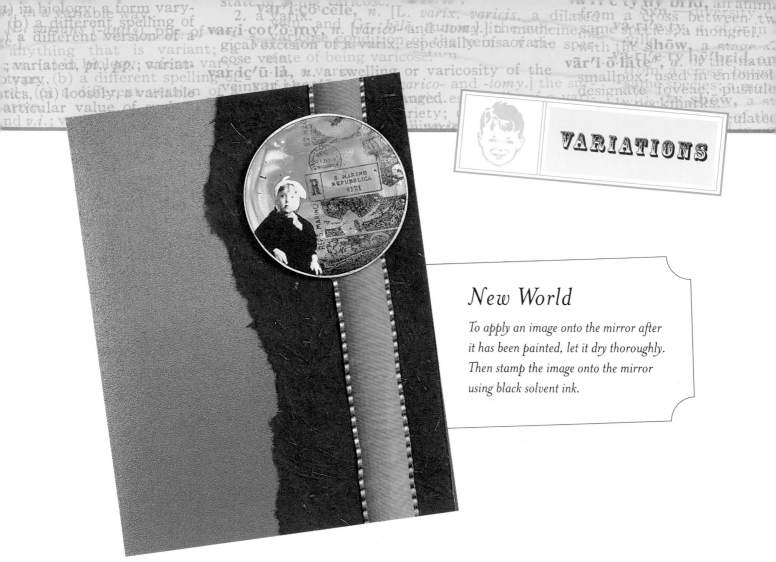

New World

To apply an image onto the mirror after it has been painted, let it dry thoroughly. Then stamp the image onto the mirror using black solvent ink.

Setting Sun

To create a mottled look on the mirror, dab off some of the wet ink with a paper towel. This lets more of the mirror show through.

MATERIALS LIST

- white or light color polymer clay
- pasta machine or acrylic clay roller
- tissue blade
- color-copied dark photo
- rolling pin
- craft knife or sharp scissors
- gold leafing pen
- page from an old book
- Omni Gel (or Diamond Glaze)
- folded cardstock
- doublestick tape
- vintage ribbon
- pearl-headed pin
- wire cutters
- game piece (or button)

Polymer clay is a great medium for greeting cards; it is lightweight, can be rolled flat and is perfect for transferring photos. I prefer Premo! clay because it remains a little flexible when dry, which is excellent for greeting cards. Use utensils kept especially for polymer clay. If you don't want to invest in a pasta machine, an acrylic clay roller is available at most craft stores.

TECHNIQUE:
Polymer Clay Photo Transfer

CREATIVE MATERIALS:
page from old book, vintage ribbon, game piece

‹ HERITAGE CLAY ›

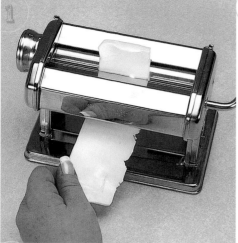

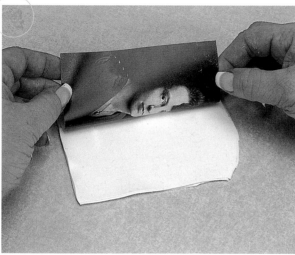

STEP ONE

Using white or a very light color of polymer clay, condition the clay by running it through a pasta machine. This process is simple. Begin by flattening one end of a block of clay. Feed the flat end into the rollers, then continue rolling until all of the clay is through.

STEP TWO

Cut the clay in half with a tissue blade. Lay one piece on top of the other, then roll through the machine again. Repeat this process several times until the clay has no visible air pockets and is soft.

STEP THREE

Change the machine to the widest setting. Cut and stack the clay as in step two, then trim away the excess clay to create a rectangle. Run this through the machine.

STEP FOUR

Select and trim a color copy of a very dark photo. The most intense photos turn out best. Cut the clay to the size of the photo. Lay the copy of the photo face down on the clay.

TIP

I LIKE TO BAKE CLAY

ON CUT-UP HEAVY

BROWN PAPER BAGS,

WHICH CAN BE

THROWN AWAY AFTER

BAKING.

STEP FIVE

Roll over the photo with a rolling pin or acrylic roller to adhere it to the clay. Bake the clay according to the package directions.

STEP SIX

Remove the clay from the oven. Immediately roll again with the rolling pin. Slowly peel off the copy paper. Let cool for five minutes, then flip the clay over and cool for another five minutes. This prevents the thin clay from curling.

STEP SEVEN

Trim the clay with sharp scissors or a craft knife.

STEP EIGHT

Use a gold leafing pen to color the edge of the clay.

STEP NINE
Tear a page from an old book. Glue the page to the front of the folded cardstock. Trim away the excess.

STEP TEN
Use glue or doublestick tape to adhere the clay to the front of the card.

STEP ELEVEN
Create a small fan with a piece of vintage ribbon and secure it with a pearl-headed pin. Snip off the sharp end of the pin with wire cutters.

STEP TWELVE
Glue the fan to the cardstock, tucking it slightly under the clay photo.

STEP THIRTEEN
Attach a game piece or button with a little glue.

‹ REMEMBER ›

Make an old-fashioned frame for photos by using a translucent polymer clay.
Translucent clay is the best to start with if you are a
beginner because it is easy to tell when the clay is fully
baked. When completely baked, this clay has a yellowish, alabaster look and
will be slightly blotchy.

TECHNIQUE:
Polymer Clay Frames

MATERIALS LIST

- color-copied photos made with carbon-based toner
- translucent polymer clay
- pasta machine or acrylic clay roller
- craft knife
- nail file
- gold leafing pen
- copper ink
- rubber stamp
- heat gun
- clear glue
- folded cardstock
- doublestick tape

STEP ONE

Select and size the images to be transferred. The photocopies must be done on a copying machine using carbon-based toner. Transfer the photo images onto white clay and the frame images onto translucent clay, as described on pages 235 and 236.

STEP TWO

Cut out the frames after baking by carefully scoring around the inside oval. Cut through the clay slowly, then score the outside edges.

STEP THREE

Trim the clay edges using a craft knife.

STEP FOUR

Smooth out any rough edges with a craft knife by carefully shaving the clay.

STEP FIVE

Sand the edges with a nail file.

STEP SIX

Color the inside and outside edges of the frame with the gold leafing pen.

STEP SEVEN

Stamp a word or decoration on the frame with copper ink. Dry the ink with a heat gun.

STEP EIGHT

Put glue on the corners of the photo pieces, then position the frame over them. Let dry.

STEP NINE

Attach the frames to folded cardstock with doublestick tape.

All in the Family

To get a more finished, professional-looking edge around the polymer clay transfers, coat the edges with paint or a colored pen.

Just Visiting

Mica works great as a background as well as an overlay, as seen in Vintage Santa on page 196.

Molding paste is a fun compound that can be textured with sand, beads, buttons, mica and more. The light version is awesome for greeting cards, since it is extremely lightweight.

Molding paste can be colored with a variety of products including inks, powdered pigment and acrylics. I prefer Golden Fluid Acrylics. They are so intensely pigmented that a little goes a long way.

TECHNIQUE:
Walnut Ink

CREATIVE MATERIALS:
*molding paste, buttons,
mica chips, tiny jewels, rickrack*

< TEXTURED PAST >

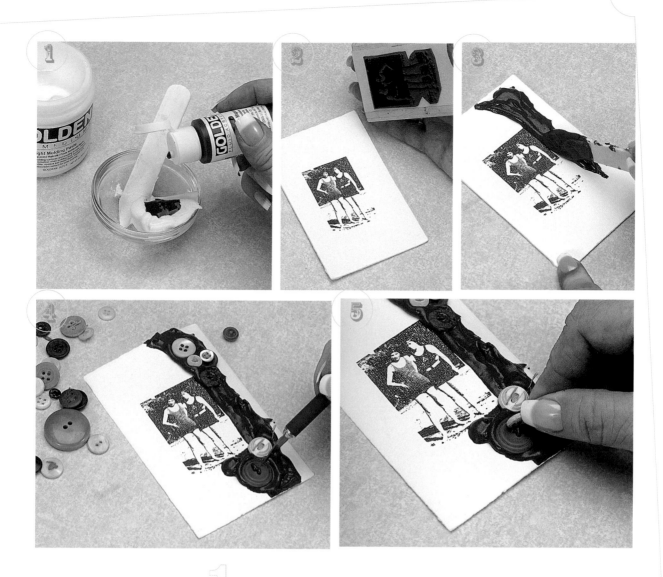

STEP ONE

Mix a couple of generous tablespoons of light molding paste with several drops of liquid acrylic or ink until you have achieved the desired color. Set aside.

STEP TWO

Stamp or photocopy an image onto heavy cardstock.

STEP THREE

Spread the molding paste along one side of the cardstock.

STEP FOUR

Apply the largest and most colorful button first. Press it firmly into the paste so the button holes fill with the paste.

STEP FIVE

Layer smaller buttons over the paste, making sure each button has enough paste for a secure bond.

STEP SIX
Place tiny jewels and sprinkle mica chips over the surface. Let dry for thirty minutes.

STEP SEVEN
Spritz the other half of the cardstock with water.

STEP EIGHT
Brush a small amount of walnut ink onto the edge of the cardstock. Let dry.

STEP NINE
Attach the piece to the folded cardstock with doublestick tape.

STEP TEN
Tie on a skinny piece of black rickrack.

Bead and Button

Be sure to use light molding paste on greeting cards. Regular molding paste is heavier and will need additional postage to mail. It will also take longer to dry.

Sisters

When using complicated embellishments, keep the main image simple so the card doesn't look too busy or over-designed.

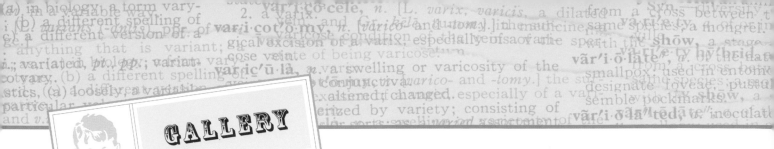

Window to Holland

The photo used in this card is a picture of my grandmother in Holland, before she and her family moved to America. I used a type-writer key ring to frame the definition of portrait. Typewriter key rings are available from Coffee Break Design (see Resources on page 252 for information).

☞ **CREATIVE MATERIALS:**
vintage napkin and typewriter key ring

Faith

Use the faux wallpaper technique on white paper. Paint the lips and eyes using colors from the wallpaper.

☞ **TECHNIQUE:**
Faux Wallpaper

246

Wild West

Instead of polishing the polymer clay, I applied a layer of Diamond Glaze over the clay to create a nice sheen.

☞ **TECHNIQUE:**
Polymer Clay Photo Transfer

American Gothic

Instead of transferring a photograph onto metal, transfer the photo onto pearlized paper to achieve a metallic look.

☞ **TECHNIQUE:**
Liquid Photo Transfer

First Love

For embellishment, I used photographic stickers (stickers made from actual photos; available at craft stores). I stained them with shoe polish to make them darker and more vintage in appearance .

☞ **TECHNIQUE:**
Liquid Photo Transfer

Beautiful View

Spread on a thin layer of molding paste with a palette knife or credit card. The background was antiqued using walnut ink.

☞ **TECHNIQUE:**
Walnut Ink

Love in Bloom

Use shoe polish to age the greeting card roses for a more vintage look.

☞ **TECHNIQUE:**
Shoe Polish Overlay

Through the Keyhole

To create a sea glass look, I filled a rubber washer (or o-ring) with Diamond Glaze.

☞ **TECHNIQUE:**
Faux Fresco

A is for Arthur

*Instead of gluing the game piece,
I adhered it with beeswax.*

☞**TECHNIQUE:**

Beeswax as Adhesive

That's My Chicken

*Don't throw away leftover scraps because you
never know when they might fit perfectly onto
another card. The circle piece used here is the
leftover cutout from the colonial money used in
Old Money on page 221.*

☞**CREATIVE MATERIAL:**

sea glass

Food for Thought

To visually unify the third layer of the card, I dipped the mica pieces and the gems in beeswax.

☞ **TECHNIQUE:**
Beeswax as Adhesive

Attic Baby

To change the color of the molding paste, I used Piñata Colors after it was dry.

☞ **CREATIVE MATERIALS:**
molding paste and buttons

RESOURCES

☞ WALNUT INK GRANULES, WORD SLAB STAMPS, STAMPS

Postmodern Design

‹☒› *Stamps used on pages 130, 134, 146, 164, 169, 238, 246*

☞ LIQUID WALNUT INK, STAMPS

Stampers Anonymous
Williamsburg Square
25967 Detroit Rd.
Westlake, OH 44145
(440) 250-9112
www.stampersanonymous.com

‹☒› *Stamps used on pages 202, 205, 206*

☞ EYELETS, SOLID HEADS, BRADS, TYPEWRITER KEY RINGS, MICA TILES

Coffee Break Design
P.O. Box 34281
Indianapolis, IN 46234
(800) 229-1824 fax

☞ GOLDEN MEDIUMS, PAINTS, MOLDING PASTES, LIQUID ACRYLICS

Golden Artist Colors, Inc.
188 Bell Rd.
New Berlin, NY 13411
(607) 847-6154
www.goldenpaints.com

☞ DIAMOND GLAZE, STAMPS, LEAFING PENS *(gold, copper, silver)*

Judi-Kins
17803 South Harvard Blvd.
Gardena, CA 90248
(800) 398-5834
www.judikins.com

‹☒› *Stamps used on pages 130, 132, 134, 140, 144, 164, 205, 222, 225, 226, 229, 230, 246, 247, 248, 249*

☞ OMNI GEL

Bearing Beads
110 Michigan
San Antonio, TX 78201
www.bearingbeads.com

☞ MICROGLAZE

Skycraft Designs, Inc.
26395 South Morgan Rd.
Estacada, OR 97023
(800) 578-5608
www.skycraft.com

☞ POLYMER CLAY, TISSUE BLADES, ACRYLIC ROLLING PINS

Polyform Products Co., Inc.
1901 Estes Ave.
Elk Grove Village, IL 60007
(847) 427-0020
www.sculpey.com

☞ BEESWAX, PIÑATA COLORS

Rupert, Gibbon & Spider, Inc.
P.O. Box 425
Healdsburg, CA 95448
(800) 442-0455
www.jacquardproducts.com

☞ PIÑATA COLORS, CLARO EXTENDER, MICA TILES, CHIPS AND GLITTER

USArtquest
7800 Ann Arbor Rd.
Grass Lake, MI 49240
(517) 522-6225
www.usartquest.com

☞ PAPER FOIL EPHEMER

Amy's Magic Leaf
173 Main St.
West Leechburg, PA 15656
(724) 845-1748

☞ GAME PIECE EMBELLISHMENTS

Wonderland Emporium, Inc.
Boca Raton, FL 33432
(561) 395-6393
www.mystampstore.com

☞ VARIOUS STAMPS

Queen of Stamps
email: queenstamp@aol.com

‹☒› *Stamps used on pages 160, 242, 245*

River City Rubber Works
5555 South Meridian
Wichita, KS 67217
(877) 735-2276
www.rivercityrubberworks.com

‹☒› *Stamp used on page 175*

Rubbermoon Stamp Company
P.O. Box 3258
Hayden Lake, ID 83835
(208) 772-9772
www.rubbermoon.com

‹☒› *Stamps used on pages 214, 222, 225*

Stampington & Company
22992 Mill Creek, Ste. B
Laguna Hills, CA 92653
(877) STAMPER
www.stampington.com

‹☒› *Stamp used on page 233*

Stampland
5033 N. Mozart Street
Chicago, IL 60625
(773) 293-0403
www.stamplandchicago.com

‹☒› *Stamps used on pages 217, 245*

CREATIVE CORRESPONDENCE

MICHAEL & JUDY JACOBS

here's some
seattle paper ephemera
for your mailart
see inside

NORTH LIGHT BOOKS
CINCINNATI, OHIO
www.artistsnetwork.com

TABLE OF

CONTENTS

Jumping In

Pocket Surprises

More Fun With Folds

Magic Up Your Sleeves

The Envelope Please

Introduction

Years ago we entered the exciting world of **mail art**, corresponding with other mail artists around the country and overseas. Our mailbox was a constant source of anticipation and surprise. And then, along came e-mail, creating instant communication with no travel time and no postage. Now, even we who make our living working with paper, reluctantly resort to sending e-mail more and more. However, we continue to send decorative mail to friends and family because we know the excitement it generates on the receiving end.

Our goal with this book is to make it possible for people who don't have a lot of time (isn't that everyone?) to make and send decorative mail. We show how easy it is to turn a piece of paper into correspondence art: a tactile messenger of good will, a colorful container for your latest news. The projects are simple yet spectacular, requiring a few basic tools, a little measuring, and some folding and cutting. The most difficult part will be choosing which beautiful paper to use with what project. The easy part will

be changing the dimensions of the foldnotes, sleeves and inserts
so you can mix and match them to suit your fancy.

And because our favorite slogan is **Reduce, Reuse,
Recycle,** we've made some of the samples in this book from used
paper. Make yours from used or new paper, or creatively combine
them. Then, add your personal touch quickly and easily with rubber
stamping, collage, colored pencils and more. We give you lots of
visual ideas and a few tips along the way.

We hope you have just as much fun as we do making these
projects. May you be inspired to use our ideas as a starting point for
your own creative correspondence.

Michael Jacobs AND *Judy Jacobs*

UNOFFICIAL
dear mom!

Tools and Materials

✉ You can create wonderful correspondence art with as few as ten tools in your basic tool kit. With these tools, you can make all of the projects in this book. Everything else listed in "Other Fun Stuff" is just frosting on your cake.

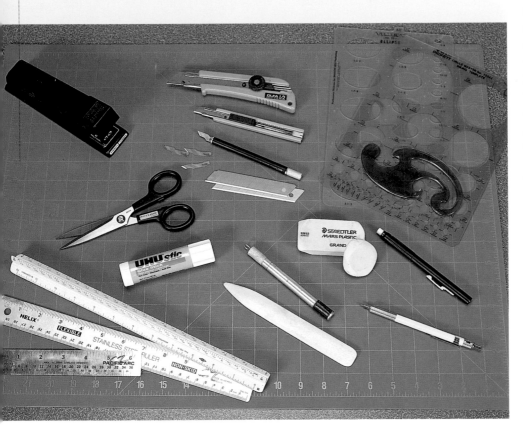

mechanical pencil We strongly recommend a 0.5mm pencil with 2H lead. The hard, narrow lead makes a thin, non-smearing line, which is best for accuracy.

rulers Rulers come in different lengths and materials, and believe it or not, they are meant to be used for different jobs. For cutting, start with a 12" (30cm) metal ruler, with or without cork on the back side to keep it from sliding around. For measuring, buy a plastic three-sided architectural ruler with a ¹/₁₆" scale—this means one of its sides has inches divided into sixteenths. We use this scale for all our projects.

knives Craft knives come in different sizes and are best for cutting paper. Utility knives, which are larger and have a heavy-duty blade, are better for cutting heavier paper, cardstock and board. Look for one with snap-off blades.

scissors We have two pairs of scissors, one large and one small. Scissors are useful for cutting curves; however, we always cut straight lines with a knife and ruler.

self-healing cutting mat Cutting mats come in different sizes. Small mats are great for traveling; however, if you're going to get only one, a medium size or larger is much more practical.

bone folder Bone folders come in handy for a number of jobs, including scoring and creasing. If the scoring end is too thick, it can be shaped with a fine grade of sandpaper to the desired thickness. You can also make your own scoring tool out of a knife handle and a jumbo paperclip (see page 264).

glue We recommend the Uhu glue stick, which is acid-free, goes on smoothly, and is water-soluble so it washes off easily. Stick to the medium or large size for the best deal.

stapler For binding, a standard hinged stapler is as complicated as we get in these correspondence projects.

templates and French curves

Plastic templates and curves come in all shapes and sizes. These are a must for transferring circles, ovals and curves quickly and easily. We use them for windows and customized flaps.

erasers Look for white vinyl erasers, which erase your pencil marks and lines cleanly, with minimal particle build-up. We like the long, tubular erasers that come in a penlike holder.

OTHER FUN STUFF

mouth atomizer This is a fun little gadget once referred to as the poor man's airbrush. Use it to create a spattered pattern on the front of a foldnote (see page 279). Cheap and portable, it's found in art supply stores.

brayer A brayer is a roller with a handle, often used to roll paint or ink onto paper. For our brayering technique shown on page 267, you'll need a softer brayer that comes apart so you can wrap the roller with rubber bands.

decorative scissors and cutters

These are perfect for creating fun decorative edges on your paper. Olfa, Fiskars and other companies also make decorative cutters that look and act like mini pizza cutters. Or dig out those old pinking shears.

punches These handy little gadgets can create beautiful corners on your paper, or you can punch out fun shapes for more decoration and embellishment.

tweezers Tweezers come in handy for picking up and positioning smaller pieces of paper, especially when you have glue on your fingers.

acrylic paints and brushes Acrylics are pigment paints that come in myriad vibrant colors. Lightfast and versatile, they can be used as is, or watered down and used as a wash. We suggest getting at least two acrylic brushes: one small and one wide.

markers We use double-ended markers with a fine point and a bullet point to address envelopes, outline labels, add bits of color, draw, etc.

crayons Wax crayons are great for adding quick color to your projects and for creating crayon-resist papers.

colored pencils We use colored pencils all the time for quick embellishing. The softer pencils color in larger areas more easily, but tend to wear down faster. Both soft and hard pencils make great squiggles.

Prismacolor Art Stix are Michael's favorite color tool. They are richly pigmented colored pencils without the wood. Use flat for a wide swath of color, or hold like a crayon to add quick squiggles.

rubber stamps Rubber stamps are tailor-made for correspondence art. We use a combination of retail stamps, hand-carved stamps, and stamps we've had made from clip art. (See page 344 for a complete list of stamp credits.)

ink pads Ink pads are one of the quickest ways to add color to your art. Use with rubber stamps, or stamp the ink pad itself directly onto the paper. Cool!

Dye-based ink is thin, dries fast and cleans up easily. Pigment ink is thicker, does not dry on coated paper, is great for embossing and resists fading.

paint scrapers You can buy paint scrapers made specifically for creating patterns in wet paint or paste. You'll find them in craft stores and paint stores.

newsprint pad A large pad of newsprint is the perfect protection for your work surface whenever you stamp or paint.

squirt bottle A must for adding water to your paint a little at a time, or for wetting your stamping-off towel.

double-stick tape Look for the kind on a roll with peel-off backing so you can work with one sticky side at a time. Excellent for closing envelopes, sleeves and foldnotes, and for attaching inserts to your correspondence projects.

sealing wax and seals Popular in the Victorian Age when correspondence was queen, sealing wax and decorative seals can be found in stationery and rubber stamp stores. What a great finishing touch for a beautiful foldnote!

Postal Regulations

Almost all of the projects in this book (with the exception, perhaps, of the Letter in a Bag project on page 320) can be safely mailed at the basic letter rate. If you design your own correspondence projects, or plan to adapt any in this book to a different size or shape, we highly recommend asking your local post office for a list of standard rates and dimensions.

The United States Postal Service also offers a Mail Dimensional Standards Template. Brilliantly designed and easy to use, this plastic template indicates the acceptable height-to-length ratios for first-class and single-piece third-class mail weighing one ounce or less. Also included are minimum and maximum postcard sizes and a cut-out slot for measuring thickness. It makes sizing mail a cinch—and it's free!

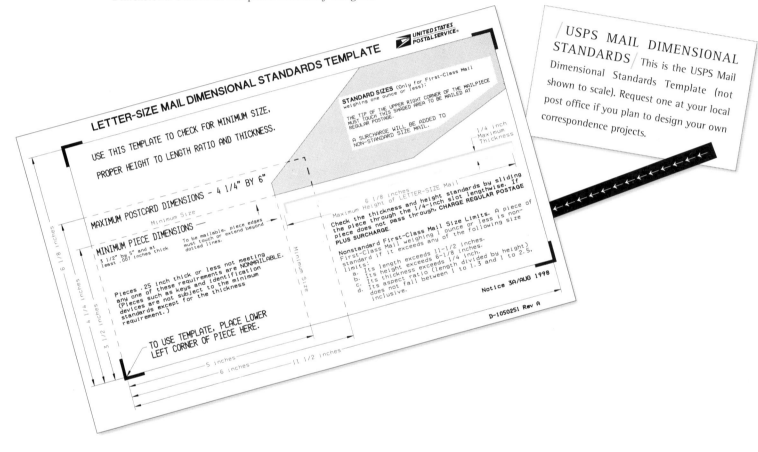

Here are a few guidelines for mailing correspondence art in the United States:

Postcards: Minimum size is 3½" x 5" (8.9cm x 12.7cm) and at least .007 inches thick. Maximum size is 4¼" x 6" (10.8cm x 15.2cm).

Letters: Minimum size is 3½" x 5" (8.9cm x 12.7cm) and at least .007 inches thick. Maximum size is 6⅛" x 11½" (15.5cm x 29.2cm) and no more than one-quarter inch (6mm) thick.

Be sure to check the height-to-length ratio of your letter. Some mail within this range is either too tall or too long to qualify as standard and will need additional postage.

For more information on postal rates and dimensions, you can visit the following Web sites:

United States: www.usps.com
United Kingdom: www.consignia-online.com
Canada: www.canadapost.ca

Choosing the Right Paper

Paper has definitely come a long way since its invention in China in A.D. 105. The abundance of types, weights, textures and colors is enough to boggle the mind. Where the heck do you start?

You start by keeping it simple. Most of our projects use commercial papers. Accessible, affordable and colorful, these papers are sold by the individual sheet so you can try them out before going on a buying spree. The remaining projects are made from hand-decorated or used papers.

Bond and Text Weight Papers

Think of papers used for stationery, photocopies and typewriters (oops! we mean printers). You can buy these papers individually or by the ream (500 sheets).

Decorative Papers

Any thin decorative paper you like is great for embellishing correspondence art. Think of wrapping paper, marbled paper, scrapbook papers, colored and designer tissue paper, Japanese lace papers, etc.

Cardstock

Students are forever e-mailing to say, "What the heck is cardstock? My store didn't know what I was talking about." Simply put, cardstock is just heavier paper. It's what greeting cards, business cards and postcards are usually made from (*cards*, get it?) Cardstock ranges in weight from 65 lb. to 110 lb. (140gsm to 235gsm); anything over 110 lb. (235gsm) and we're talking cardboard or mat board.

You can buy large sheets of cardstock and cut them down to size, or purchase a ream of 250 letter-sized sheets. When buying by the ream, read the end label. For our projects, when the materials list says cardstock, anything from 65 lb. to 80 lb. (140gsm to 170gsm) will be perfect.

Used Papers

Seattle, where we live, is one of the most recycle-conscious cities in the country. Everywhere you go you see the words *Reduce, Reuse, Recycle.* Used paper is our favorite source for mail art. It's abundant, it's free, and it comes in a humongous variety of colors, sizes, printed designs and textures. You probably have some of these around the house even as we speak: old maps and atlases, calendar pages, wrapping paper, junk mail, shopping bags, posters, brochures, envelopes, paper promotions, colorful newsprint and architectural drawings.

Local printers can also be a great source of paper and cardstock. They often sell or give away leftovers from print jobs.

Basic Paper Techniques

THE BEST WAY TO MEASURE, SCORE AND CUT PAPER

The simple truth is—it takes no more time to be precise when measuring and cutting than it does to be sloppy. In fact, these few techniques will make your life in paper easier and will save you time in the long run.

Honest. Even students with extensive papercraft experience have told us they improved their skills with these techniques.

❶ CHOOSE A GOOD RULER

The best ruler for measuring is a triangular architectural ruler (shown at bottom). Its angled surface has skinnier lines which rest right on the paper, so you can accurately transfer measurements to your paper.

When measuring, make sure your ruler is lined up properly and parallel to the top and bottom edges of the paper. Be sure you know where the zero point is before you begin measuring. In this photo, the top ruler's zero point is right at the end of the ruler, but the middle ruler's zero point is set in from the end.

❷ MEASURE AND MARK THE TOP OF YOUR PAPER

Whenever you need to draw, score or cut a line, first align your ruler properly, then measure over from the left and make small pencil marks. First mark your measurements toward the top of your paper, to indicate any lines. If using a metal ruler, tilt the ruler up to simulate an architectural ruler for greater accuracy.

❸ MARK THE BOTTOM OF YOUR PAPER

Now do the same thing at the bottom of your paper, measuring from the left and making small pencil marks.

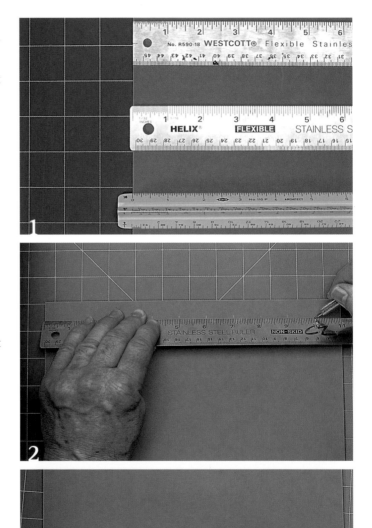

RULERS: WHICH SIDE IS UP?

The cork on the back of your metal ruler keeps the ruler from sliding around. However, the thickness of the cork lifts the ruler off the paper and your pencil (or scoring tool or knife) tends to wander underneath the raised edge. Draw a line with the cork side down and see how easy it is to wiggle your pencil back and forth.

To solve this problem, flip your ruler over. If you hold your ruler firmly, corkside up, and use the edge simply as a guide, your lines will be straight. Just one note of caution: We prefer cutting with our ruler corkside up to keep the blade from wandering. However, you may prefer cutting corkside down for greater safety.

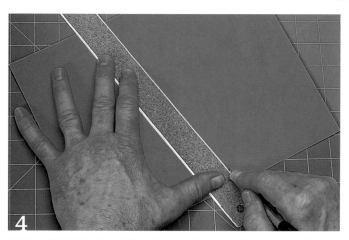

4 POSITION YOUR TOOL

After you've made marks at the top and bottom of your cardstock, stab the very center of the bottom mark with your pencil (or knife or scoring tool if you are cutting or folding) and slide the lower end of a metal ruler firmly against it.

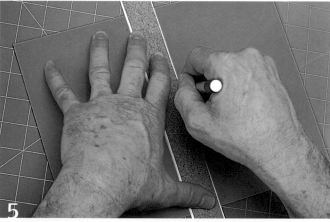

5 ALIGN THE RULER WITH THE MARKS

Now slide the top end of the ruler to the top mark, then back off just a hair to account for the thickness of your pencil, knife or scoring tool. With practice, this stabbing and sliding will increase accuracy and save you time.

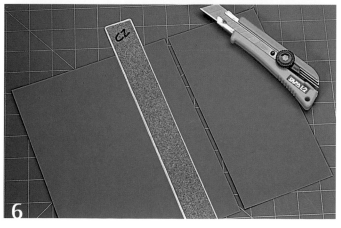

6 CUT OR SCORE YOUR PAPER

Press down firmly on your ruler. Draw the pencil, scoring tool or knife blade toward you, keeping it at a steady angle. If you are cutting thicker paper or cardstock, use a heavy knife and make several swipes with the blade.

HOW TO MAKE GREAT FOLDS

Cardstock and heavier paper fold easily and cleanly when they have been scored first. When you score your paper with a bone folder or a scoring tool, you compress the fibers so they will bend more readily.

Follow the basic measuring guidelines on page 262 to make your scoring accurate. The object is to score down the very center of your pencil marks, so adjust your ruler placement to account for the thickness of your scoring tool.

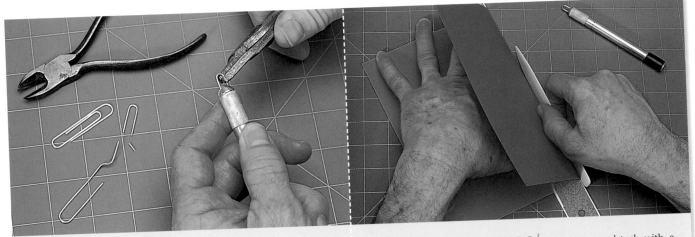

/ MAKING YOUR OWN SCORING TOOL / Here's how to create our preferred scoring tool. Unfold a large paper clip and snip off the smaller inside rounded end, about 3/4" (2cm) long, with wire cutters. Lightly hammer the cut ends to flatten slightly. With your pliers, push the cut ends into the open end of a medium craft knife handle, then tighten the chuck. This lifetime tool is ideal for scoring cardstock and heavy paper.

/ MAKING CLEAN FOLDS / Score your cardstock with a ruler and scoring tool. Keeping your ruler in place, run your bone folder along the crease on the back side of the cardstock. The cardstock will bend easily along the edge of the ruler. (This only works if you score with the ruler placed cork side up.)

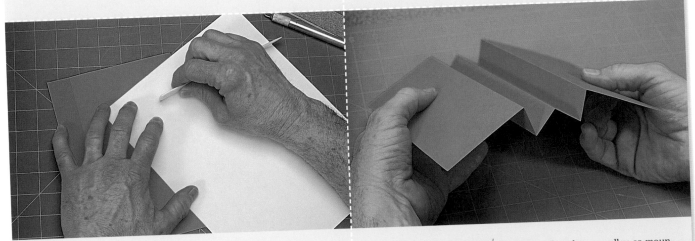

/ CREASING YOUR FOLDS / When you fold cardstock, line up the edges, then lay a clean sheet of scrap paper on top of the fold to protect it. Crease heavily with your bone folder.

/ TYPES OF FOLDS / Folds are referred to as valley or mountain folds. A score line made on the front of your cardstock creates a valley fold. A score line made on the back of the cardstock creates a mountain fold.

How Grain Direction Affects Folds

Machine-made paper, cardstock and cardboard all have a grain direction. This simply means that the fibers from which the paper is made all lie in one direction. Why is this important? Because paper folded against the grain—across the direction of the fibers—is weaker, tends to crack, and will not lie as flat. And we wouldn't want that to happen to you.

For the best results as you make these projects, watch for notations in the materials lists and tip boxes stating whether your paper should be *grain short* (with the grain running parallel to the width of the paper), or *grain long* (with the grain direction running parallel to the length). When specified, this indicates the correct

grain direction after you've cut out your project papers or cardstock. Trim your paper accordingly and your folds will be crisp and lie flat. However, take these directions with a "grain of salt"—these projects will look good and function well even if you occasionally go "against the grain."

If you like to buy paper by the ream, the label will sometimes indicate the grain direction. If the *11* on a label of 8½" x 11" paper is underlined, then the paper is grain long. If the *8½* is underlined, then the paper is grain short. When in doubt, test your paper using the techniques below, and always try to crease your paper in the same direction as the grain.

Quick Tricks for Determining Grain Direction

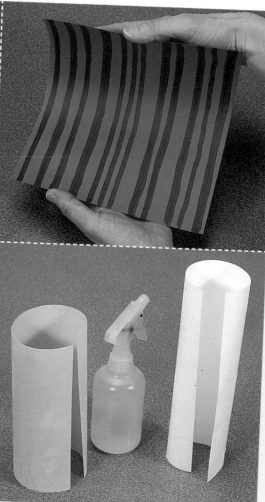

/WEAK FOLDS GO AGAINST THE GRAIN/ If you bend the same piece of cardstock across the width, you will feel more resistance because you are bending against the direction of the grain. Your folded edge will be weaker and visually rough.

/TRY THE SPRAY TEST/ If you can't tell the grain direction by feeling the resistance, then lightly spray your paper with a fine mist of water and see which way it curls—it will curl around the direction of the grain.

Both pieces of cardstock at left are 8½" x 11" (21.6cm x 28cm). The curled blue cardstock is grain short and the white cardstock is grain long.

/GOOD FOLDS GO WITH THE GRAIN/ The black lines show the direction of the grain in this piece of cardstock. If you fold the sheet lengthwise, your fold will run the same direction as (parallel to) the grain. The cardstock will bend more easily and when folded, the edge will be smooth.

Decorating Paper by Hand

With the incredible choice of decorative papers on the market, why would anyone spend time decorating her own? Because it's easy and fun and creative and . . . well, some of us need to express ourselves this way. And, like the correspondence projects coming up, hand-decorated papers can be prepared in quantity and customized to fit the occasion. The following techniques are super simple, yet the results are simply super!

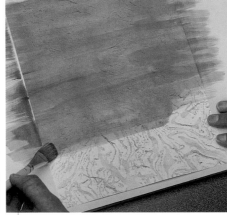

Stamping with Netting Wadded-up nylon netting, such as this bath sponge, creates a beautiful, delicate pattern when used as a stamp. Choose light-colored or metallic pigment inks for best results on black paper. For a fun variation, try stamping with bubble wrap or plastic wrap.

Texture Rubbing with Wax Resist Almost anything can be used as a rubbing surface to create interesting texture. We use crayons to create a waxed rubbing of a piece of textured vinyl wall covering, then paint over it with a wash of watered-down acrylic paint. The wax resists the paint for a beautiful two-tone surface effect.

Lace Stencils Create beautiful lace paper by stamping ink through a piece of lace with a make-up sponge. We started with white paper and moved a small piece of lace around the paper. Better yet, find a piece of lace larger than your paper and tape it down for quicker results.

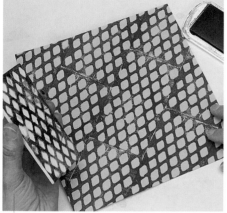

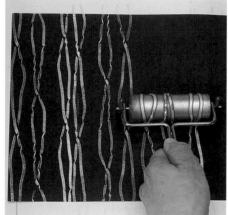

Foam Tray Stamping Save textured foam trays from the grocery store and cut out shapes to use as texture stamps. Here, we stamped a diagonal pattern on yellow paper. You can also trace your own patterns into a foam plate with a ballpoint pen.

Rubber Band Brayering We use ordinary household rubber bands twisted around a soft rubber brayer to create a simple line pattern. Roll the brayer over a metallic ink pad. Silver ink layered on black turns this paper into a rich dimensional texture.

Apple Printing Firm fruits and vegetables such as apples and potatoes make wonderful prints. Begin by stamping a light background color in a random pattern, turning the apple as you go. Stamp over the first layer in a contrasting color. Shaped wooden blocks also work well with this technique.

EASY PASTE PAPER

Paste paper usually involves a bit of preparation, like following a recipe and cooking the paste. This is why we've avoided it in the past, and why we're so excited about this recipe—there's no cooking! A student of

Michael's gave us this art paste to try. All you do is add cold water, stir, and let it sit for 15 minutes. Now, that's our kind of cooking!

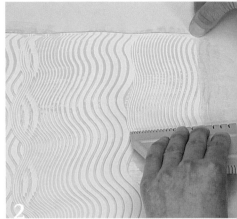

❶ MIX THE PASTE
Use approximately one quarter of the bag of dry paste and add one quart (946ml) of cold water. Mix your main batch in a container with a cover and let it sit according to directions. Then, dole out smaller amounts for each color and stir a gob of acrylic paint into each one. The consistency should be that of thick buttermilk.

MaTeRiaLS NEEDED

- covered container
- measuring cup
- 2 oz. (57gm) box of Ross Paper Mache Art Paste
- cold water
- small plastic containers
- acrylic paints
- stir sticks
- paper to decorate (HEAVIER IS BETTER)
- wide paint brush
- paint scrapers

❷ COMB THE PASTE TO MAKE PATTERNS
Paint the first color on a sheet of paper. If it doesn't spread easily, add more water and stir well. Holding down the edge of the paper, pull your paint scraper toward you while making squiggly lines. If it's not what you want, paint over it and start again.

❸ ADD A SECOND LAYER FOR CONTRAST
When the first layer is dry, paint a second color over the first and comb through it with your paint scraper. The first layer of color will combine with the second to create interesting patterns.

For a fun variation, use colored paper and layer it with paste of a different color on top.

BUBBLE MARBLING

We tried several recipes for bubble marbling, and this one from the Scribes of Central Florida makes nice, dark bubbles. The secret ingredient is the sugar, which helps bind the coloring to the paper. A little bit goes a long way—one bottle of bubbles will decorate lots of paper. And your leftovers will be just as willing to make bubbles the following day.

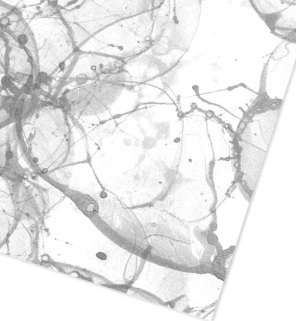

1 MIX THE BUBBLE SOLUTION
Pour some bubble solution into three small containers. Add ten to twelve drops of a different color of food coloring to each one and stir thoroughly. Add one teaspoon (5g) of sugar to each color and stir until dissolved.

2 BLOW BUBBLES TO FILL THE BOWL
Start with your lightest color. With a straw, blow bubbles that come up higher than the edge of your bowl.

If your bubbles are too light on the paper, add more drops of food coloring.

3 POP THE BUBBLES WITH THE PAPER
Hold your paper or cardstock over the container and gently pop the bubbles without hitting the rim of the container. Blow more bubbles and repeat the process until you have a random pattern on your paper.

Add a second or third layer, overlapping the first layer with increasingly darker colors.

MaTeRiaLS NEEDED

- bubble solution
  (FOUND IN TOY STORES)
- small bowls
- food coloring
- sugar (1 tsp. [5g]
  to each color)
- stir sticks
- plastic straws
- paper or cardstock
  to decorate

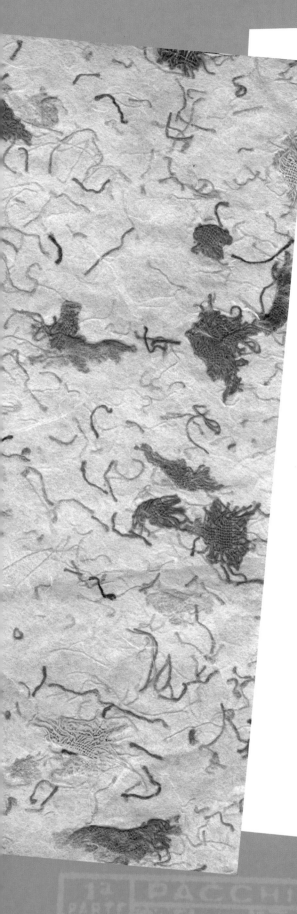

Jumping In

The real art of creative playing around is knowing how to jump right in. Children do it every day; we big kids sometimes need a little nudging to actually do something that's… well, just for fun. Luckily, paper makes it easy to play around because it invites you to look at its beautiful colors and patterns, to feel its textures, to bend it and shape it into something more than what it is, something dimensional. And it is just this interactive nature of paper that gives us the nudge to jump in and rediscover that "child as artist."

Even if you're new to paper arts—even if you don't know a craft knife from a corner punch—all you have to do is pick up a piece of paper, make a few folds, add some colorful paper scraps, and your creative play has begun. These first few projects include stationery made from reused envelopes and handmade postcards. We'll also introduce you to *foldnotes*, a clever correspondence format in which the paper and the envelope are rolled into one. They are so simple and so fun, you'll wonder why you ever waited so long to jump in and let the good times unfold.

chapter one

MaTeRiaLS NEEDED

- assorted cardstock cut into pieces at least 3½" x 5" (8.9cm x 12.7cm) in size

- ruler

- scissors or craft knife

- cutting mat

- decorative paper scraps

- glue stick

- bone folder

- colored pencils

- sealing wax and seal (OPTIONAL)

- metallic ink (OPTIONAL)

Postcards are the perfect canvas for getting your feet (hands) wet in the creative process; they're too small to be intimidating. We make them up in batches, all using a similar theme, and often stamp the word *postcard* on the back to make them look official.

Artful Collage Postcards

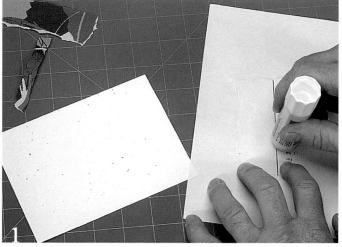

4

❶ APPLY GLUE TO ASSORTED COLLAGE PIECES

Cut your cardstock into an acceptable size for the regular postcard rate. In the U.S. that would be a minimum 3½" x 5" (8.9cm x 12.7cm); maximum 4¼" x 6" (10.8cm x 15.2cm). (See page 10 to find information for the U.K. and Canada.) Grab colorful scraps of different sizes—small, medium and large—and begin gluing.

❷ PLACE THE COLLAGE ELEMENTS ON THE CARD

For a quick and colorful collage, start with the largest piece of paper and glue it to your postcard at an interesting angle.

❸ BURNISH WELL TO FLATTEN

Lay a clean piece of scrap paper over the glued paper and use your bone folder to smooth out any bubbles or wrinkles.

❹ ADD EXTRA DETAILS

Finish layering your paper scraps—smallest pieces on top—and add other embellishments. In this example you see a red ink pad stamped over the collage, quick lines made with colored pencils, and finally, sealing wax stamped with a seal that was first pressed in metallic ink.

- used envelopes
- bone folder
- glue stick
- decorative paper scraps
- colorful string or yarn
- crayons or colored pencils
- rubber stamps
- ink pad

Used paper is our favorite source for mail art; it's abundant and it's free. You can make and decorate a whole stack of used envelope stationery in just a couple of hours, and either side of an envelope can be used. Keep some on hand for those occasions when you need to send a quick note.

Inside-Out Envelope Stationery

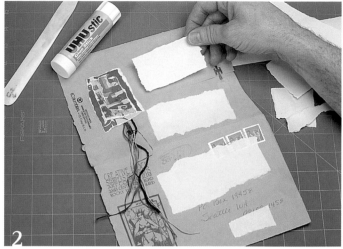

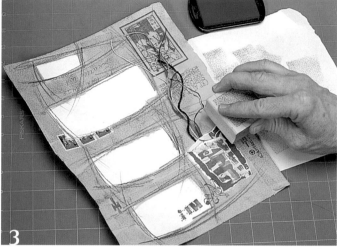

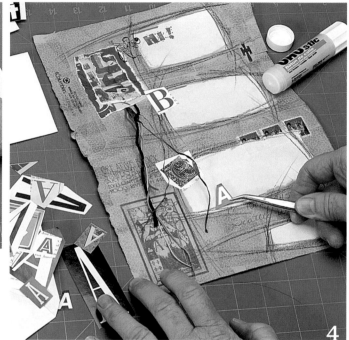

1 SLIT THE ENVELOPES OPEN

Slit the envelopes down each side with your bone folder and save for decorating.

Decide which surface of the envelope you want to use as your letter. We like the image and printing on the outside of our envelope, as well as the colorful postage stamps.

2 ADD A WRITING SPACE

Start embellishing. Paper scraps, colorful threads and yarn can be attached easily with a glue stick.

If your surface is busy, add writing areas by gluing in torn shapes of paper.

3 ADD COLOR AND TEXTURE

Outline the writing areas with crayons or colored pencils and stamp your salutation.

Next, add dimension and tie everything together by stamping a texture design over the entire surface, except for the writing areas.

4 ADD COLLAGE LETTERS

Add cut-out letters from magazines to the beginning of each writing area. Let the letters determine how you start each paragraph; or write your paragraphs first, leaving off the first letter until you know what you're saying.

COLLAGE TIP

Keep a collection of cut-out letters and words in separate envelopes, ready for collaging at a moment's notice. Save used or foreign postage stamps, too. They add exotic interest to any correspondence art.

MaTeRiaLS NEEDED

- 8½" x 11" (21.6cm x 28cm) sheet of decorative paper
- bone folder
- ruler
- pencil
- scissors or craft knife
- cutting mat
- glue stick
- decorative paper scraps
- crayons or colored pencils
- rubber stamps
- ink pads
- double-stick tape (OPTIONAL)

What's a foldnote? It is a single sheet of letter-size paper, cleverly folded so that the stationery and envelope are one and the same. This project is a great place to discover the fun of foldnotes. Because you'll find this one quick and easy, make up multiple notes, decorate the whole bunch, and keep them handy for future occasions. When you're really crunched for time, everything will be done but the writin'!

Simple Centered Foldnote

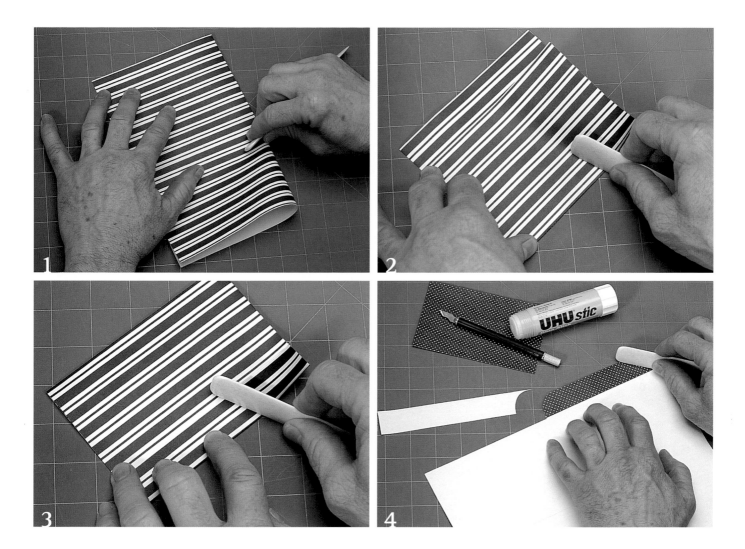

○ FOLD YOUR PAPER IN HALF WIDTHWISE

With your paper horizontal and the decorative side face down, fold the paper in half across the width and crease well with a bone folder.

○ FOLD THE BOTTOM UP

Fold the bottom edge up to within 1" (2.5cm) of the top and crease.

○ FOLD THE TOP DOWN

Fold the top over to create the flap and crease.

○ MAKE THE TOP FLAP

Open your note and cut away the top-left flap section. Shape the remaining flap and cover it with contrasting paper. We've covered both sides of our flap.

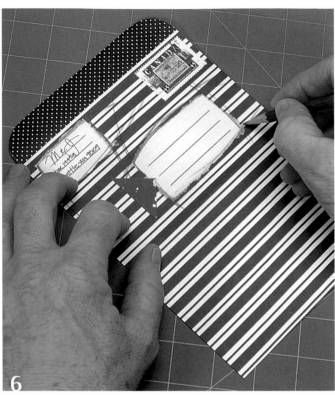

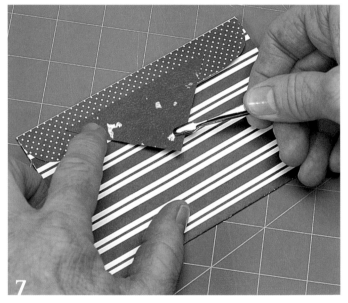

DECORATE AND WRITE YOUR LETTER
Decorate the inside of your foldnote with paper scraps, crayons and rubber stamps, then write your letter.

ADD AN ADDRESS LABEL
Tear out address labels from light-colored paper and glue them to the front of the foldnote. Add color to the edges of the labels with colored pencils or crayons.

SEAL WITH A HANDMADE STICKER
Make your own decorative sticker: cut out a shape from contrasting paper and glue it part-way onto the flap. When you're ready to seal the note, finish gluing the sticker closed, or use a piece of double-stick tape.

TRY A FUN VARIATION GET CREATIVE BY ADDING A MASKED ADDRESS LABEL TO THE OUTSIDE OF YOUR FOLDNOTE. JUST FOLLOW THE INSTRUCTIONS ON THE NEXT PAGE. →

DECORATE FIRST!

We're firm believers in "Decorate first, write later!" Often, your collage or design elements define a more interesting writing area than if you write first and then try to squeeze in some visual decoration.

ADDING A MASKED ADDRESS LABEL

Masking is an easy alternate way to create address labels directly on the front of a plain foldnote. By masking off an area and decorating around the mask, you define a perfect focus for the address. Fun and versatile, masks can be made in different shapes and sizes to fit the theme of any special day.

MaTeRiaLS NEEDED

- plain foldnote
- removable sticky notes
- removable tape
- scissors or craft knife
- cutting mat
- acrylic paint
- mouth atomizer (OR BLOW PEN)
- long-handled paint brush

❶ MASK YOUR ADDRESS SPACES
Make a Centered Foldnote from white or colored paper. Cut sticky notes to your desired size and shape. Use the sticky edge or a small piece of removable tape to adhere the masks to the front of the note.

❷ PLACE THE ATOMIZER IN THE PAINT
Put a gob of acrylic paint in a little cup, add water and mix. Open the atomizer fully and place the long skinny tube in the paint.

❸ BLOW FINE SPATTERS
With the foldnote propped up in front of a large sheet of paper, hold the cup and blow through the large tube. Keep blowing as you move around to cover the entire surface.

❹ ADD BIGGER SPATTERS
To create more visual interest, add bigger spatters with a paint brush and the remaining acrylic paint. Holding one hand over the paper, bring the wet brush up against the bottom of your wrist.

❺ LET DRY AND ADD THE ADDRESS
Allow the spatters to dry, then remove the masks and address the note.

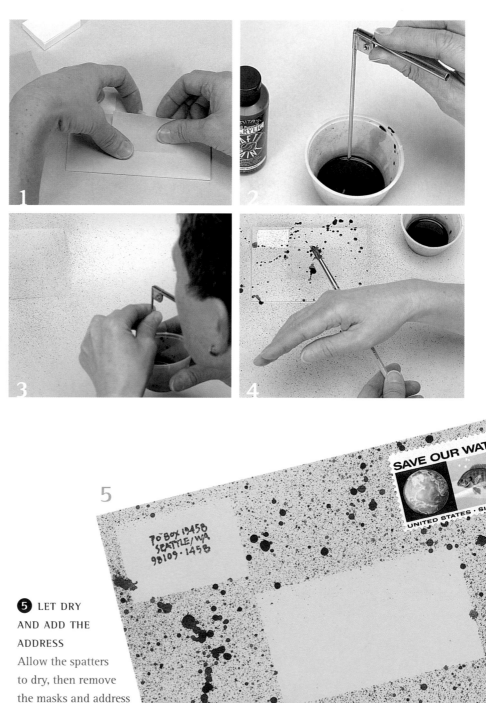

- 8½" x 11" (21.6cm x 28cm) sheet of decorative paper
- bone folder
- ruler
- pencil
- scissors or craft knife
- cutting mat
- glue stick
- decorative paper scraps
- colored pencils
- rubber stamps
- ink pads

Imitating French doors that open from the center and swing out to the sides, this foldnote (also known as a gatefold) has the added advantage of secured sides. Write your note, then enclose bits and pieces of paper ephemera like photos, tickets, recipes or newspaper clippings, knowing that everything will safely reach the intended destination.

French Door Foldnote

1 FOLD IN HALF AND PINCH THE TOP EDGE

Place your paper horizontally with the decorative side down. Bring one side over to the other as if folding in half and pinch at the top; this is the easy way to find the center without measuring.

2 FOLD THE EDGES IN TOWARD THE CENTER

Open the paper flat. Fold the left edge to the center pinch mark and crease with a bone folder. Then fold the right edge to the center and crease.

3 FOLD UP THE BOTTOM EDGE

Fold the bottom up to within 1" (2.5cm) of the top and crease.

CHANGING DIMENSIONS

You can adjust the size of this French Door Foldnote by adjusting the side flaps. When folding the sides in toward the center, simply leave a space between the two edges. The finished height of any foldnote must be at least 3½" (8.9cm) if you plan to mail it in the U.S. at the basic rate.

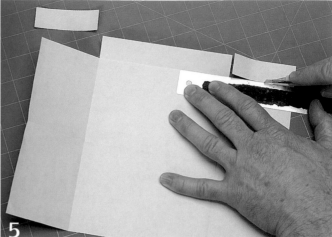

4 MAKE A TOP FLAP

Fold the top over to create a flap and crease.

5 CUT AWAY THE EXCESS PAPER

Open your foldnote and cut out the two upper corners with scissors or a craft knife.

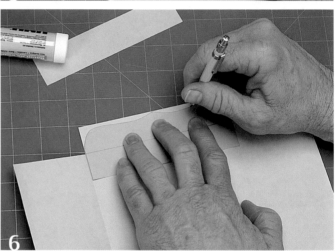

6 SHAPE THE FLAP

Shape the remaining flap either freehand or by tracing a flap template. (See the instructions on page 284.)

7 ADD COLORED PAPER FOR CONTRAST

To make your foldnote more interesting, glue contrasting paper to one or both sides of the flap if desired. First, apply glue to the flap. You can protect the rest of your note from stray glue if you first lay the straight edge of a piece of scrap paper down at the fold of the flap.

Next, using a contrasting paper strip that is slightly larger than the flap, lay the straight edge of the strip along the flap's fold and glue it down.

8 TRIM THE DECORATIVE PAPER

Trim off the excess contrasting paper with scissors, following the shape of the original flap.

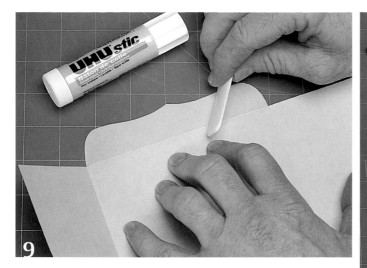

9 BURNISH THE FINISHED FLAP

Burnish and smooth out the completed flap with your bone folder one more time. This will keep the decorative paper from coming unglued.

10 DECORATE THE INSIDE

Decorate the inside of your note with colored pencils, rubber stamps and paper scraps.

Remember that the French Door flaps will keep any cards or photos safe inside, so feel free to add something extra to your correspondence.

11 ADD THE ADDRESS LABELS

Glue torn paper scraps to the outside of your note to make a clean space for writing the addresses. The outer flap can be further accented with a second decorative layer of paper smaller than the first.

TWEEZER TIP

If you are gluing small pieces of paper onto your foldnote, try holding them with a pair of flat-tipped tweezers. They make the job of positioning sticky little scraps much easier, while keeping your fingers clean.

The Creative Zone
P.O. BOX 19458
SEATTLE, WASHINGTON
98109-1458

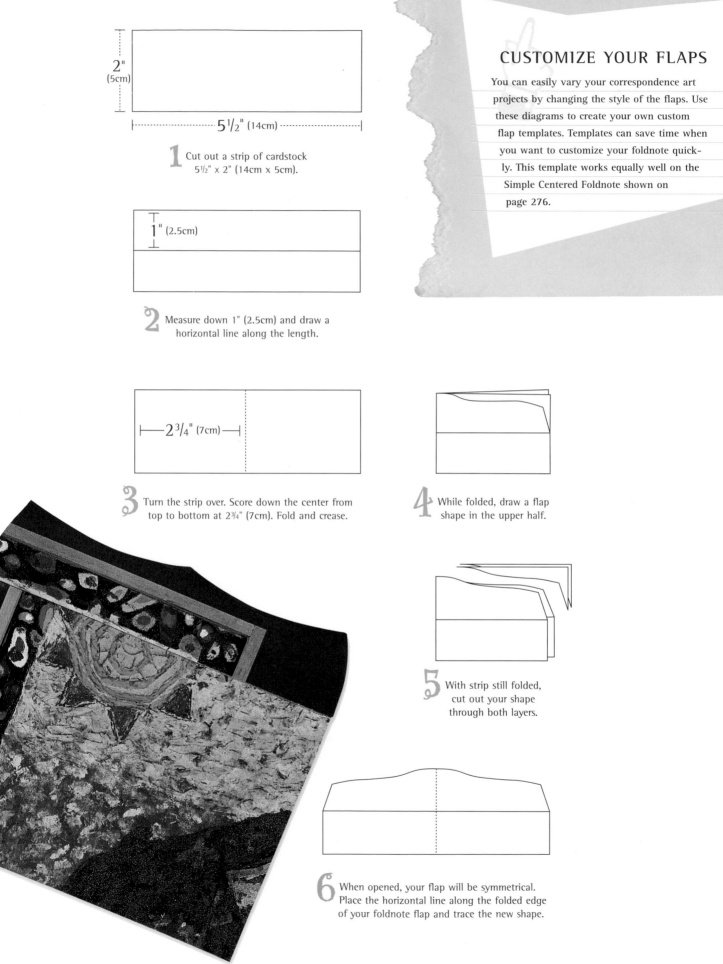

1 Cut out a strip of cardstock 5½" x 2" (14cm x 5cm).

2"
(5cm)

5½" (14cm)

CUSTOMIZE YOUR FLAPS

You can easily vary your correspondence art projects by changing the style of the flaps. Use these diagrams to create your own custom flap templates. Templates can save time when you want to customize your foldnote quickly. This template works equally well on the Simple Centered Foldnote shown on page 276.

1" (2.5cm)

2 Measure down 1" (2.5cm) and draw a horizontal line along the length.

2¾" (7cm)

3 Turn the strip over. Score down the center from top to bottom at 2¾" (7cm). Fold and crease.

4 While folded, draw a flap shape in the upper half.

5 With strip still folded, cut out your shape through both layers.

6 When opened, your flap will be symmetrical. Place the horizontal line along the folded edge of your foldnote flap and trace the new shape.

INTERESTING Variations

/ADD A COLLAGED CARD/ Salvaged papers and old photographs combine to make interesting collages in this quick note to a friend. Trim pieces of cardstock to fit the inside of a French Door Foldnote and embellish them to your heart's content. Wavy scissors add a decorative touch to the flap.

/FUN WITH WINDOWS/ Give your readers a surprise peek at what's inside. A window or door cut into the flaps of your foldnote adds a visual focal point.

/ADDRESS LABELS WITH A HEART/ Cut heart-shaped masks and place them over the address areas. Then stamp around the edges to turn a plain foldnote into a special greeting.

PocketSurprises

In this chapter we'll introduce you to the Perfect Pocket Foldnote. The element of surprise makes this foldnote as fun to give as it is to receive. What arrives looking like a simple envelope, unfolds to show two pockets just waiting to reveal their hidden secrets. The challenge for you, the sender, is deciding how to tailor your foldnote to that special someone, and what to hide in those two little pockets.

We'll show you how to make four different pocket inserts—from mini pages and paper wreaths to stapled booklets—all from one little pattern. But really, the sky's the limit here. You can stick just about anything into one of these foldnotes. Think about sending lottery tickets for an extra birthday boost. Got some theater tickets you can't use? Send them across town tucked away in a pocket foldnote. Coupons, a clipped article, paper holiday decorations and jokes all make wonderful pocket surprises for those special occasions—or for any time at all.

chapter two

MaTeRiaLS NEEDED

- **foldnote:** 8½" x 11" (21.6cm x 28cm) sheet of decorative paper (GRAIN SHORT)

- **pages:** two sheets of 8½" x 11" (21.6cm x 28cm) colored text-weight paper

- 8½" x 11" (21.6cm x 28cm) sheet of colored cardstock

- ruler

- pencil

- bone folder

- pocket insert pattern (ON PAGE 289)

- scissors or craft knife

- cutting mat

- glue stick

- decorative paper scraps

- rubber stamps

- black ink pad

The element of surprise makes this foldnote especially fun to send and receive. Unfold the note to discover hidden pockets just waiting to share their secrets. Perfect receptacles for mini pages or booklets (see the insert ideas on pages 293–297), these pockets might also hold tickets or coupons for that special some-one's special day.

Perfect Pocket Foldnote

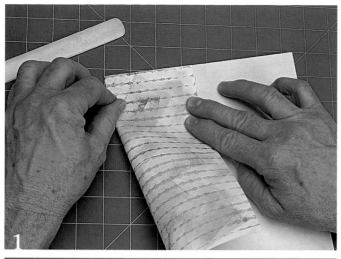

1 MEASURE AND FOLD
THE LEFT EDGE OF THE PAPER
Place the foldnote paper horizontally on
your work surface, decorative side down.
Starting from the left edge, measure over
and make pencil marks at 4" (10.2cm)
and 7" (17.8cm) close to the top edge.
Fold the left edge of the paper to the 7"
(17.8cm) mark, aligning the top edges.
Crease the fold with a bone folder and
open it up.

2 FOLD THE RIGHT
EDGE OF THE PAPER
Fold the right edge of the paper to the 4"
(10.2cm) mark, align the top edges, then
crease and open.

This is the pattern for custom
pages you can tuck into your
pocket foldnote. To use this template, copy it at 100% onto a
piece of cardstock and cut it out.

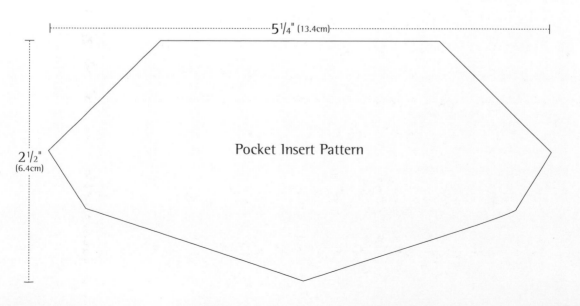

5¼" (13.4cm)

2½"
(6.4cm)

Pocket Insert Pattern

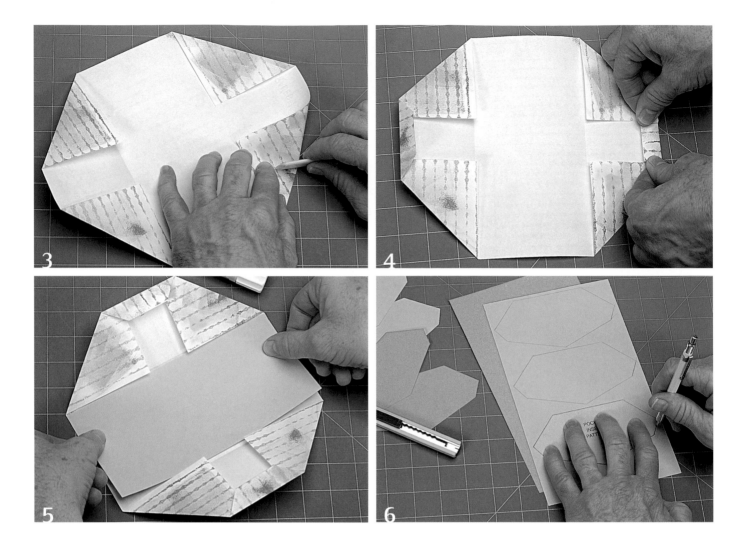

3 FOLD THE CORNERS

Fold each corner in to the nearest fold line and crease them with a bone folder.

4 FOLD IN FLAPS ON BOTH SIDES

With your foldnote still in a horizontal position, make pencil marks 1 1/2" (3.8cm) in from each side. Fold both sides in to the pencil marks, creating 3/4" (1.9cm) flaps and crease them well.

5 GLUE CARDSTOCK INTO THE CENTER SECTION

Cut a strip of cardstock 8 1/2" (21.6cm) x 3 7/8" (9.8cm) and glue it to the center section of the foldnote for stiffness and color contrast.

6 TRACE YOUR NOTE PAGES

Photocopy the pocket insert pattern on page 289 to a piece of cardstock and cut out carefully. This pattern will be used for each pocket insert. Trace your pattern on colored paper for individual note pages.

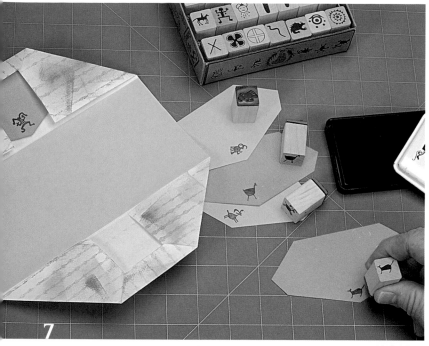

7 DECORATE YOUR PAGES WITH STAMPS
Decorate your pocket note pages. When you're done writing your letter, tuck the pages snugly inside the pockets.

8 ADD A STICKER TO THE FLAPS
Close your foldnote and add a handmade sticker to seal the flap.

9 THE FINISHED POCKET FOLDNOTE
The side pockets can hold any number of surprises. Jot down a short poem, or send a series of humorous pictures.

TAKE IT A STEP FURTHER NEED MORE SPACE FOR WRITING? ADD A STAPLED BOOKLET INSERT TO YOUR POCKET FOLD-NOTE BY FOLLOWING THE INSTRUCTIONS ON PAGE 292. →

CREATIVE INSERTS

Add some further excitement by using your pocket insert pattern for more than just making loose pages. Go wild with one of the four different pocket insert variations found on pages 293–297.

STAPLED BOOKLET INSERT

The beauty of the Pocket Foldnote is that there's plenty of room to play around with enclosure variations. When you have lots to say, make a stapled booklet and glue it to the middle section of your foldnote for added writing space. Make your covers from two pieces of cardstock cut to 8½" x 3⅞" (21.6cm x 9.8cm) grain long. Choose a light-colored text-weight paper and cut four inside pages to 8" x 3⅝" (20.3cm x 9.2cm). Trim a scrap of decorative paper to 1½" x 8½" (3.8cm x 21.6cm) to wrap around the booklet spine.

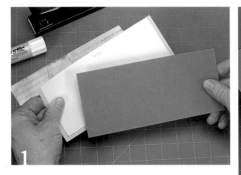

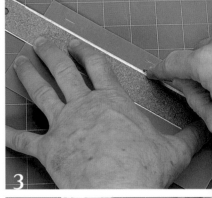

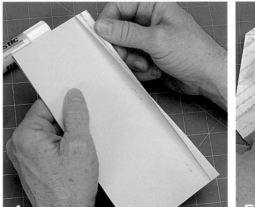

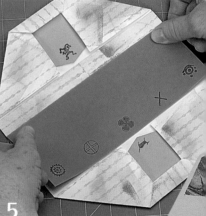

1 STAPLE THE INSIDE PAGES
Square up your pages, then put one staple in the middle of the spine area, close to the top edge, to hold the pages together. Center your pages inside the covers, flush with the top edge.

2 ATTACH THE COVERS
Place three staples along the spine, ¾" (1.9cm) from the top edge. Gently flatten the staples by tapping with a small hammer or the blunt end of a round-handled craft knife.

3 SCORE THE COVER FLAP
Measure down 1" (2.5cm) from the edge of the spine and score your top cover. Fold and crease. This will make it easier to open your booklet.

4 ADD A DECORATIVE STRIP
Glue up the inside surface of your decorative paper strip. Starting at the score line on the front cover, adhere the paper and wrap it around the spine to the back cover as shown. Burnish the spine well.

5 INSERT THE BOOKLET INTO YOUR FOLDNOTE
Glue the back surface of your booklet and adhere it to the middle section of your Pocket Foldnote. We've added stamped images from Ivory Coast.

POCKET INSERTS

One little pattern, so many creative combinations! The next four inserts are all made from the basic pocket insert pattern on page 289, but depending on how you fold your paper, where you place the pattern, or what you do with the pages, each one lends new meaning to "variety is the spice of correspondence art." Instructions for each one begin on page 294.

stapled POCKET INSERT

A few staples and decorative paper scraps will turn loose pages into mini-booklets. Send separate letters to your niece and nephew in the same foldnote; or write your letter in one and a teeny weeny story in the other. Our booklets have four pages, but there's certainly room for more. (See page 294.)

folded POCKET INSERT

For this insert, tracing the pattern to a folded piece of paper creates a whole different animal, so to speak. Colored pages can be trimmed and nested inside one another to create layered letters as fun to look at as they are to read. (See page 295.)

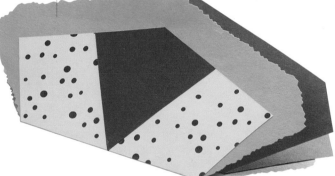

wreath POCKET INSERT

There's something very inviting about a circular wreath. Our Wreath Insert can definitely be decked out for the holidays, or delight your friends and family at any time of the year. (See page 296.)

accordion POCKET INSERT

Accordion folds are among the most popular folds, perhaps because they're so versatile and dramatic. You start with something that is one size and when you open it, end up with so much more. (See page 297.)

HEY HOWDY!

stapled POCKET INSERT

For each stapled pocket insert you will need colored cardstock for the covers, colored text-weight paper for the inside pages and decorative paper to wrap around the spine. These booklets have four pages, but there's always room for more.

1 TRACE THE PAGES AND COVERS
Trace the pocket insert pattern from page 289 eight times on contrasting colored paper for your pages and four times on cardstock for your covers. When tracing the pattern, be sure to have the longest (top) edge of the pattern parallel to the grain of the paper or cardstock.

Cut out your pages and covers. Next, measure and score the top covers with a bone folder ½" (1.3cm) from the long straight edge.

2 STAPLE THE PAGES
Place four pages between two covers and staple twice in the middle of the spine area. Repeat for your second booklet, then flatten all the staples.

3 ADD A DECORATIVE SPINE WRAP
Fold both pieces of decorative paper in half along the length, decorative side out, and crease. Glue up the inside surface of one and slip it over the spine of one booklet to cover the staples. Make sure the wrap is snug, then burnish it on both sides with your bone folder. Repeat these steps for the second booklet.

4 ADD THE FINAL TOUCHES
Trim the ends of your wraps flush with the angled edges of the inserts.

Make a coordinating Pocket Foldnote, and tie everything together with matching spine wraps and cardstock for a truly sophisticated mail-art package.

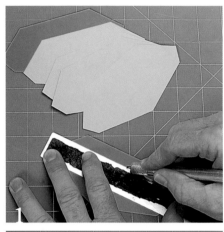

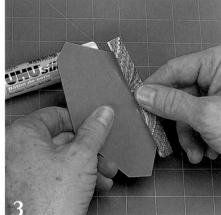

folded POCKET INSERT

Nest different colored pages inside one another for a dramatic layered effect. This insert is easy to make and fun to embellish. For these pages you will need four colored text-weight papers each cut to 5¼" (13.3cm) square.

1 FOLD EACH SQUARE
Fold your colored squares in half with the fold parallel to the grain and crease with a bone folder.

2 TRACE THE PATTERN
Place one folded square inside another, then trace the pattern from page 289 with the longest straight edge on the fold. Repeat these steps for the remaining squares.

3 CUT OUT THE SHAPES
With the pages still folded and nested, cut out the traced shapes. Trim the edges of your outer covers with decorative scissors if desired, to expose the colored edges of your inner pages.

4 DECORATE THE COVERS
Decorate the outer covers with simple geometric paper shapes.

5 ADD FURTHER EMBELLISHMENTS
There are numerous ways to add flair to your foldnotes. Here, we've added a deckled edge to the black cardstock in the center, which ties it visually to the inserts. It's subtle, but effective.

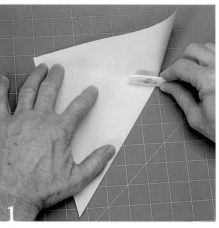

wreath POCKET INSERT

With a wreath, you can write your letter in each folded section, or in a circle around and around the center. For each wreath you make, you will need a sheet of colored text-weight paper cut to 8½" (21.6cm) square.

① FOLD ON THE DIAGONAL
Fold one square in half diagonally and crease the fold with a bone folder.

② FOLD IN HALF AGAIN
Fold it in half again, bringing the points at either end of the folded edge together and crease.

③ TRACE THE PATTERN
Place your folded triangle with the open edges facing you, then trace the pattern from page 289 as shown.

④ CUT OUT THE WREATH
Remove the pattern and cut the traced lines through all layers. Repeat these steps for your second wreath.

⑤ DECORATE THE WREATH PAGES
We've used our foldnote paper again to frame the wreath opening and to add decorative touches around the outer edge. Consider stamping or writing on the inside of the pocket.

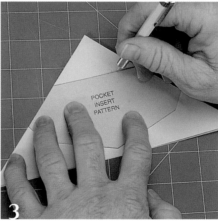

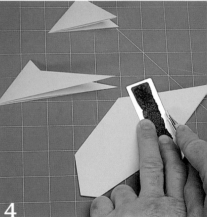

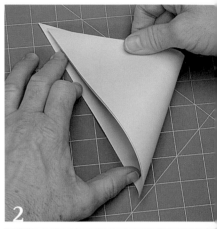

5

accordion POCKET INSERT

For this project, make the same insert look totally different just by combining your papers in different ways. You will need a 5½" x 9½" (14cm x 24.1cm) piece of colored text-weight paper (grain short) for each insert.

❶ FOLD PAPER IN HALF
Place your paper horizontally. Fold one side over to the other and crease well with a bone folder. Open the paper and flip it over.

❷ MARK AND FOLD OVER THE EDGES
Measuring from the left edge, make pencil marks at 4" (10.2cm) and 5½" (14cm) close to the top edge.
   Fold the left edge over to the 5½" (14cm) mark, aligning the top and bottom edges, then crease and open. Fold the right edge over to the 4" (10.2cm) mark, align the edges, crease and open.

❸ ACCORDION FOLD THE PAPER
Accordion fold the paper. Notice that the center fold is recessed—that's intentional. Place the longest edge of the pattern from page 289 on the folds and trace.

❹ CUT OUT THE PATTERN
Cut out the pattern shape through all the layers. Repeat these steps for the second piece of paper. Then decorate each accordion insert with colorful scraps of paper.

❺ COORDINATE THE PAGES AND THE FOLDNOTE
Decorative edge cutters are a nice optional tool when working with paper. Here, the small wavy edges on the decorative papers add contrast to the straight edges on the rest of the foldnote.

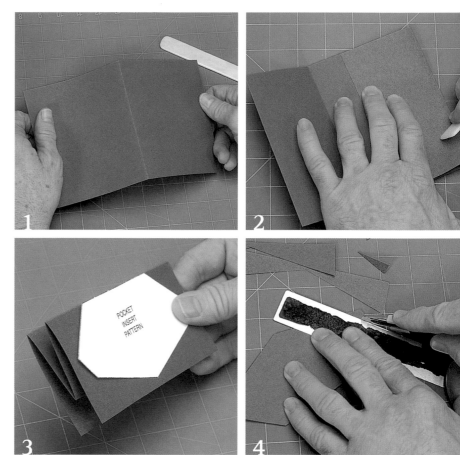

HELLO,

MoreFunWithFolds

So much to do, so little time. Real or imagined, time does seem to be speeding us faster and faster. Yet, nieces and nephews still have birthdays, friends still invite us to special events, life still keeps happening, whether we have time for it or not. So what do you do when time is of the essence and you need to send a thank you? Or you want to say "Hey, howdy!" to your sister and an e-mail just won't cut it? We say, make more foldnotes!

Foldnotes are so quick and easy that a lack of time is really not an issue. Simply make a few folds in a piece of paper and you have the note and envelope all in one. Want more substance? Add a creative insert. Or photos. Or see-through address windows. The following projects show you how. And in the making, we hope you discover the best reason of all for sending foldnotes—they're just plain fun! Really, in these times of hurry, hurry, hurry, couldn't we all use just a little more fun?

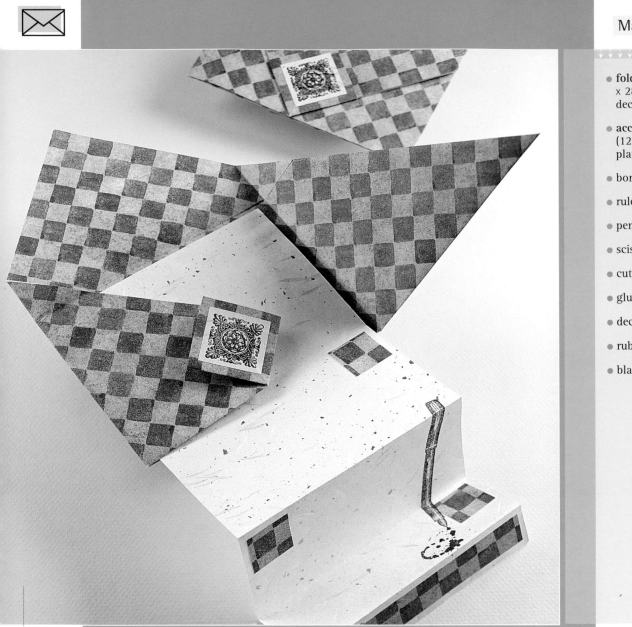

- **foldnote:** 11" x 11" (28cm x 28cm) square sheet of decorative paper

- **accordion insert:** 5" x 11" (12.7cm x 28cm) sheet of plain paper (GRAIN SHORT)

- bone folder

- ruler

- pencil

- scissors or craft knife

- cutting mat

- glue stick

- decorative paper scraps

- rubber stamps

- black ink pad

Of all the projects in this book, the Diamond Foldnote is like the "hostess with the mostest" who always has room for one more at the table. Made from the largest piece of paper, the finished note offers the most writing surface and plenty of opportunity to add even more writing surface and more surprises. Like its name, this one is a true gem.

Diamond Foldnote

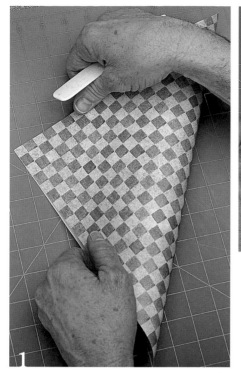

① FOLD THE SQUARE ON THE DIAGONAL
Fold an 11" x 11" (28cm x 28cm) square in half diagonally and crease the fold well with a bone folder.

② MEASURE AND FOLD THE SIDE FLAPS
Place your ruler along the folded edge. Measuring from the left, make pencil marks at 5½" (14cm) and 10" (25.4cm). Fold the right point over to the left pencil mark and crease heavily, then unfold. Now fold the left point over to the right mark, crease heavily and unfold. Erase your pencil marks.

③ FOLD BACK THE TIP OF THE LEFT FLAP
Fold both points over again with the left point on top. Then take the tip of the left point and fold it back to the left so that the new vertical fold is at the bottom of the V formed by the overlapping sections of the foldnote. Crease this fold hard with your bone folder.

④ OPEN UP THE DIAMOND POCKET
Take the left point and raise it to a standing position. Holding both sides of the point open between your thumbs and forefingers, push the point forward to create a diamond pocket. Crease the folds with your bone folder.

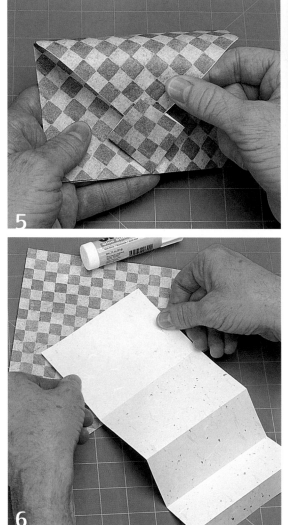

WRITING SPACE OPTIONS

Your letter can be written on the accordion letter pasted into the Diamond Foldnote, or you can open up the entire inside surface of the foldnote and write on the additional blank space inside—an unexpected surprise.

5 TUCK THE TOP FLAP INTO THE POCKET

Fold the remaining top point of the foldnote down to the bottom center of your foldnote and crease heavily. Now lift the top flap and stick the point into the diamond pocket. Your Diamond Foldnote is ready to decorate.

6 ADD AN ACCORDION LETTER

To add more writing surface inside, lay your plain paper in the center rectangle of the triangle and begin accordion pleating. No measuring is necessary—the sections of your accordion letter can be different sizes as long as it all fits inside the foldnote. Then run your glue stick along the top edge on the back side of the accordion letter and glue it into the rectangle.

7 ADD THE FINAL TOUCHES

In our foldnote, the panels of the accordion get smaller and smaller. We use the last panel as the hand-pull that opens the letter. A few rubber stamps and pasted scraps of decorative paper complete the elegant look of this design.

TAKE IT A STEP FURTHER TRIANGLE POP-OUTS ARE A CLEVER WAY TO ADD SOME DIMENSION TO YOUR DIAMOND FOLDNOTE. ADD A FEW TO YOUR FOLDNOTE BY FOLLOWING THE INSTRUCTIONS ON THE NEXT PAGE. →

triangle POP-OUT INSERT

With all that writing surface inside the Diamond Foldnote, we still can't resist adding more. This simple triangular pop-out can be positioned anywhere inside your fold-note to create a truly surprising piece of interactive mail. For each pop-out you will need a 5" x 5" (12.7cm x 12.7cm) square piece of colored text-weight paper.

❶ FOLD A SQUARE ON THE DIAGONALS
Fold a 5" (12.7cm) square diagonally, crease and unfold. Now fold it diagonally the other way on the same side of the paper. Your diagonal folds should intersect in the middle.

❷ FLIP THE SQUARE OVER AND FOLD IN HALF
Turn your square over. Fold it once in half, bringing the bottom edge of the square up to the top edge. Crease well and unfold.

❸ PUSH IN THE CENTER
Turn your square over again and with one finger, push down at the center. The ends of the horizontal fold should pop up.

❹ BRING IN THE ENDS TO MAKE A TRIANGLE
Bring the opposite ends of the horizontal fold together, then lay it down and flatten your triangle. Crease the folds well. Your pop-out is ready to be added to your foldnote.

❺ DECORATE AND GLUE IN YOUR POP-OUTS
Once you've finished making your pop-outs, decorate and write on them, then glue them into any available section of your Diamond Foldnote. If you wish, you can even open up the entire inside of your foldnote and paste a few pop-outs in there as well!

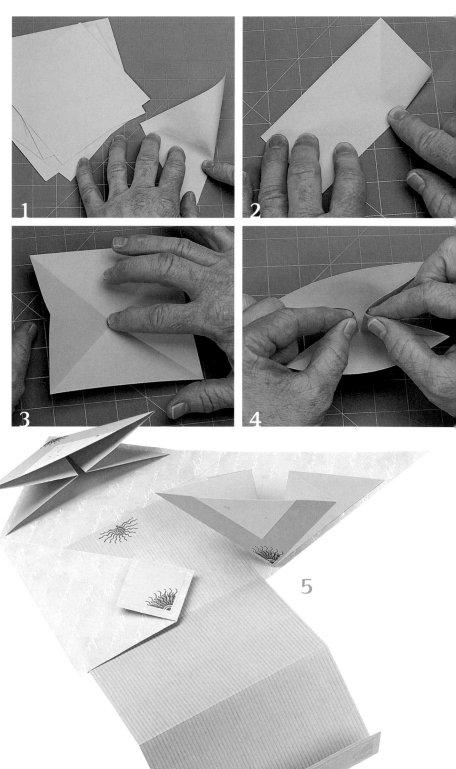

- **foldnote:** 8½" x 8½" (21.6cm x 21.6cm) square sheet of decorative paper

- **insert:** 11" x 4⅛" (28cm x 10.5cm) piece of cardstock (GRAIN SHORT)

- ruler

- pencil

- bone folder

- glue stick

- decorative paper scraps

- rubber stamps

- black ink pad

- oval template for insert

- photos or images for insert

The Square Foldnote is one of our most practical. Quickly made, it easily adapts to handle different enclosures—like the French Door insert we include for you here. Dress it up or leave it plain, write on the inside surface, cut individual pages for your letter, or include a special address window on the outside (see page 307). There's no end to this note's versatility.

Easy Square Foldnote

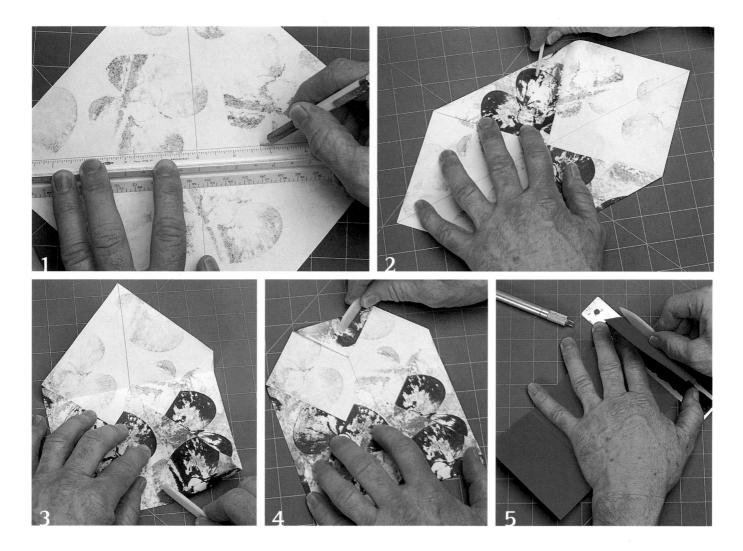

1 MARK THE DIAGONALS

Place your paper decorative side down and draw two light diagonal pencil lines that intersect in the center of your paper. Place the paper in front of you so the pencil lines run north/south and east/west. Make two pencil marks on the horizontal (E/W) line 1³/₄" (4.5cm) to the left and 1³/₄" (4.5cm) to the right of the center point.

2 FOLD IN THE TOP AND BOTTOM

Fold the north and south points in to the center and crease them with your bone folder.

3 FOLD IN THE REMAINING POINTS

Turn your paper so the remaining points are north and south. Fold the top point down to the bottom pencil dot, crease and open. Fold the bottom point up to the top pencil dot, crease it and leave it folded.

4 FOLD THE TOP FLAP DOWN

To finish the foldnote, fold the top point down approximately 1 to 1¹/₂" (2.5cm to 4.5cm) and make a second crease. Now fold the entire top flap down. Your foldnote is complete and ready for contents and decorative touches.

5 CREATE A FRENCH DOOR INSERT

Place an 11" x 4¹/₈" (28cm x 10.5cm) piece of cardstock horizontally, plain side up. For smoother folds, cut this cardstock with the grain running parallel to the short edge of the paper.

Measure from the left and make pencil marks at the top and bottom, at 2⁵/₈" (6.7cm) and 8³/₈" (21.3cm). Align your ruler with each set of marks and make a valley score. Fold and crease each line.

6 ADD PICTURE WINDOWS
TO EACH PANEL
Trace appropriate-sized ovals on one or
both door panels, then cut out the shapes.

7 INSERT YOUR PHOTOS
Glue or tape your photos or images
behind the window openings. If
you're using double-stick tape,
place all the pieces before peeling
off the top protective paper. Then
attach the photo.

8 COVER THE PHOTO BACKS
WITH DECORATIVE PAPER
Line each window panel with paper
to cover the back of the photo and
give your insert a finished look.

9 DECORATE THE FRENCH DOORS
Add faux photo corners to the front of the
doors for a decorative touch. Here, we've
used different photos of our nephew and
stamped below the words *Now* and *Then*
on decorative paper scraps.

Write a note inside your French Door
insert, tuck it into your Square Foldnote
and send it on its way.

TRY A FUN VARIATION ADD A SEE-THROUGH ADDRESS WIN-
DOW TO YOUR FOLDNOTE BY FOLLOWING THE INSTRUCTIONS ON
THE NEXT PAGE. →

ACETATE ADDRESS WINDOWS

We like address windows because they add dimension to correspondence. Put a window on the front of your Square Foldnote and you invite the viewer to "C'mon in and visit with me a spell." Try layering different colored windows for even more dimension. For the acetate windows, you will need one or more contrasting papers and a piece of acetate or polyester film, all 4¼" x 6" (10.8cm x 15.2cm) in size.

❶ CUT OUT AN ADDRESS WINDOW
Make a Square Foldnote. With your foldnote open, trace a window shape on the center rectangle and cut it out. Leave at least a ¾" (1.9cm) border on all sides. Trim the inside pages and acetate.

❷ TRACE THE WINDOW
Place a piece of 4¼" x 6" (10.8cm x 15.2cm) colored paper inside your foldnote and close it, then trace the address opening on the inside paper.

❸ ADDRESS THE SPACE
Remove the paper and stamp or write the address within the drawn shape. If you plan to add another layer, leave some space between the address and the traced opening.

❹ ADD A CONTRASTING FRAME
To create a layered frame, trace the original opening on a different colored paper, then cut out a slightly smaller opening.

❺ ASSEMBLE THE LAYERS
To send, place the acetate window in first, then the address paper. You may find it easier to cut out and layer your windows, then stamp your address in the space left over. You can also save time by making cardstock templates, so all you have to do is trace the different-sized openings on future foldnotes.

- **foldnote:** 8½" x 11" (21.6cm x 28cm) sheet of decorative paper
- ruler
- bone folder
- glue stick
- decorative paper scraps
- rubber stamps
- black ink pad
- postage stamp

The story we've been told over the years is that the Mennonites designed this foldnote to eliminate the cost of an envelope. While their motives may have been thrifty, the resulting foldnote is worth its weight in gold. Simple, clever and beautiful, it requires no measuring or cutting, and we especially like the way the postage stamp does extra duty as the sticker that seals the note.

Mennonite Foldnote

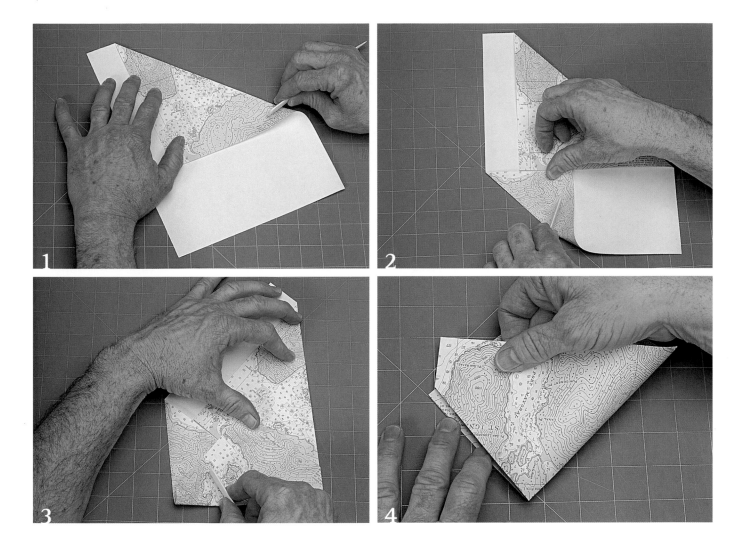

1 FOLD THE TOP-RIGHT CORNER DOWN

With your paper placed vertically and decorated side down, fold the top-right corner down leaving approximately a 1½" (3.8cm) margin on the left side. Make sure your edges are parallel, then crease the fold with your bone folder.

2 FOLD THE BOTTOM-LEFT CORNER UP

Fold the bottom-left corner up to meet the edge of the first folded corner and crease.

3 TURN THE NOTE AND FOLD THE BOTTOM CORNER UP

Turn your note slightly so that the bottom-right corner now points south. Fold the bottom corner up approximately 4" (10.2cm), keeping the side edges parallel, and crease the fold.

4 FOLD LAST CORNER UP OVER TOP EDGE

Swing the note around 180 degrees so the remaining corner now points south. Fold this last corner up so the top part of the point is sticking above the top edge of your foldnote and crease.

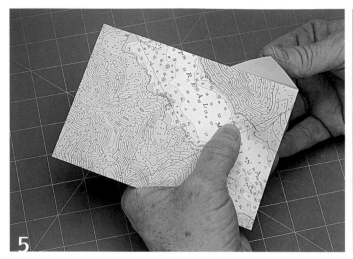

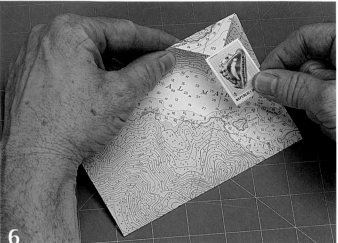

5 FLIP THE NOTE OVER AND FOLD THE TIP DOWN

Flip the note over and fold the little triangle down.
Unfold your note and you're ready to decorate.

6 WRITE YOUR LETTER
AND SEAL WITH A STAMP

You can write directly on the foldnote, or create individual stationery
pages. When you're done writing
your letter, close it up, fold the last
little triangle down and seal the
foldnote with your postage stamp.

We show a decorative foreign
stamp here, but of course you will
want to use correct postage to mail
your Mennonite Foldnote.

7 DECORATE THE FOLDNOTE

Finish by cutting paper into
organic shapes to create address
labels that mimic the shapes
found on the nautical map.

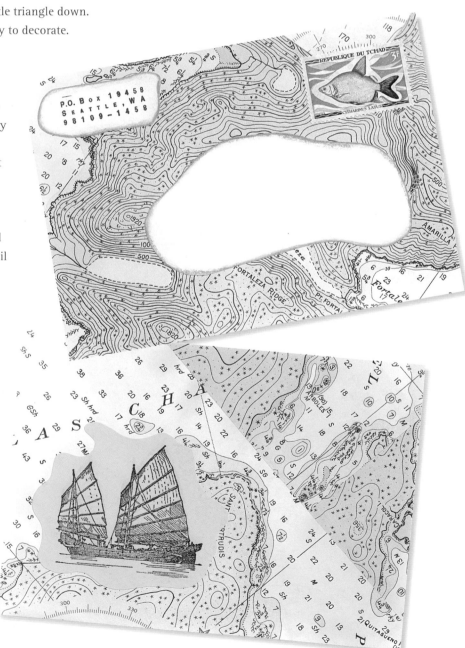

/ DROP IN A BOOKLET / Instead of loose pages, why not put in a booklet with French Door flaps? We adjusted the sides of this Square Foldnote to make a wider foldnote. Then we created a booklet just the right size to drop inside.

/ ELEGANT DIAMONDS / A hand-carved stamp lends a touch of oriental elegance to this Diamond Foldnote. Inside, yellow pop-outs provide a brilliant contrast to the red and black exterior.

/ MORE FUN WITH WINDOWS / Acetate windows can be used for more than just addresses. They also make perfect frames for a piece of art or a holiday greeting.

MagicUpYourSleeves

Like a magician making objects appear and disappear, these cardstock mail-art sleeves will surprise and delight your audience with the paper magic they perform. Versatile and venerable in their simplicity, they make the perfect foil for creative combinations of inserts and embellishments—mix and match your favorite inserts or decorating ideas from any other project with a sleeve and see what happens. And because sleeves are so accommodating, they can be transformed quick as a wink to a different size simply by slicing off one end.

In this chapter, we conjure up the basic sleeve from a single piece of cardstock that has been decorated with food coloring and blown bubbles, then show you how to add decorative flaps to keep your creative contents from doing a disappearing act. We follow that with four multitalented inserts: an accordion letter, a shopping bag letter that doubles as art, and two variations of a photo frame letter. Start sending out correspondence magic like this and you'll have everyone begging for more.

MaTeRiaLS NEEDED

- **sleeve:** 8½" x 11" (21.6cm x 29.2cm) sheet of card-stock (GRAIN SHORT)
- ruler
- pencil
- bone folder
- scissors or craft knife
- cutting mat
- decorative cutter (OPTIONAL)
- hole punch
- glue stick
- decorative paper scraps

Think of the sleeve as the workhorse of mail art. Made from cardstock, a sleeve provides a sturdy platform from which to launch interactive letters that run the gamut from simple to complex, funky to trés elegant. Choose cardstock from a wonderful variety of colors and designs, or decorate your own as you see here.

Basic Correspondence Sleeve

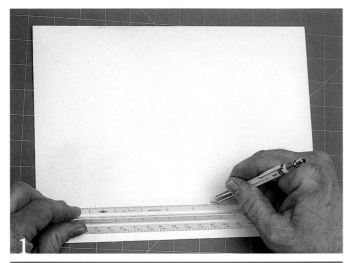

1 MEASURE AND MARK YOUR FOLDS

Place your large cardstock horizontally with the decorated side down. Measuring from the left, make pencil marks at the top and bottom at 2¼" (5.7cm) and 6¾" (17.2cm).

2 SCORE YOUR FOLDS

Score with a bone folder or scoring tool, fold the cardstock and crease at the pencil marks.

3 ADD A SEAL

Glue a colorful handmade seal to the top flap to complete your sleeve.

TAKE IT A STEP FURTHER YOUR BASIC SLEEVE IS NOW READY TO BE FILLED. IF YOU PLAN TO INSERT LOOSE PAGES, TURN THE PAGE TO LEARN HOW TO ADD DECORATIVE SIDE FLAPS.

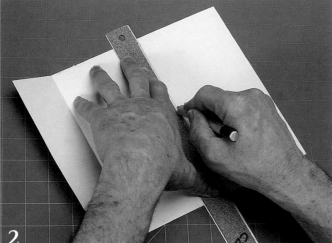

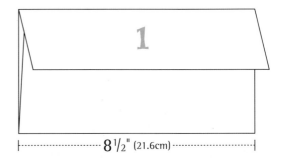

1

8½" (21.6cm)

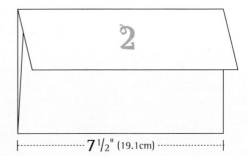

2

7½" (19.1cm)

SLEEVES OF ALL SIZES

The basic sleeve is made from 8½" x 11" (21.6cm x 28cm) cardstock. Score and fold according to the directions above, then trim one end to vary the width. You can make custom sleeves by varying the width and height. All three of the widths shown here meet standard U.S. postal regulations.

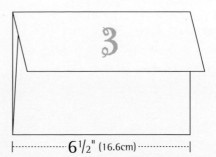

3

6½" (16.6cm)

Adding flaps is a great way to dress up a basic correspondence sleeve. Better yet, flaps will keep any note pages or other enclosures from falling out. To create flaps for this sleeve you will need a 4¾" x 11" (12.1cm x 28cm) piece of cardstock (grain short) and some decorative paper scraps.

❶ MEASURE AND MARK YOUR FLAPS
With your 4¾" x 11" (12.1cm x 28cm) piece of cardstock placed horizontally, measure from the left and make pencil marks at the top and bottom at 1¼" (3.2cm), 5½" (14cm) and 9¾" (24.8cm).

❷ SCORE AND FOLD THE FLAPS
Align your ruler with each outer set of marks. With your scoring tool, valley score and crease these two outer lines.

❸ CUT THE FLAPS APART AND SHAPE THEM
Cut the flaps apart at the middle line, then shape your flaps at either or both ends if desired. We've used straight lines coming to a point, but you could round the ends or cut them with a decorative cutter.

FOLDING PERFECT FLAPS

How can you make your flaps fold easily and lie flat? Cut this piece of cardstock grain short, with the paper grain running parallel to the short edge of the cardstock. (See page 265 for more on grain direction.)

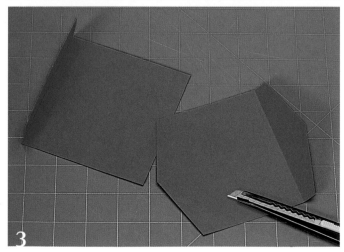

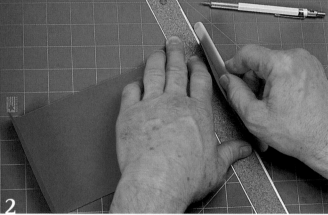

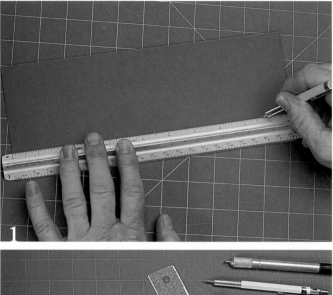

4 DECORATE THE FLAPS

It's much easier to decorate your flaps before you attach them to the sleeve. Try cutting out contrasting paper that mimics the shape of the flap, then add wavy edges and punched holes for visual interest.

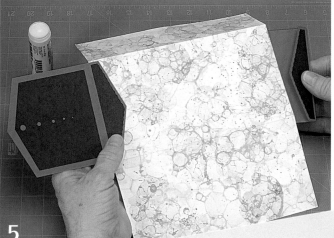

5 ATTACH THE FLAPS TO THE BASIC SLEEVE

Flaps can be glued to the inside or the outside of a sleeve. We're gluing the short section of our flaps to the outside surface of the sleeve so that the large sections wrap around to the inside.

6 ADD MATCHING STATIONERY

Our sleeve with flaps holds stationery with crayon rubbings of found objects. Notice how the flap sections glued to the outside become a design element for the address surface.

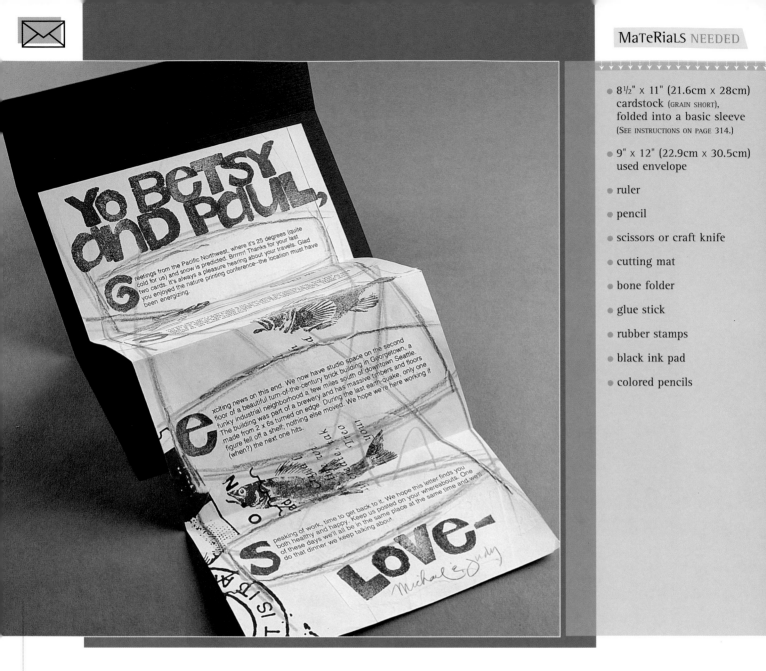
- 8½" x 11" (21.6cm x 28cm) cardstock (GRAIN SHORT), folded into a basic sleeve (SEE INSTRUCTIONS ON PAGE 314.)

- 9" x 12" (22.9cm x 30.5cm) used envelope

- ruler

- pencil

- scissors or craft knife

- cutting mat

- bone folder

- glue stick

- rubber stamps

- black ink pad

- colored pencils

Envelopes are one of our favorite sources of earth-friendly stationery, which is why you see a lot of them in our projects. Here's a simple way to reuse a large envelope. Open one up and you have a piece of paper approximately 24" (61cm) long, perfect for the accordion fold and more exciting than plain paper, especially if you include the outside printing and postage in your letter.

Recycled Envelope Insert

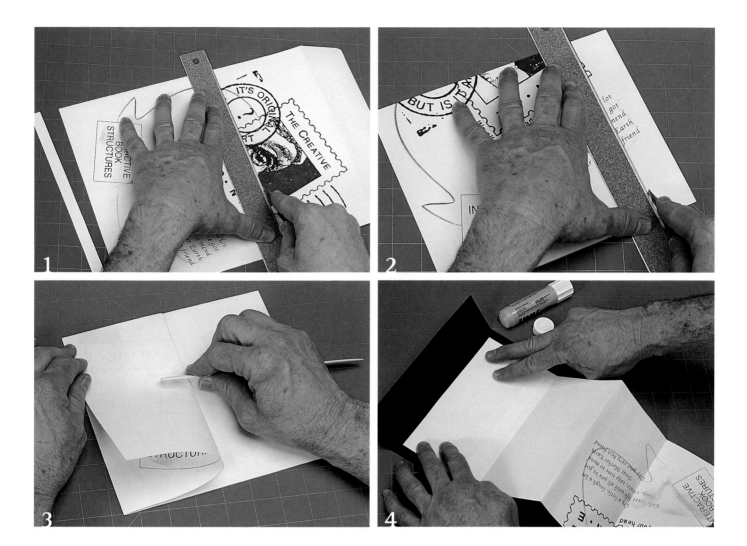

1 CUT OFF THE TOP AND BOTTOM

Choose a large, colorful envelope, at least 9" x 12" (22.9cm x 30.5cm). Place it horizontally, with the bottom of the envelope facing left. Measure from the left and draw vertical lines at ½" (1.3cm) and 8" (20.3cm). Cut through both layers of paper on these lines.

2 CUT OFF ONE FOLDED EDGE

Turn what's left of your envelope so the folded edges are on the sides. Measuring from the left, make pencil marks at the top and bottom at 8" (20.3cm). Align your ruler with these marks and cut through both layers of paper on this line.

3 FOLD THE PAPER LIKE AN ACCORDION

Leaving your paper in the same position, fold the top cut edge on the right over to the folded edge on the left and crease. Then flip your paper over and fold the remaining cut edge back to the fold and crease.

4 ATTACH IT TO A BASIC SLEEVE AND WRITE YOUR LETTER

Apply glue to the back of the top panel and adhere it to the middle section of your sleeve. Then, embellish and write your letter. Our letter was printed from the computer, then torn apart and pasted onto the accordion panels. The large letters were stamped with Michael's 37-year-old hand-carved eraser set, then the letters were colored in with pencil.

MaTeRiaLS NEEDED

- 8½" x 11" (21.6cm x 28cm) cardstock (GRAIN SHORT), folded into a basic sleeve (SEE INSTRUCTIONS ON PAGE 314.)
- used paper bag
- ruler
- pencil
- scissors or craft knife
- cutting mat
- bone folder
- glue stick
- decorative paper scraps
- rubber stamps
- black ink pad
- colored pencils

Whoever invented shopping bags with handles gets our vote of thanks. When slit down the sides and opened up, a paper bag is the perfect canvas for correspondence art. Write on the clean inside of the bag, or incorporate the outer bag design into your letter. And the really fun part? The handle acts as a hanger, just in case your letter ends up on the wall. And you thought shopping bags were just for shopping!

Letter In a Bag

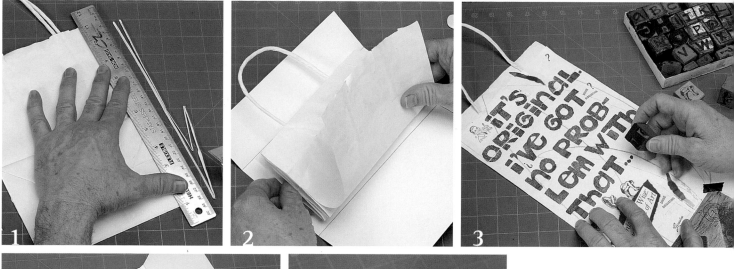

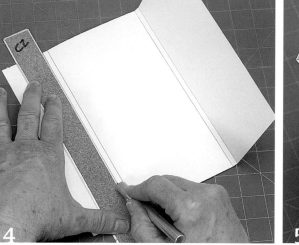

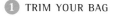

1 TRIM YOUR BAG

You will be inserting this bag into a basic sleeve (see page 314), so trim off both sides of the bag to fit the width of your sleeve. Open the bag up and cut off the handle at the bottom.

2 FOLD THE BAG TO FIT THE SLEEVE

Place the top edge of the bag in the middle section of your sleeve. Pleat the bag back and forth accordion style so that the sections are about 4¼" (10.8cm) high. Continue pleating until you run out of bag.

3 WRITE YOUR MASTERPIECE

Now comes the fun part: create your paper bag masterpiece. Ours has everything but the kitchen sink—hand-carved letters, clip art images, word stamps, collage and colored pencil.

4 ADJUST THE OUTER SLEEVE

Because this letter tends to be thick, your sleeve must be adjusted to accommodate it. To do this, measure over ¼" (6mm) to the outside of each existing fold and mark these lines. Score and crease these two additional folds.

5 GLUE IN THE PAPER BAG

Glue the back surface of your handle section to the inside center of the sleeve and burnish. When folded up, the sleeve now has the capacity to hold the paper bag and whatever you add to it.

6 ADD THE FINAL TOUCHES

Notice here how the back of the bottom panel of our letter ends up on top when the accordion is folded up—providing one more surface to decorate.

Our families spend a lot of time both behind and in front of the camera, so we enjoy finding ways to showcase photos for mail travel. This picture-perfect project requires only two folds and a little cutting to create a frame letter that holds one or two photos, and can be shaped and decorated to fit your fancy.

Doubletake Photo Flaps

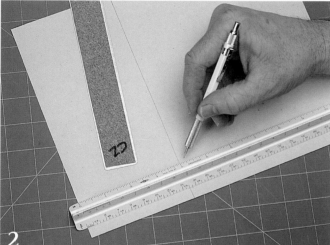

1 FOLD THE CARDSTOCK
IN HALF LENGTHWISE

Place your 8½" x 11" (21.6cm x 28cm)
cardstock for the insert vertically on your
work surface. Measure from the left and
make pencil marks top and bottom at
4¼" (10.8cm). Score and fold your cardstock in half lengthwise. Crease well with
a bone folder.

2 DRAW A LINE PERPENDICULAR
TO THE FOLD

Open up your cardstock and place it horizontally on your work surface, decorated
side down. Measuring from the left edge,
make pencil marks at the top and bottom
at 4" (10.2cm) and draw a light vertical
line to connect them.

3 CUT OUT THE LOWER-LEFT SECTION

Cut out the lower-left section formed by
the pencil line and the fold. Save this
piece as a liner.

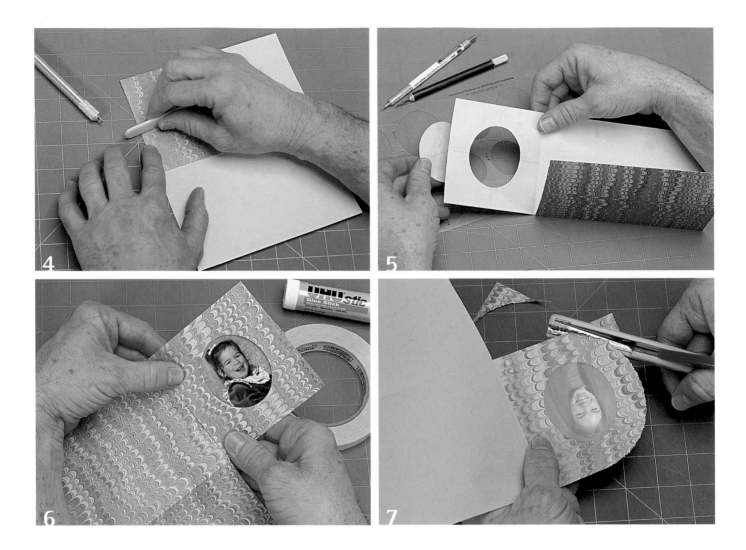

4 FOLD BACK THE SMALL FLAP

Score and crease the remaining line, then fold the left section over and crease it.

5 CUT OUT A PICTURE FRAME

Trace your desired picture shape on the inside of this top-left corner flap, then cut out the window.

6 PLACE YOUR FIRST PHOTO IN THE FRAME

Glue or tape your photo behind the frame opening. We've taped one of our niece's childhood photos in first.

7 ADD A SECOND PHOTO TO THE BACK

At this point, you can line the inside of the frame panel with the cut-out corner section. Or, as we've done, glue another photo back-to-back with the first one (the teen photo) and then glue or tape your extra panel on top to frame this inside photo. Shape the photo flap if desired.

8 WRITE YOUR LETTER AND DECORATE THE SLEEVE

Embellish and write your letter before you attach the insert to your sleeve (it's easier that way). Then, glue up the back of the top panel and adhere it to the middle section of your sleeve. Dress up your sleeve with matching decorative paper and trim the edges with decorative scissors.

8

DEAR GRANDMA,

DOUBLETAKE PHOTO IDEAS

This multifaceted foldnote offers plenty of clever possibilities. Here are a few to consider:

- Show a baby with a birthday cake followed by the child's face covered with icing.
- Insert before-and-after pictures of someone wearing a costume or makeup.
- Place a wedding photo outside and a 25th anniversary photo inside.
- Show pictures of the same house or tree in two different seasons.

If you want to take this idea a step further, glue an additional frame flap to the right side of the foldnote before gluing it into the sleeve.

MaTeRiaLS NEEDED

- 8½" x 11" (21.6cm x 28cm) cardstock (GRAIN SHORT), folded into a basic sleeve (SEE INSTRUCTIONS ON PAGE 314.)

- insert: 8½" x 14" (21.6cm x 35.6cm) piece of decorative paper

- bone folder

- pencil

- scissors or craft knife

- cutting mat

- glue stick or double-stick tape

- photo

- decorative paper scraps

- rubber stamps

- black ink pad

- colored pencils

Still have more photos than you know what to do with? This next frame insert is so simple that it needs no measuring. We start with a long piece of paper, so there's a generous writing surface, do a little more folding, and end up with plenty of interaction.

Folded Photo Frame

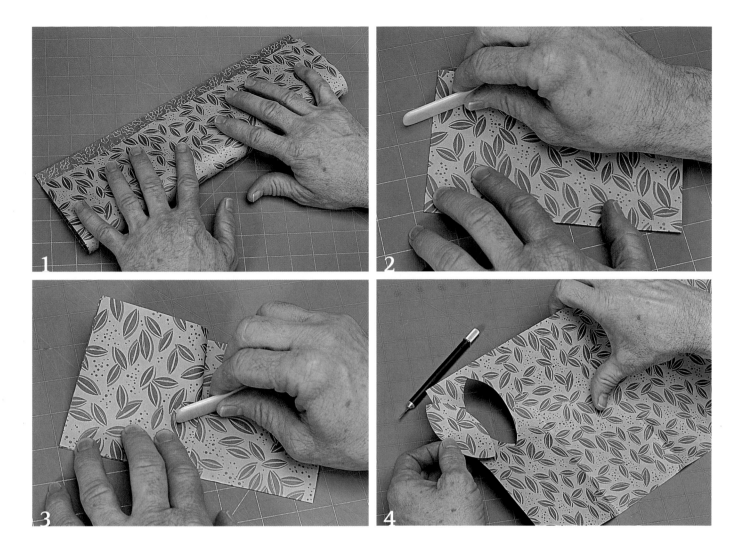

1 FOLD THE BOTTOM EDGE UP

With your paper placed horizontally, fold the bottom edge to the top and crease. We chose a paper that is decorated on both sides. If only one side of your paper is decorated, start with the paper decorated side down.

2 FOLD THE LEFT EDGE OVER TO THE RIGHT

Fold the left edge over to the right edge and crease.

3 FOLD THE RIGHT EDGE BACK

Now fold the right edge of the top section back to the left folded edge and crease.

4 ADD A PICTURE WINDOW

Open your paper completely, with the decorated side up, and cut out a window shape from the top-left section. Our shape mimics the shape of the leaves on our paper.

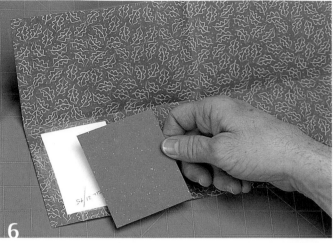

5 ADD A FAVORITE PHOTO
Glue or tape your photo behind the frame opening.

6 COVER THE BACK OF THE PHOTO
Line the back of the photo panel with contrasting or matching paper.

7 MAKE A COLORFUL WRITING SURFACE
If both sides of your paper are decorated, create writing surfaces by gluing in sections of paper and decorate accordingly. We're coloring in one of our favorite nature print stamps. The surprise element of this letter is the ample writing space that is revealed as the letter unfolds.

Finish by attaching the Folded Photo Frame into the center of a basic sleeve.

INTERESTING VariaTioNs

/MORE FUN WITH ACCORDIONS/ If one accordion fold is fun, are three accordion folds three times the fun? We think you'll have fun playing around with the possibilities for this insert. Cut all three panels the same width and stagger them as we do, or cut each one a different width, or attach them in a straight line, or turn the middle panel upside down, or have each panel open in a different direction, or... well, you get the picture.

bonjour paula
thanks for the postage
stamps from paris.... i
absolutely love 'em!

your letter was great.
those parisian flea mar
kets sound incroyable!

here's some
seattle paper ephemera
for your mailart
see inside

/A BRILLIANT IDEA / We added our own green ribbon handle to this reused accordion envelope letter. Then we tied in a mini accordion with bows and added a triangle pop-out to the bottom for a package that's full of surprises.

/PHOTO NOT REQUIRED / The interesting thing about photo frames is that you don't have to put in a picture to get an interesting effect. Here we have used the empty frame to accent the beautiful Japanese paper behind it.

TheEnvelopePlease

Junk mail in general, and return envelopes in particular, inspired our last three projects. We've always had a hard time throwing away perfectly good gummed envelopes, even though they're preprinted with someone else's address. So, the challenge was to retain the enclosure element of the envelope and to make use of the gummed flap if possible. These envelope pockets fit the bill on both counts, and perhaps—just perhaps—collecting return envelopes will help take the edge off receiving all that unsolicited mail (well, maybe).

Like many of our correspondence projects, envelope pockets are adaptable—a favorite characteristic of ours, in case you hadn't noticed. Pick a theme for the sleeve and carry it onto the envelope pockets. Create a collage with colorful paper or images on the outside and the inside of your sleeve; hide images inside the pockets along with stamped or collaged or hand-painted notes. Cut your pockets into different lengths, angle the cut edges, number your pockets or letter them. Reuse decorated envelopes that someone else sends you, or get rid of left-over envelopes from unused holiday cards. Oh, how the mind reels! Isn't it time to decorate and send the envelope, please?!

chapter five

MaTeRiaLS NEEDED

- 8½" x 11" (21.6cm x 28cm) cardstock (GRAIN SHORT), folded into a basic sleeve (SEE INSTRUCTIONS ON PAGE 314.)
- one return envelope, approximately 8" x 4" (20.3cm x 10.2cm)
- ruler
- pencil
- bone folder
- scissors or craft knife
- cutting mat
- glue stick
- decorative paper scraps
- decorative scissors
- rubber stamps
- black ink pad

At the risk of sounding redundant, but because it bears repeating, folding is the *fun*damental step that turns paper into something more than what you see. For the Instant Envelope Pocket, we take the existing fold and reverse it, use the gummed flap to attach the envelope to a sleeve, and then dress up the plain back of the envelope—which is now the front. Got that?

Instant
Envelope Pocket

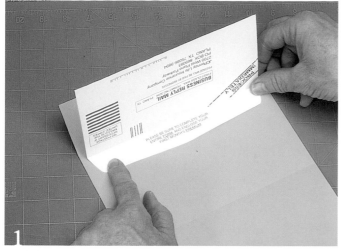

1 ATTACH THE ENVELOPE TO A SLEEVE

First, make a basic sleeve out of cardstock by following the instructions on page 314. Take an envelope, open the flap and bend it backwards. Then lick the flap and use it to adhere the envelope to the middle section of your sleeve, centering it from side to side approximately ¼" (6mm) down from the fold.

2 DECORATE THE ENVELOPE

Glue decorative paper over the front surface of your envelope and trim it if necessary. Make a finger pull—a cut-out section in the front of the envelope. This finger pull is rounded, but you can make yours any shape you like.

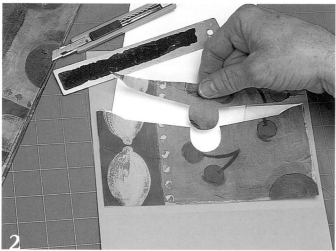

3 DECORATE THE OUTER SLEEVE

Using images from the decorative paper, create a collage on the inside and outside of your sleeve to tie the piece together. Add collage elements to the individual note pages and stamp them with numbers to indicate the proper sequence of the correspondence.

3

HELPFUL TIP

Finger pulls are notches cut away from the front of the envelope that make it easier for you to pull out your letter. To assist you, place a piece of cardboard or tag board inside the envelope as a surface to cut against.

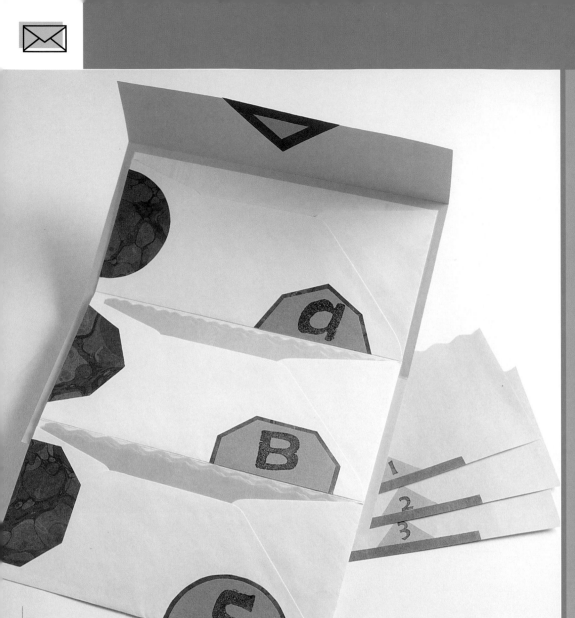

- 8½" x 11" (21.6cm x 28cm) cardstock (GRAIN SHORT), folded into a basic sleeve (SEE INSTRUCTIONS ON PAGE 314.)
- three unused envelopes
- ruler
- pencil
- scissors or craft knife
- cutting mat
- bone folder
- glue stick
- decorative paper scraps
- rubber stamps
- black ink pad
- decorative scissors

All paper is fair game for the accordion fold, and envelopes are no exception. We use three envelopes for our Cascading Pockets, but you could easily add more. Slice off the ends to fit any size sleeve, then add decorative paper wraps to the cut ends to keep the contents in their pockets.

Cascading Envelope Pockets

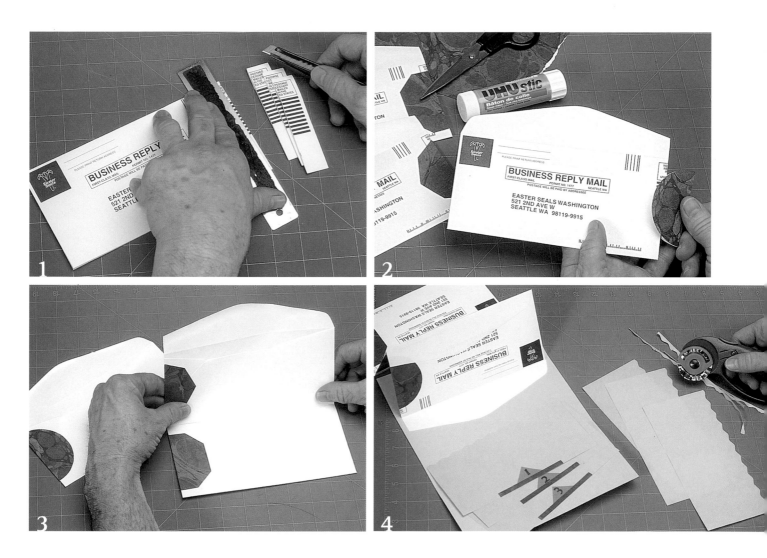

① CUT OFF THE ENVELOPE ENDS

Many envelopes are too long to fit in a standard sleeve. To solve this problem, cut off the ends. On one envelope, measure from the left and make pencil marks at 8" (20.3cm). Then stack all three envelopes and cut off the right ends. Your envelopes will now fit the sleeve.

② SEAL THE CUT ENDS

Open the envelope flaps. Glue decorative paper (any shape) around the open ends of each envelope to secure them.

③ CONNECT THE ENVELOPES

Lick the flap of one envelope and place the envelope on your work surface, gummed side up. Take a second envelope and lay it on top of the first envelope flap, keeping the bottom edge of the second envelope flush with the flap fold. Burnish with a bone folder. Repeat these steps for the third envelope.

④ ATTACH THE ENVELOPE POCKETS TO THE SLEEVE

Lick the remaining flap and bend it backwards, then attach the entire envelope unit to the middle section of your sleeve. Accordion fold the pockets. Your basic structure is done and ready to be decorated.

Next, make your note pages. Create greater visual interest by cutting one edge with a wavy cutter or scissors.

MaTeRiaLS NEEDED

- 8½" x 11" (21.6cm x 28cm) cardstock (GRAIN SHORT), folded into a basic sleeve (SEE INSTRUCTIONS ON PAGE 314.)

- flap: 4⅜" x 6" (11.1cm x 15.2cm) cardstock (GRAIN SHORT)

- three unused business envelopes

- hinges: three 2" x 4" (5.1cm x 10.2cm) pieces of decorative paper (GRAIN LONG)

- pages: colored text-weight paper

- ruler

- pencil

- bone folder

- scissors or craft knife

- cutting mat

- glue stick

- decorative paper scraps

- cork

- black ink pad

- stickers

We've pulled out all the stops on our last project to show you just how elegant plain envelopes can be when combined with a simple sleeve, a window flap and some beautiful paper. And therein lies the true magic of creative playing around—simple combinations that create correspondence as inspiring as the person who sends it. That's *you*.

Hinged Envelope Surprise

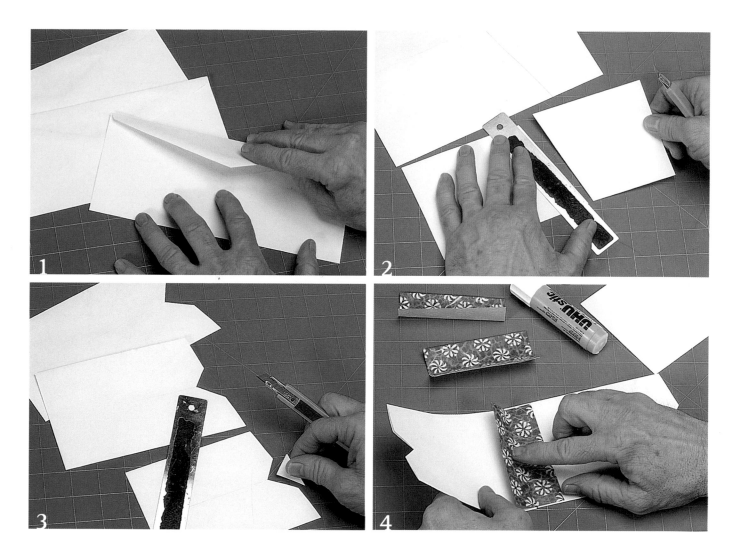

1 SEAL THE ENVELOPES

In this project, you will access the pockets from the side, not the top flap. So lick the flaps of all three envelopes, close them and burnish them with a bone folder.

2 TRIM OFF THE ENVELOPE ENDS

Cut off the right ends of your envelopes, one at 8" (20.3cm), one at 7" (17.8cm) and one at 6" (15.2cm). You can add greater visual interest by cutting the ends at an angle or rounding them.

3 CREATE THE FINGER PULLS

Cut a decorative notch out of both layers of each envelope. This finger pull will make it easier for you to remove the pages of correspondence from each pocket.

4 ATTACH THE HINGES

Fold your hinges in half lengthwise, decorative side in. Then, glue up the outside of one hinge. Place the 6" (15.2cm) and 7" (17.8cm) envelopes end to end and attach them with the hinge. Fold them together and then hinge the 8" (20.3cm) envelope to the 7" (17.8cm) envelope in the same way. Burnish the hinges flat.

5 ATTACH THE POCKETS TO THE SLEEVE
Glue the remaining hinge and attach the
three-pocket unit to the middle section of
your sleeve. Leave a ¼" (6mm) border at
the left edge and center your pockets
from top to bottom. Burnish the hinges
with a bone folder.

6 CREATE THE SIDE FLAP
Next, you need to add a side flap to your
sleeve. With your cardstock flap horizontal, score the inside surface 1½" (3.8cm)
from the left edge, crease and fold.

7 ATTACH THE FLAP TO THE SLEEVE
Apply glue to the outside surface of the
small section of the flap and attach the
flap to the right side of your sleeve. This
flap will keep pages or hundred dollar
bills from falling out.

MAKING A NICER FLAP

Your side flap will open more easily if
you cut your cardstock grain short,
with the paper grain running parallel
to the short edge of the cardstock. If
you need help, see page 265 for
tips on grain direction.

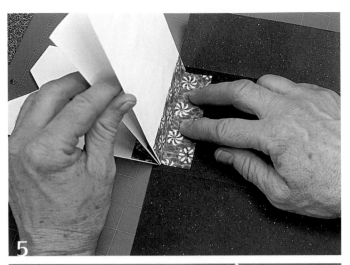

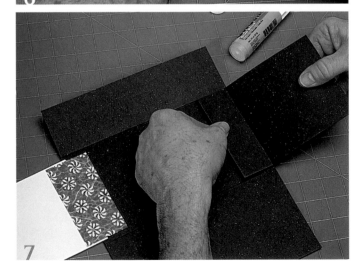

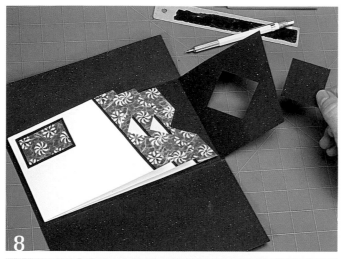

8 **DECORATE THE POCKETS**
Line the open edges of the pockets with decorative paper, then cut a window in the flap to create another layer of visual excitement.

9 **CREATE THE INSIDE STATIONERY**
Continue the oriental theme by embellishing inside pages to match. Even a simple wine cork stamped in black ink looks elegant when accented with beautiful paper strips.

10 **ADD THE FINAL DECORATIVE TOUCHES**
Finish by decorating the outer sleeve with paper scraps and a coordinating address label. No one will ever guess you started with ordinary plain envelopes when they receive your colorful, creative correspondence.

YO FRANCES!! to answer your question—Judy and I go out for coffee just about every day, seven days a week (are we addicted, or what?!).

Anyhoo, it's mostly at these morning coffee klatches that we brainstorm and come up with kit ideas, projects, new workshops, etc. we are happiest when we are solving creative problems.

design and work out construction techniques for 3-D projects and Judy plays with words and concepts. however, sometimes we switch roles.

We can't imagine not having fun when we work. isn't that the way it's supposed to be? if you're having fun, then it isn't really work.

/A GIFT THAT KEEPS ON GIVING/ Looking for other ways to reuse that growing stack of used envelopes? This is an interesting twist on the Recycled Envelope Insert on page 68. Here we connect some of those envelopes in a series of hinged pages. Scraps of gift wrap make colorful hinges and perfect collage accents. It's a great way to turn waste paper into a very playful piece of correspondence.

e hope this letter finds
you healthy and creatively
happy! LOVE,

Michael & Judy

/ TROPICAL FLAVORS / This is a colorful variation on the Instant Envelope Pocket on
page 332. Instead of just one envelope, we've
stacked three envelopes cut to different lengths.
The tropical wrapping paper ties all the colors
together nicely. Finally, for more writing space,
we pasted a folded sheet of paper below.

/ CHANGING CHARACTERS / This variation on the last project shows how a change in
colors, shapes and styles can create an entirely different look. Think about giving each piece of your
creative correspondence a personality all its own.
Change the flaps, the inserts, the paper. There's
always a new combination to explore.

Resources

BOOKS

Collage Art
by Jennifer L. Atkinson
Rockport Publishers, Inc.
ISBN 1-56496-215-6

Color on Paper and Fabric:
A Wealth of Techniques for
Applying Color
by Ruth Issett
Hand Books Press
ISBN 1-893164-02-0

The Crafter's Recipe Book
by Jessica Wrobel
Rockport Publishers, Inc.
ISBN 1-56496-445-0

MAGAZINES AND PERIODICALS

RubberStampMadness
P.O. Box 610
Corvallis, OR 97339-0610
(541) 752-0075
www.rsmadness.com

Somerset Studio Magazine and
Stampers' Sampler
22992 Mill Creek, Suite B
Laguna Hills, CA 92653
(877) 782-6737
www.somersetstudio.com

Expression Magazine
12345 World Trade Drive
San Diego, CA 92128
(858) 605-0251
www.expressionartmagazine.com

RUBBER STAMPS AND ACCESSORIES

CLEARSNAP, INC.
P.O. Box 98
Anacortes, WA 98221
(888) 448-4862
www.clearsnap.com
• Inkpads, stamps and accessories,
  penscore

FRED B. MULLETT STAMPS
FROM NATURE PRINTS
P.O. Box 94502
Seattle, WA 98124
(206) 624-5723
www.fredbmullett.com

RANGER INDUSTRIES
15 Park Road
Tinton Falls, NJ 07724
(800) 244-2111
www.rangerink.com
• Inks and accessories

STAMP FRANCISCO
1248 Ninth Avenue
San Francisco, CA 94122
(415) 566-1018
www.stampfrancisco.com
• Ivory Coast and Fruit Basket
  Upset rubber stamps

STEWART SUPERIOR CORP.
2050 Farallon Drive
San Leandro, CA 94577
(800) 558-2875
www.stewartsuperior.com
• Stamp pads and accessories

TSUKINEKO
17640 NE 65th Street
Redmond, WA 98052
(800) 769-6633
www.tsukineko.com
• Stamp pads, pens and inks

TOOLS AND MATERIALS

AIKO'S ART MATERIALS
IMPORT, INC.
3347 North Clark Street
Chicago, IL 60657
(773) 404-5600
• Art supplies and Japanese papers

AMERICAN TOMBOW, INC.
2000 Newpoint Place Pkwy,
Atlanta, GA 30303
(678) 442-9224
(800) 835-3232
www.tombowusa.com
• Art supplies and pens

AMSTERDAM ART
1013 University Avenue
Berkeley, CA 94710
(510) 649-4800
• Art supplies and papers

COLOPHON BOOK ARTS SUPPLY
3611 Ryan Street SE
Lacey, WA 98503
(360) 459-2940
home.earthlink.net/~colophon
• Papers, tools, binding supplies

DANIEL SMITH
P.O. Box 84268
Seattle, WA 98124-5568
(800) 426-7923
www.danielsmith.com
• Art supplies and papers

DIANE MAURER HAND
MARBLED PAPERS
P.O. Box 78
Spring Mills, PA 16875
(814) 422-8651
• Marbling, paste paper, and
  Boku Undo dye supplies,
  decorative papers

DICK BLICK ART MATERIALS
P.O. Box 1267
Galesburg, IL 61402-1267
(800) 828-4548
www.dickblick.com
• Art supplies and papers

FEBRUARY PAPER
P.O. Box 17043
Salem, OR 97305
www.febpaper.com
• Fibers and papers

FISKARS SCHOOL, OFFICE &
CRAFT
7811 W. Stewart Avenue
Wausau, WI 54401
(800) 500-4849
www.fiskars.com
• Scissors and paper cutters

HOBBYCRAFT
7 Enterprise Way
Aviation Park
Bournemouth International
Airport
Christchurch
Dorset BH23 6HG
United Kingdom
0800 272387
www.hobbycraft.co.uk
• Retail craft stores

JOHN NEAL, BOOKSELLER
1833 Spring Garden Street
Greensboro, NC 27403
(800) 369-9598
www.johnnealbooks.com
• Books, tools and calligraphy
supplies

LA PAPETERIE ST. ARMAND
3700 St. Patrick
Montreal, Quebec
H4E 1A2 Canada
(514) 931-8338
• Papermaking supplies

MARVY-UCHIDA
3535 Del Amo Blvd.
Torrance, CA 90503
(800) 541-5877
www.uchida.com
• Markers, dye inks and supplies

NASCO ARTS & CRAFTS
4825 Stoddard Road
P.O. Box 3837
Modesto, CA 95352-3837
(800) 558-9595
www.enasco.com
• Huge selection of art materials
and tools

NEW YORK CENTRAL ART
SUPPLY CORP.
130 E. 12th St.
New York, NY 10003
(800) 950-6111
www.nycentralart.com
• Art supplies

THE ORIGINAL PAPER-YA
9-1666 Johnston Street
Granville Island,
Vancouver, BC
V6H 3S2 Canada
(604) 684-2531
• Papers

PAM BAKKE PASTE PAPERS
1419 37th Street
Bellingham, WA 98226
(360) 738-4830
• Hand-decorated papers

PAPER & INK ARTS
3 North Second Street
Woodsboro, MD 21798
(800) 736-7772
www.paperinkarts.com
• Art and calligraphy supplies,
papers, tools and books

PAPER SOURCE, INC.
232 W Chicago Avenue
Chicago, IL 60610
(312) 337-0798
• Papers

PEARL PAINT CO. INC.
308 Canal Street
New York, NY 10013-2572
(800) 221-6845
www.pearlpaint.com
• Art supplies and papers

SKYCRAFT DESIGNS, INC.
26395 S. Morgan Road
Estacada, OR 97023
(800) 578-5608
www.skycraft.com
• Hand-decorated papers and
supplies

THINK INK
7526 Olympic View Drive
Edmonds, WA 98026-5556
(800) 778-1935
• Gocco Printing Supplies

USARTQUEST, INC.
7800 Ann Arbor Road
Grass Lake, MI 49240
(800) 200-7848
www.usartquest.com
• Unique art materials, Perfect
Paper Adhesive

WEB SITES

www.silverfoxstamps.com
• Huge listing of rubber stamp
stores in the U.S.

www.thecreativezone.com
• Papercraft kits, book arts and
papercraft workshops throughout the U.S.

www.art-e-zine.co.uk
/artemalluk.html
• Listing of rubber stamp suppliers
in the United Kingdom.

STAMP CREDITS

Stenciling
&Embossing
GREETING CARDS

18 Quick, Creative, Unique & Easy-to-do Projects   **Judith Barker**

Basic Stenciling & Embossing Techniques

Stenciling Projects

Stenciling & Embossing

Cutting and Piercing

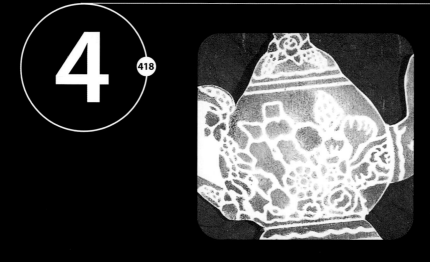

4 (418)

Special Effects

5 (438)

Stenciling and embossing are so easy and relaxing. Stamp pad ink and oil sticks are foolproof! You can make a card in minutes. Everyone loves to receive handmade cards and the giver personally benefits from the satisfaction of creating a beautiful card.

A stencil can be cut quickly from any paper or plastic material with an art knife or manicure scissors. We've provided designs for your convenience. You may enlarge them on a copier and cut stencils from the photocopies. Stencils may be found in many stores, including rubber stamp stores, art and craft supply stores, and home decorating centers. Each type of material has its specific traits. American Traditional's blue laser stencils are extremely durable with fine detail. You can use them to stencil with any paint and on any surface. You can also use them for embossing.

There are so many ways to use stencils to decorate not only greeting cards but your whole world! Begin with a card for a friend and progressively pursue more extravagant projects. Soon your entire house could be a work of art!

Happy stenciling!

You will need the same basic materials for all stenciling projects. First, you'll need a stencil. For these examples, we used American Traditional stencil MS-84 Iris. There are many types of paint used in stenciling, including some paints made specifically for this purpose. Throughout this book, I have used oil sticks and bottled acrylic paints. You also need brushes with which to apply the color through the stencil. I use ⅜6-inch stencil brushes, which should be available in your local art and craft supply store. You can use many different materials for your palette: a foam plate for acrylics, wax paper for oil sticks or even scrap paper. Keep paper towels on hand for rubbing extra color out of your stencil brush and use masking tape to secure your stencil to the stenciling surface. Be sure to tap the tape against your clothing a few times before adhering the stencil to paper; this decreases the adhesive strength of the tape and prevents it from tearing your paper.

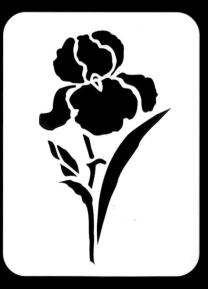

a

BASIC STENCILING

Basic stenciling materials include stencil, cardstock or other stenciling surface, stencil brushes, palettes, acrylic paints, oil sticks and ink pads.

Stencils

MS-84. To make a stencil, photocopy this image at 80 percent and use a sharp craft knife to cut out the design.

Stenciling With Oil Sticks

This exercise uses Shiva Paintstiks in Azo Yellow, Naphthol Red and Ultramarine Blue. These three colors come together in Shiva's primary colors kit. Use wax paper for a palette when stenciling with oil sticks.

1 Prepare palette

Remove the skin from the tip of an oil stick with a paper towel. Rub the stick on a wax paper palette to create a smear of color.

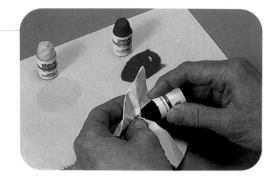

Load brush 2

Rub brush into the lightest color—in this case, Azo Yellow.

3 Start stenciling

Tap brush through stencil. You can also rub gently in a circular motion.

Add red 4

Tap or rub in accents in red.

Mix purple ⑤

Mix colors by blending on palette. Red and blue make purple.

⑥ **Add purple**

Tap or rub in purple.

Mix green ⑦

Yellow and blue make green.

⑧ **Add green**

Stencil green last because it can turn other colors muddy. A little green in the center of the iris will add depth.

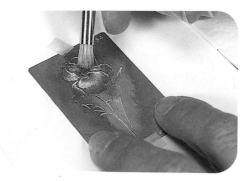

Finished iris ✳

Remove your stencil, then clean it with a dry cloth or paper towel.

Stenciling With Acrylics

You'll need a small container of water and a foam palette when using acrylics. For this exercise, we used DecoArt Americana acrylics in Yellow Light, Brandy Wine, Wedgewood Blue and Avocado.

1 **Moisten brush**

Dip brush in water to moisten bristles.

Dry the brush **2**

Squeeze out excess water on a paper towel.

3 **Pick up paint and rub out**

Squeeze a small dollop of each color onto a foam plate (or other suitable palette). Dip brush into the lightest color first, Yellow Light. Rub out on paper towel to remove all but a trace of paint from the brush.

Begin stenciling **4**

Tap or rub yellow into the stencil. Rinse brush between colors and dry with paper towel.

Mix purple ⑤

To make purple, first tap into red paint and rub out.

⑥ **Mix purple**

Then tap into blue and rub out, mixing colors on the brush.

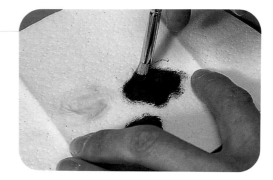

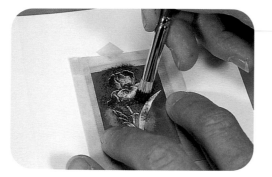

Add purple ⑦

Tap or rub purple into stencil.

⑧ **Add green**

As usual, finish with green.

Finished iris ✳

Remove the stencil, then clean with hot water and a nylon scouring pad.

Stenciling With an Inkpad

A multicolored ink pad is a convenient stenciling tool. Here I'm using Color Box's Primary pigment stamp pad. Use a separate brush for each color, except when mixing.

1 Load brush

Tap brush into pad. Start with the lightest color.

Rub out 2

Tap off or rub out excess color on scrap paper or paper towel.

3 Add color

Tap or rub color through stencil.

Mix color 4

To mix colors, tap into one color and then the other. Mix on the brush by rubbing in a circular motion on scrap paper or paper towel.

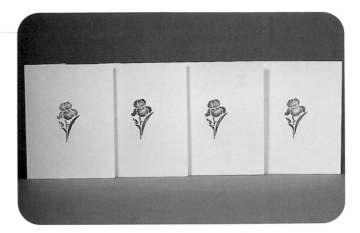

Iris stenciled in four different color combinations.

BASIC EMBOSSING

I used American Traditional stencil BL-35 Rose for this exercise. It's easiest to emboss using a light box because you can see the outline of the stencil under your paper. You can also emboss by feel without a light box. A stylus or embossing tool has a ball tip at one end for outlining. You'll also need masking tape to adhere the stencil to your cardstock.

(a)

✳ Emboss

Attach the stencil to the front of the card with two ¼-inch pieces of masking tape. Flip the card over onto the light box (or use a lamp under a glass table or a piece of clear plastic ware). Rub your fingers over the paper before embossing; the oil from your hand will help the stylus glide more easily. From the back of the paper, trace the entire outline of the stencil with the stylus.

Stencils

(a) BL-35. To make a stencil, photocopy this image at 167 percent and use a sharp craft knife to cut out the design.

2

Now that you understand the basic principles of stenciling, it's time to get creative. These cards feature many types of stencils and several different stenciling mediums. You'll learn a few techniques to jazz up your designs—stenciling is more than just paint on paper! I have provided stencil patterns for every project in this book. Photocopy them to the proper size, then cut out with a sharp craft knife or scissors. Cuticle scissors work well. Once you have the design cut out of paper, you can use it as is or transfer it to heavier plastic, acetate or Mylar. See the resources guide at the end of the book for information on where you can purchase stencils and stenciling supplies. Stencil away!

Glittery Star Card

This glittery card sure looks impressive, but it couldn't be easier. Instead of stenciling with paint, stencil the stars with glue and then top with glitter. Don't be afraid to try this project with different colors and types of paper and with all sorts of different stencils.

Materials

* American Traditional stencil
  BL-445 Hearts, Stars, and Dots
* Paper
  5½" x 4¼" white notecard
  5½" x 4¼" shiny black paper
  5½" x 4¼" shiny gold paper
* tacky glue
* copper, emerald and purple glitter
* ³⁄₁₆" stencil brush
* Fiskars decorative edging scissors
* glue stick
* eraser pencil (for correcting errors
  and cleaning up edges)

(a) BL-445. To make a stencil, photocopy this image at 111 percent and use a sharp craft knife to cut out the design.

(a)

1 Prepare cardstock and paper

Glue the shiny gold paper to the front of your white cardstock to cover entire front of card. Trim the edges of the shiny black paper with the decorative edging scissors so it is about ¼-inch smaller on each side than the size of the cardstock.

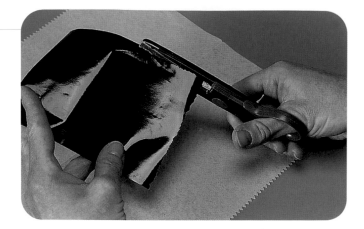

Add glue to palette 2

Squeeze out small amount of glue onto wax paper.

3 Stencil star

Stencil a star in the size of your choice on the black paper with glue.

Add first glitter color 4

Sprinkle glitter liberally over the wet glue while stencil is still on top of the paper.

5 Make multicolored star

Make a multicolored star by sprinkling half with one color of glitter and half with another color (shake off excess between colors). You can repeat this process several times with different sizes of stars. Stencil and glitter one star at a time.

Glue star to notecard 6

Carefully remove stencil. Allow to dry thoroughly. Attach the black paper with star to the front of the notecard with glue stick.

✳ The finished card

Halloween Watercolor Card

This card is simple enough that older children can make it. Zig 2-Way glue has a no-mess applicator that makes it easy to get creative with glitter accents.

Materials

* American Traditional stencil:
  BL-172 Halloween Memories
* Paper
  5½" x 4¼" white notecard with
  matching envelope
* watercolor paints in basic colors
* foam makeup applicator sponge
* ³⁄₁₆" stencil brush
* small container of water
* Zig 2-Way glue
* light-colored glitter
* masking tape

a BL-172. To make a stencil, photocopy this image at 80 percent and use a sharp craft knife to cut out the design.

a

1 Affix stencil to notecard

Center stencil on front of notecard.
Tap a piece of masking tape on
your clothing several times to make
it less sticky, then tape the stencil
in place.

2 Prepare sponge

Wet sponge and squeeze out
excess water.

3 Load sponge

Dip sponge into yellow watercolor.

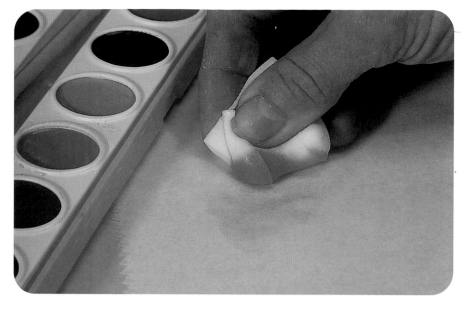

Test paint consistency ④

Test paint consistency on scrap paper. You don't want the paint so heavy or runny that it will bleed under the stencil. Add more paint or water as needed, keeping in mind that only a very small amount of paint should remain on the sponge.

Add color with sponge ⑤

Tap the nearly dry sponge along the edge of the stencil to make a colored border.

Load brush with black ⑥

Dip the stencil brush in water, tap dry on a piece of scrap paper, and dip it into black watercolor. Test the consistency on scrap paper and add paint or water as needed.

7 Stencil black

Stencil as desired in black, and add a little black around the stencil border.

8 Remove stencil

9 Load brush with orange

Rinse brush in water and add orange, blotting out on paper towel. Drybrush orange over witch's face, pumpkin, witch's brew and words.

Add glue accents (10)

Apply glue to select areas, such as eyes, cauldron bubbles and words.

Add glitter (11)

Sprinkle glitter over the glue and shake off excess.

The finished card ✳

Chinese Character Card

Chinese characters are as beautiful as they are meaningful. This card features the character for love. The colors, simplicity, and class of this card make it perfect for a man or woman.

Materials

* American Traditional stencil:
  BL-167 Love
* Paper
  10¾" x 6" black cardstock
  folded to 5⅜" x 6"
  5½" x 4¼" red cardstock
  5½" x 4¼" white linen paper
  5½" x 6" white mulberry paper
* Shiva Paintstik in Black
* tacky glue
* gold embossing powder
* ³⁄₁₆" stencil brushes
* heat gun
* wax paper
* masking tape

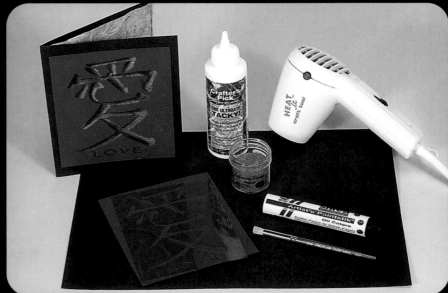

(**a**) BL-167. To make a stencil, photocopy this image at 61 percent and use a sharp craft knife to cut out the design.

(a) -LOVE-

1 Stencil black

Center your stencil on red cardstock with masking tape. Stencil using black oil stick. Remove the stencil and clean it with a paper towel. Allow stenciling to dry.

Reposition stencil 2

Reapply stencil over lettering, but offset by about ⅛ inch down and to the right.

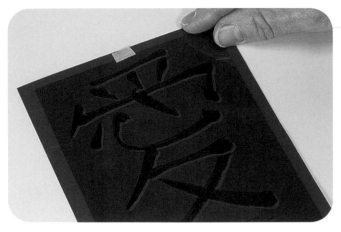

3 Stencil with glue

Squeeze a small amount of glue onto wax paper or scrap paper. Brush the edges of the character and lettering with glue. Remove stencil.

Add gold powder 4

Apply gold embossing powder. Shake off the excess and return it to the jar.

5 Heat

Heat the embossing powder with the heat gun until it melts.

Reposition stencil 6

Tape stencil to the cardstock in its original position.

7 Blend in black

Stencil in black along the top edges of the lettering, blending from black to gold.

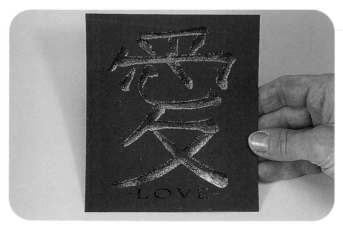

Remove stencil 8

Lettering should appear three-dimensional with gold highlights.

9 Add stenciling to black cardstock

Fold black cardstock in half to measure 6" x
5⅜". Center and glue the stenciled red card
onto the black cardstock.

Line notecard 10

Open card. Apply a thin line of glue down
the center of the left flap and attach a sheet
of mulberry paper.

11 Deckle the linen paper

Carefully tear the edges of the linen paper to
get a deckled edge.

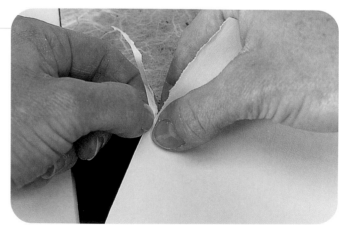

Drybrush with black 12

Drybrush the deckled edges with the stencil
brush and the black oil stick.

13 Line the right side of the card

Glue the linen paper into the inside of the
card to create a writing surface.

✻ The finished card

Glossy Snowflake Card

Use clear embossing powder on this card to add a subtle glint to the design. The embossing powder creates a glossy surface that contrasts with the matte paper surrounding the snowflakes.

Materials

* American Traditional stencils
    FS-957 Snowflake Ornament
    GS-139 Merry Christmas
* Paper
    5½" x 4¼" white note card with
        matching envelope
* Shiva Paintstiks
    Azo Yellow
    Naphthol Red
    Prussian Blue
    Sap Green
* four ³⁄₁₆" stencil brushes
* clear embossing powder
* heat gun
* scissors
* Fiskars scallop decorative
    edging scissors
* wax paper
* masking tape

(a)   F-957. To make a stencil, photocopy this image at 70 percent and use a sharp craft knife to cut out the design.

(b)   GS-139. To make a stencil, photocopy this image at 70 percent and use a sharp craft knife to cut out the design.

(a)

(b)

1 Stencil first snowflake

Stencil snowflake in Prussian Blue on bottom center of card front.

2 Add more snowflakes

Repeat process on both sides of center snowflake, positioning the additional snowflakes slightly higher.

3 Add embossing powder

Sprinkle embossing powder over snowflakes. Shake off excess powder and return it to container.

Heat (4)

Melt embossing powder with
heat gun.

Stencil message (5)

Position "Merry Christmas" stencil
(or a stencil with a message of your
choice) on the center of the card
front, overlapping snowflakes
slightly. Tape into place and stencil
with a mixture of Azo Yellow,
Naphthol Red and Sap Green.

Add embossing powder and heat (6)

Sprinkle embossing powder over
the lettering, returning excess to jar.
Melt the powder with a heat gun.

7 Trim

Trim around snowflakes along bottom edge of card.

8 Create snowflake mask

To create a wax paper mask from the snowflake stencil, begin by stenciling a snowflake lightly onto wax paper. Carefully cut out the snowflake.

9 Drybrush blue

Place wax paper snowflake over snowflakes on card and drybrush with Prussian Blue around the edges of the snowflakes. The mask keeps paint from getting on the snowflakes themselves.

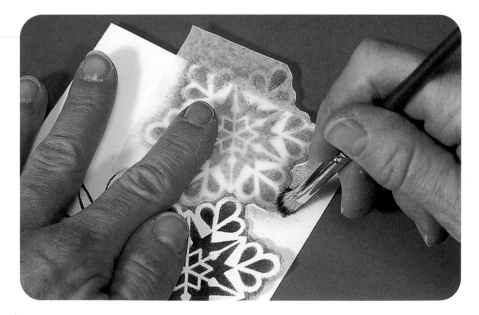

Decorate envelope flap to match the card. Use scallop edging scissors to trim the edge of the flap.

Glossy Snowflake Card

Overlay Rose on Handmade Paper

The stencil for this project comes in three parts, each of which is stenciled separately. On the purchased stencils, you will notice a triangular hole in each corner. These registration marks allow you to position each stencil exactly in line with the others. Place small pieces of masking tape on your stenciling surface underneath the registration marks, then trace inside the registration marks. Align the registration marks for the next stencil overlay with your first marks, and voilà! You're ready to stencil.

Materials

* American Traditional stencil
  CS-7 Three-Part Rose
* Paper
  5" x 6" white mulberry
  handmade paper
  6" x 7" dark teal textured paper
* Shiva Paintstiks
  Azo Yellow
  Naphthol Red
  Prussian Blue
  Sap Green
* four ³⁄₁₆" stencil brushes
* masking tape
* wax paper

(a) CS-7. Part 1. To make a stencil, photocopy this image at 133 percent and use a sharp craft knife to cut out the design.

(b) CS-7. Part 2. To make a stencil, photocopy this image at 133 percent and use a sharp craft knife to cut out the design.

(c) CS-7. Part 3. To make a stencil, photocopy this image at 133 percent and use a sharp craft knife to cut out the design.

a

b

c

1 Fringe handmade paper

To "fringe" the edges of the handmade paper, start by dipping a brush or rolled-up paper towel in water. Wet a ¼-inch border around the handmade paper.

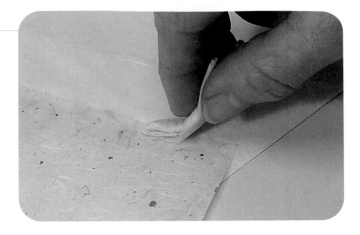

Pull fringe 2

Allow the water to soak in for several seconds, then pull edges gently with fingernails.

3 Position stencil

Attach part 1 of the rose stencil to the hand-made paper with masking tape. If you are using a purchased stencil, you will see a triangular registration opening in the corners of each part of the stencil. Place small pieces of tape on the handmade paper under the registration openings.

Mark registration 4

Mark the masking tape with pencil through the registration openings.

5 Begin stenciling

Use the image on page 387 as a color guide and begin stenciling the image. Your first color should be the lightest, Azo Yellow.

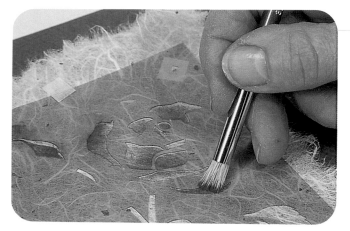

Add red and green 6

Continue stenciling with red, then move on to green. Remember that green should always be stenciled last. To make different shades of green, use green alone or over yellow or blue. You can also blend your own green on the palette from Prussian Blue and Azo Yellow.

7 Remove part 1

Remove part 1 of the rose stencil, leaving masking tape with registration marks in place.

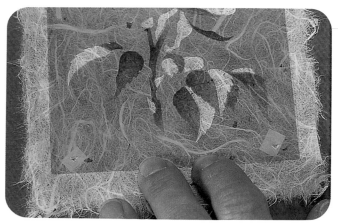

Stencil part 2 8

Position part 2 of the rose stencil so that the registration openings fall directly over the registration marks on the masking tape. Tape in place. Stencil with yellow, then red and green.

Overlay Rose on Handmade Paper

9 Remove part 2

Remove the second part of the stencil, again
leaving the masking tape registration marks
on the paper.

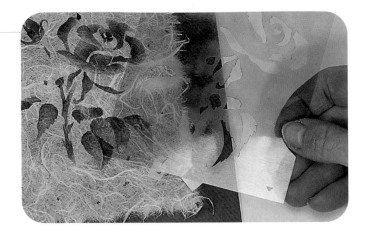

Stencil part 3 10

Position part 3 of the stencil and align the
registration marks. Stencil with yellow, red,
then green. Remove the stencil when done.

11 Remove registration marks

Carefully remove the masking tape registration marks from the handmade paper. Glue
the stenciled paper to teal background paper.

✳ **Color guide for rose**

The earth laughs with flowers.

Ralph Waldo Emerson

3

Stenciling and Embossing Projects

It's time to add another element to our stenciled greeting card projects. Embossing creates a raised image that may or may not be stenciled as well. An embossing tool, with its rounded tip, is essential for good results; it embosses the paper without tearing it. You should be able to find this tool in art and craft supply stores and rubber stamp stores. Some paper stores may also carry this tool. Most stencils can be used for embossing, as long as they are cut from a thicker, relatively stiff material. If you are cutting your own stencils for embossing, be sure to choose a heavy plastic or acetate for your stencil material rather than paper. A woodburning tool or other hot-tipped cutting tool is useful for cutting stencils from plastic. Most of these projects call for a light box. Since the stencil is placed under the paper for embossing, working over a light box makes it easier to see the pattern you will be embossing. If you do not have a light box, place a small lamp under a glass table. You can also emboss without a light box, being careful to feel the outline of the stencil as you are following it. This is necessary when using dark, opaque papers.

Dried Floral Embossed Card

The dried flowers add an elegant touch to this embossed card—or is it the embossing that adds an elegant touch to this floral card? You'll be pleased with the way both elements work together to create a colorful and soft impression.

Materials

* American Traditional stencil
    MS-213 Blossoms & Ivy
* Paper
    5½" x 4¼" white notecard
* embossing tool
* light box
* clear-drying glue
* clear contact paper
* scissors
* dried small pressed flowers
    and greens
* pen or rubber stamp (optional,
    for lettering)
* masking tape

(a) MS-213. To make a stencil, photocopy this image at 50 percent and use a sharp craft knife to cut out the design.

a

1 Write message and position stencil

Hand-write or stamp your message at the bottom of the card front. Tape the stencil at the top of the card as shown. We will use only the blossom portion of the stencil for this project.

Emboss cardstock 2

Once stencil is taped in place, flip the card-stock and stencil over and place on light source. Rub your fingers over the area to be embossed; the oil from your hands will make the embossing tool glide more easily. With your embossing tool, trace inside all the stencil openings.

3 Form border

Reposition stencil and emboss three more times, creating a frame for the dried flowers.

e earth laughs with flowers.

Ralph Waldo Emerson

Add flowers 4

Glue the dried flowers in a pleasing arrangement inside the embossed frame. Use a brush to apply the glue.

5 Finish flower arrangement

Glue the greens down first, then add the flowers. Continue adding flowers until you get an attractive bouquet.

Seal with contact paper 6

Cut clear contact paper to the size of the card and adhere it to seal and preserve the dried flowers.

✳ The finished card

The earth laughs with flowers.

Ralph Waldo Emerson

Dried Floral Embossed Card

Gold-Embellished Fleur-de-lis

The fleur-de-lis on this card is stenciled in yellow, covered with gold embossing powder, then bordered with embossed lines and diamonds. Embossing powder creates a raised glossy surface in imitation of the old-fashioned engraving of wedding invitations and calling cards. The matte finish of the black cardstock balances the fleur-de-lis design.

Materials

* American Traditional stencil
    BL-155 Fleur d'lis
* Paper
    5½" x 4¼" black notecard
    4" x 5" red cardstock
    5½" x 4¼" white paper (optional,
    for inside of card)
* Shiva Paintstik in Azo Yellow
* ³/₁₆" stencil brush
* gold embossing powder
* heat gun
* embossing tool
* scissors
* glue stick
* wax paper
* masking tape

(**a**) BL-155. To make a stencil, photocopy this image at 59 percent and use a sharp craft knife to cut out the design.

(a)

1 Stencil the fleur-de-lis

Rub the yellow oil stick onto your wax paper palette. Center the stencil and tape in place on the red cardstock. Tape off the lines and diamonds in the design to prevent paint from getting in these areas. Stencil the fleur-de-lis in yellow. Remove stencil.

Add embossing powder 2

Pour gold embossing powder over the stenciled fleur-de-lis while the paint is still tacky. Remove excess powder and return to jar.

3 Heat

Heat the embossing powder, holding the heat gun about an inch above the design. The powder will melt and shine.

Cut out fleur-de-lis 4

Cut out the fleur-de-lis, leaving a narrow border of red paper.

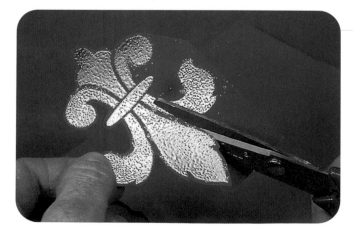

5 Emboss the black notecard

Remove the tape from the lines and diamonds of the fleur-de-lis stencil. Center and attach the stencil to the front of the black notecard. Trace over the lines and diamonds. (Light won't show through the black paper, so you don't need a light box here.) Flip card over and emboss using your trace lines as a guide. Remove stencil.

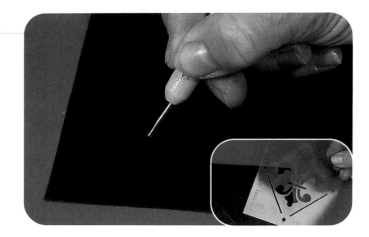

Apply glue stick 6

Apply glue stick to the edges on the back of the gold-and-red fleur-de-lis.

7 Attach fleur-de-lis to card

Center the fleur-de-lis inside the line-and-diamond embossed border and affix to the black cardstock.

Finish card ✳

To create a nice place to write your message, apply glue stick to the edges of the back of the white paper. Open the card and affix the paper to the right side.

Angel Watercolor Card With Matching Envelope

Creating this colorful card with watercolor paints is easier than it looks. There's no need to buy tubes of artist-grade watercolor—a child's watercolor set will work fine. For the envelope, you can decorate the plain white envelope that probably came with your notecard, or make your own using vellum and the envelope template and paint it to match your angel. The vellum envelope will remain transparent and is a unique touch.

Materials

* American Traditional stencils
    BL-89 Angel
    BL-442 Envelope Template
* Paper
    5½" x 4¼" white notecard
        and envelope
    5½" x 4¼" white vellum
    5½" x 4¼" lavender tissue paper
    8" x 10" white vellum
        (for envelope)
* watercolor paints in basic colors
* makeup applicator sponge
* small container of water
* small watercolor brush
* large watercolor brush
* embossing tool
* light box
* glue stick
* hole punch
* scissors
* 12" length of ½"-wide
    lavender ribbon
* masking tape

(**a**) BL-89. To make a stencil, photocopy this image at 125 percent and use a sharp craft knife to cut out the design.

(**b**) BL-442. To make a stencil, photocopy this image at 167 percent and use a sharp craft knife to cut out the design.

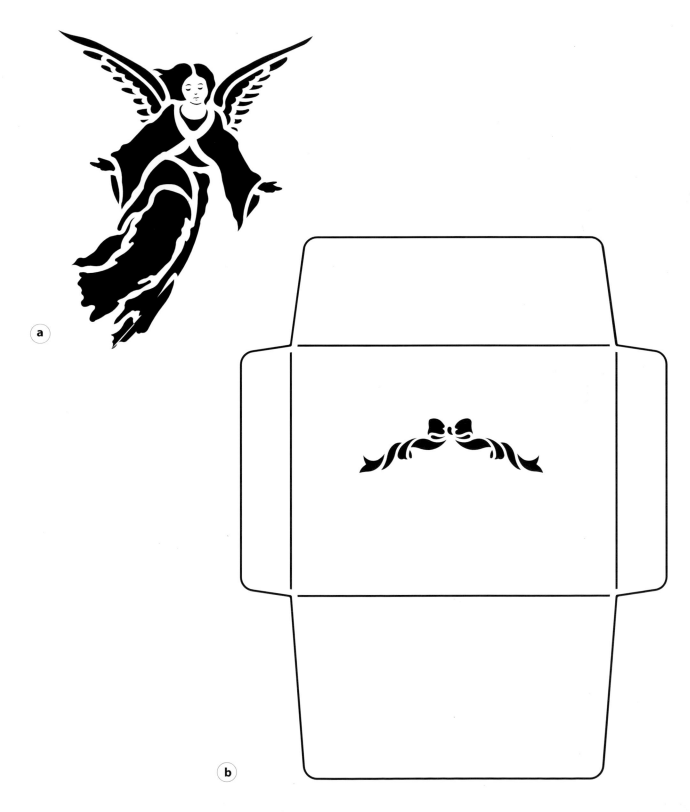

(**a**)

(**b**)

1 Position stencil

Position the angel stencil in the center of the small vellum sheet and attach with masking tape.

Emboss border 2

Flip stencil and vellum over and emboss around the edge of the stencil. (If you made your own stencil, cut it to 4" x 5" and emboss.)

3 Emboss angel

Emboss the angel. Remove stencil.

Trim vellum 4

Trim the vellum to the embossed border.

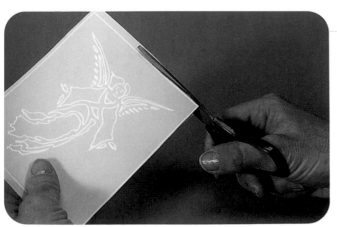

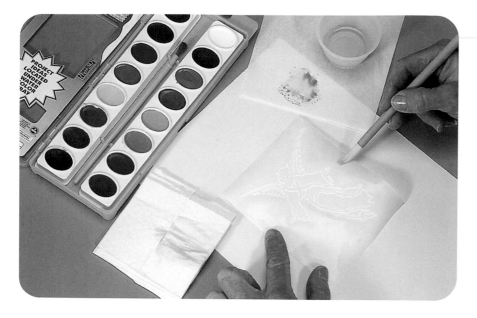

Paint background 5

Turn the vellum over and use a brush and plain water to evenly moisten the paper around the angel. Using the watercolors, paint the background in random pastels up to the embossed angel. Thin colors with water to make them lighter, blotting the brush to prevent drips. You can paint on scrap paper to practice.

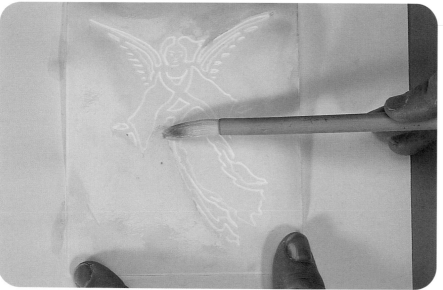

Finish background 6

Once you have filled the background around the angel, paint lightly on the angel itself.

Paint the angel 7

Turn the vellum over so the front side is up. Using the small watercolor brush, apply vibrant colors to the angel, staying within the embossed lines. To get a three-dimensional look, place the lightest colors in the center of each section and blend into the darkest colors at the edges.

8 Choose intense colors

The angel should be painted in more vibrant, intense colors against a muted pastel background.

9 Attach vellum to notecard

Apply glue stick to the back of the vellum, center the vellum on the front of the white notecard, and stick down.

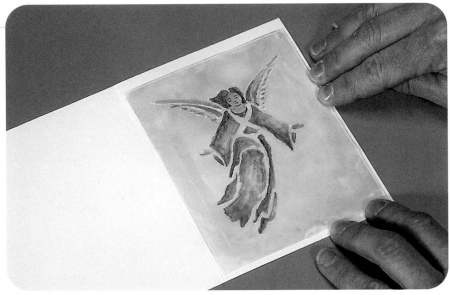

10 Attach liner

Glue the piece of lavender tissue on the inside left of the notecard. Press firmly to secure.

Add ribbon (11)

Close the card and punch holes along the fold. Thread ribbon loosely through the holes and knot the ends.

The finished card ✳

12 Trace envelope template

Trace the envelope template onto the large sheet of white vellum. Do not transfer the ribbon pattern. Remove stencil and cut out the envelope.

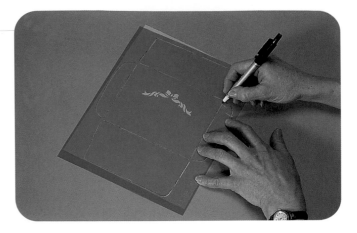

Fold envelope 13

Fold vellum along the lines to form the envelope.

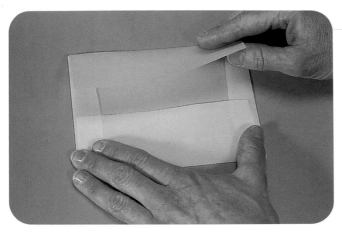

14 Paint the vellum

Using a damp makeup sponge, sponge the vellum with random pastel watercolors.

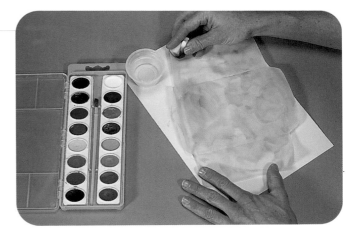

Glue envelope 15

Fold the sides of the envelope in first, then the bottom flap. Glue the edges, pressing firmly.

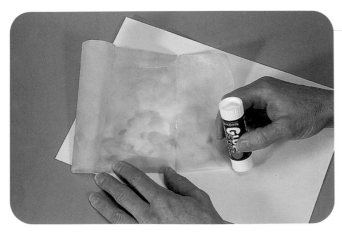

16   Add white envelope

Slide the white envelope that came with the
card into the vellum envelope.

Glue envelopes together   17

Glue the vellum envelope flap to the white
envelope flap. Trim as needed.

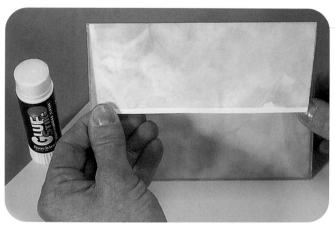

❋   The finished card and envelope

Hummingbird Music Card

This card has a cozy feel because of the dried flower accents and antiquing on the sheet music. If your sheet music or photocopy looks too white, try dipping it in a glass of hot tea until it reaches the desired color. Press the wet sheet music between paper towels so it will dry flat.

Materials

* American Traditional stencil
  FS-913 Hummingbird
* Paper
  3" x 4" white cardstock
  5½" x 4¼" ivory cardstock
  and envelope
  sheet music (original
  or photocopy)
* Shiva Paintsticks
  Azo Yellow
  Burnt Umber
  Naphthol Red
  Ultramarine Blue
* ³⁄₁₆" stencil brushes
* dried flowers
* embossing tool
* light box
* glue
* scissors
* wax paper

(a) To make a stencil, photocopy this image at 50 percent and use a sharp craft knife to cut out the design.

(a)

1. Position stencil

Center and tape stencil on the white cardstock.

Emboss 2

Flip stencil and cardstock over and place on a light box. Emboss the border and complete image.

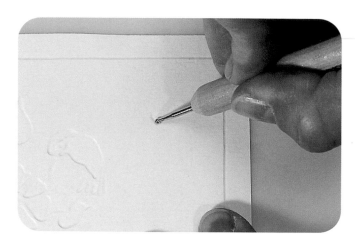

3. Stencil hummingbird

With stencil still in place, flip cardstock over and stencil the hummingbird and flowers with nicely blended yellow, red and blue oil stick colors (blend blue and yellow to make green; blue and red to make purple). Remove the stencil.

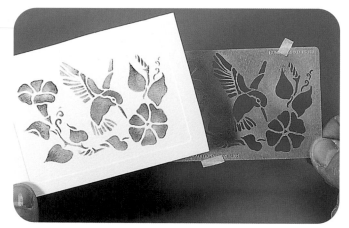

Cut out hummingbird 4

Cut out the stenciled image, following the outline of the raised embossed border.

5 Drybrush sky

Drybrush around the hummingbird with blue oil stick to create a sky.

6 Drybrush notecard

Reposition the hummingbird stencil over the stenciled image so that only the embossed border shows around the edges. Using the stencil as a mask, drybrush with Burnt Umber oil stick around the edge of the stencil to add color to the embossed border.

❊ The finished hummingbird

7 · Prepare sheet music

Tear the sheet music to form an irregular and interesting shape. Drybrush the edges with Burnt Umber to create an aged appearance.

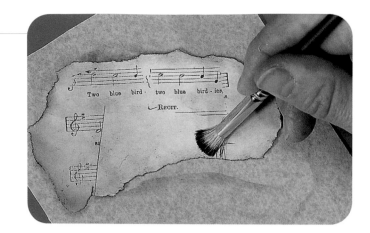

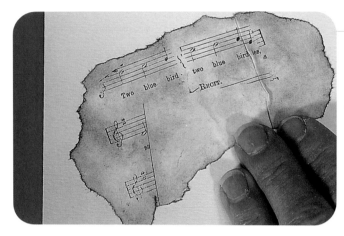

Glue music to card · 8

Add glue to the back of the sheet music and spread glue to edges. Using the ivory cardstock, attach the sheet music to the card front, slightly off center and toward the upper left.

9 · Add hummingbird

Glue the hummingbird card to the card front, overlapping the sheet music.

Add drybrushed color · 10

Drybrush blue oil stick along the edges of card front. Then drybrush Burnt Umber near the sheet music and hummingbird.

(11) Add flowers

Arrange and glue dried flowers in upper left
and lower right corners.

❋ The finished card

Sponged Vellum Tulip Card

When sponged together, the colors used for this card created a harmonious, muted effect. Choose your own color scheme according to the mood you want to convey: pale yellow, blue, pink and green for a springtime feel; white and grey sponging with bright tulips for a vibrant, zingy feel.

Materials

* American Traditional stencil
  BL-13 Double Border
* Paper
  5½" x 4¼" ivory notecard with
  matching envelope
  5½" x 2" sheet of white vellum
* DecoArt Americana acrylic paints
  Base Flesh
  Brandy Wine
  Wedgewood Blue
* clear embossing powder
* ³⁄₁₆" stencil brushes
* embossing tool
* light box
* heat gun
* Fiskars Victorian decorative
  edging scissors
* toothbrush
* glue
* sea sponge or similar sponge
* bookmark tassel
* small container of water
* wax paper
* foam plate
* masking tape

(a) To make a stencil, photocopy this image at 67 percent and use a sharp craft knife to cut out the design.

(a)

1 Trim vellum

Trim the vellum with the decorative edging scissors.

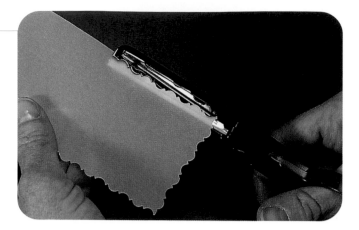

Sponge Base Flesh 2

Squeeze a small amount of each paint color onto the foam plate. Dip the sea sponge in water and wring it out. Then dip it in Base Flesh and dab off the excess. Sponge Base Flesh over vellum, allowing sponge texture to show.

3 Sponge Brandy Wine

Repeat the sponging process with Brandy Wine, allowing some Base Flesh to show through.

Sponge Wedgewood Blue 4

Repeat sponging with Wedgewood Blue, making sure the blue is consistent over the vellum but that Base Flesh and Brandy Wine colors still show through. Allow to dry (the paint will dry quickly).

5 Position stencil

Center the tulip pattern of the stencil over the vellum and tape in place.

Emboss 6

Flip stencil and vellum over onto a light box. Emboss the tulip pattern.

7 Stencil tulip pattern

Flip the vellum over to the front and stencil the tulip pattern in Brandy Wine.

Add Wedgewood Blue 8

Stencil again in Wedgewood Blue, allowing the red and blue to mix in places but preserving some mottled color.

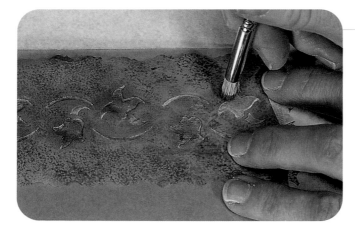

Squeeze a small amount of glue onto the foam plate. Stencil a final layer of glue into the tulip pattern. Remove the stencil.

Add embossing powder **10**

While the glue is still wet, pour clear embossing powder over the design. Shake off the excess.

11 **Heat**

Heat the embossing powder until it melts.

Spatter card background **12**

Open the notecard onto a sheet of wax paper so the front faces away from you. Place the envelope face up and with the flap out. Protect the back of the notecard and the front of the envelope with wax paper. Dip the toothbrush in water, blot on paper towel, and dip into Brandy Wine paint. Tap off the excess. Scrape your finger across the bristles to spatter paint on the card front and envelope flap.

(13) Trim envelope flap

Trim the envelope flap with the decorative edging scissors.

Attach vellum to card (14)

Apply glue to the back of the vellum and attach it to the front of the card approximately ¼-inch from the fold.

(15) Add tassel

Slide the tassel over the card until it is positioned in the fold so that the tassel hangs on the outside of the card. Adjust length if necessary.

The finished card and envelope ✳

Get out a fresh blade for your craft knife! You'll use it in these projects to create decorative cutouts, pierced paper and paper tole, a three-dimensional layered effect. Cutouts can be backed with contrasting paper or used as photo frames for those special snapshots you just have to share. Paper piercing adds depth, interest and elegance to your design. Paper tole is a way of layering elements of your design to create what is almost a paper sculpture. You may just want to frame the card for yourself when you're done! You'll soon see how the techniques in this chapter can be applied to many different designs.

Cutout Teapot Notecard

This colorful teapot is embossed, stenciled, cut out and backed with contrasting paper to form an eye-catching design. Who would be able to guess that you made it yourself? This technique can be adapted to any design, as long as the stenciled image has enough contact points with the border to keep the stenciling attached to the card.

Materials

* American Traditional stencil
  GS-132 Posh Tea Pot
* Paper
  5½" x 4¼" white notecard with
    matching envelope
  5½" x 4¼" cranberry handmade
    mulberry paper
* Shiva Paintstiks
  Azo Yellow
  Naphthol Red
  Prussian Blue
  Sap Green
* ³⁄₁₆" stencil brushes
* embossing tool
* light box
* Fiskars scallop decorative
  edging scissors
* Zig 2-Way glue
* craft knife
* wax paper
* masking tape

(**a**) To make a stencil, photocopy this image at 50 percent and use a sharp craft knife to cut out the design.

(a)

1 Position stencil

Position stencil on center front of white notecard and tape in place.

2 Emboss border

Flip paper and stencil over onto a light box. After rubbing your fingers across the area to be embossed to make the tool slide more easily, trace along the outside edge of the stencil to form a border.

3 Stencil teapot

Flip paper and stencil to front and stencil the teapot with oil sticks in the colors of your choice.

Cut out teapot background (4)

With a sharp craft knife, cut around the teapot inside of the embossed border, leaving the teapot attached to the card at the top, spout, handle and base. You may want to slip a piece of glass or cardboard under the notecard as you're cutting.

Use the stencil border as a guide (5)

To make straight edges and perfect corners, use the stencil as a cutting guide around the border.

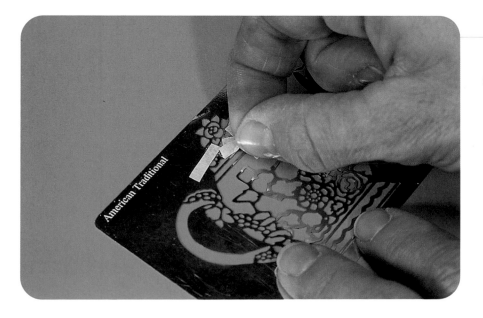

Mask off flower (6)

Use masking tape to shield off the flower at the top of the teapot. This will make it easier to stencil just the flower design.

7 Emboss and stencil flower

Emboss and stencil the flower in a few places around the edges of the card. Use red, yellow and blue and mixtures of these colors.

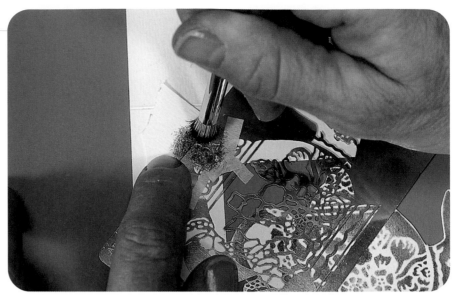

8 Attach contrasting paper

Apply glue to the edges of the handmade paper. Secure the paper to the inside of the card on the left side, behind the teapot.

9 Drybrush border

Using red oil stick, drybrush a ¼" border on the bottom inside edge of the card. Use the straight edge of scrap or wax paper as a guide.

Trim the bottom edge of the card front with decorative edging scissors.

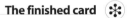

The finished card ❊

Cut-and-Pierce Tulip Wreath Photo Card

Do you have a snapshot that you can't wait to share? This card is a great way to do it. Not only is the card an elegant presentation device, but it can be used by the recipient as a frame for display.

Materials

* American Traditional stencils
    BL-72 Oval Frame
    BL-31 Triple Border
* Paper
    5½" x 4¼" white notecard
        and envelope
    5½" x 4¼" cranberry handmade
        mulberry paper
* Sakura Cray-Pas oil pastels in
    pink and green
* 3" x 5" photograph
* ³⁄₁₆" stencil brushes
* embossing tool
* light box
* craft knife
* glue
* wax paper
* masking tape

(**a**) BL-72. To make a stencil, photocopy this image at 100 percent and use a sharp craft knife to cut out the design.

(**b**) BL-31. To make a stencil, photocopy this image at 100 percent and use a sharp craft knife to cut out the design.

(**a**)

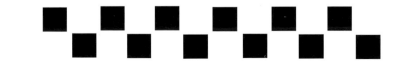

(**b**)

1 Create palette

Wax paper makes an excellent palette for oil pastels. Rub smears of each color onto your palette.

2 Emboss Oval Frame

Use tape to attach the Oval Frame stencil to center of notecard front. Flip over on light box and emboss.

3 Stencil Oval Frame

Flip the notecard back to the front and stencil with the pink and green oil pastels.

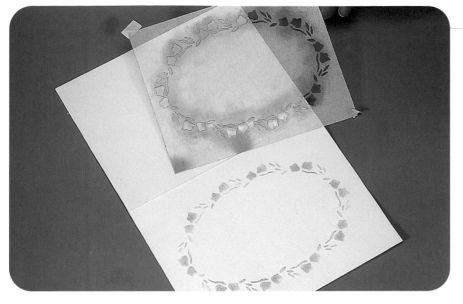

Remove stencil (4)

Emboss and stencil tulips (5)

Position a tulip design from the border stencil in a corner of the card front. Emboss and stencil using red, yellow, blue and mixtures of those colors. Repeat in all corners.

Trim corners and cut frame (6)

Use a craft knife to trim all four corners following the tulip design. Cut two straight edges at fold of card and connect the cutout in upper corners as shown. Cut out the center oval by following the tulip wreath pattern. Slip cardboard, glass, or a cutting mat under the card before you start cutting.

7 Cut and pierce

Transform the tulip corners into "cut-and-pierce" designs by making small slices with a craft knife along one side of the buds and leaves.

8 Glue photo in frame

Apply glue to the back of the oval opening in the wreath frame. Center the photo in the frame, trimming edges if necessary. Press firmly to secure.

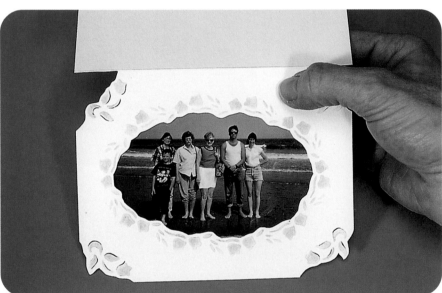

9 Glue in backing

Apply more glue to the back of the photo and the edges of the card. Affix the contrasting handmade paper, trimmed to the original size of the notecard.

Stencil an envelope to match the card.

Paper Tole Tulip

Paper tole is a process by which several identical images are cut and layered to create a three-dimensional paper sculpture. This paper tole tulip makes an impressive card that can be framed and hung as a piece of art.

Materials

* American Traditional stencil
  CS-21 Three-Part Tulip
* Paper
  5½" x 4¼" white, ivory or
    beige notecard with
    matching envelope
  8½" x 11" white cardstock
* Shiva Paintstiks
  Azo Yellow
  Naphthol Red
  Ultramarine Blue
* DecoArt Americana acrylic paint
  in Black Green
* three ³⁄₁₆" stencil brushes
* craft knife or small straight scissors
* double-sided foam tape
* toothbrush
* wax paper
* masking tape

(a) CS-21 Part 1. To make a stencil, photocopy this image at 133 percent and use a sharp craft knife to cut out the design.

(b) CS-21 Part 2. To make a stencil, photocopy this image at 133 percent and use a sharp craft knife to cut out the design.

(c) CS-21 Part 3. To make a stencil, photocopy this image at 133 percent and use a sharp craft knife to cut out the design.

1 Spatter card

Open the notecard and place on scrap paper facing up. Speckle the background by putting a small amount of Black Green acrylic paint on a toothbrush, tapping onto paper towel, then flicking bristles with fingers.

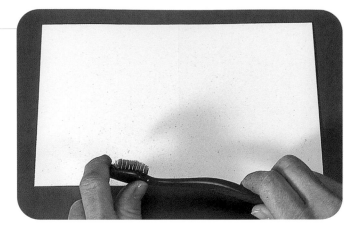

Stencil tulip 2

Center and attach part 1 of the tulip stencil on the front of the notecard. Trace registration marks. Use oil stick colors to stencil all three parts of the tulip, mixing Azo Yellow and Ultramarine Blue for varying shades of green. Control your shades of pink by using more or less red. See the images on page 437 for a color guide.

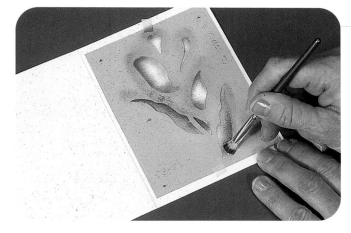

3 Repeat stenciling

Stencil the tulip four more times on the 8½" x 11" sheet of cardstock.

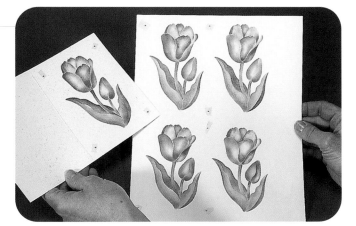

Cut tulip layers 4

Using small sharp scissors or a craft knife, cut the parts of the tulip for the four layers. See the guide on page 437 for which elements to cut for each layer. You will layer the tulip elements from back to front, with the parts that would be furthest away from the viewer in the back. This creates a three-dimensional effect.

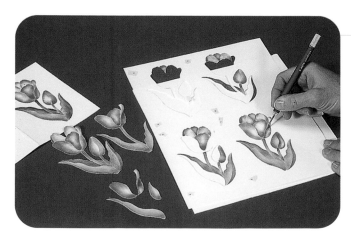

5 Add foam tape

Cut ⅛" x ¼" pieces of double-sided foam tape and mount the pieces on the back of the tulip elements. As you add each layer, peel the protective layer off the foam tape. You will need about twenty-four pieces of foam tape. Use as many pieces as necessary to hold each element of the design securely in place.

Add first layer 6

Place the first layer on top of the stenciled tulip on card front. This layer is the whole pattern, less one small tulip petal in background.

7 Add second layer

Repeat with the second layer, aligning the tulips exactly on top of one another.

Add third layer 8

❋ **The finished card**

The finished card makes a lovely framed piece.

1. The dotted lines indicate which sections to cut for the first (bottom) layer.

2. The dotted lines indicate which sections to cut for the second layer.

3. The dotted lines indicate which sections to cut for the third layer.

4. The dotted lines indicate which sections to cut for the fourth (top) layer.

5

Special Effects

Some of the preceding projects have used special materials such as glitter and embossing powder. Here are some more projects that use nontraditional materials—including foil, polymer clay, shrink plastic and a woodburning tool—for creating special effects with your stencils.

Foil Ornament Card

In addition to glitter and embossing powder, you can use foil to add shine to your stenciled greeting cards. Look for foil in your local art and craft supply store. I've chosen Crafter's Pick, The Ultimate Tacky! glue for this project, but you can also use any quick-drying foil glue.

Materials

* American Traditional stencil
  BL-79 Ornaments
* Paper
  5½" x 4¼" white notecard with
  matching envelope
* gold foil
* Crafter's Pick, The Ultimate
  Tacky! glue or other suitable glue
* ³⁄₁₆" stencil brushes
* embossing tool
* light-colored glitter
* heat gun or hair dryer (optional)
* wax paper
* Fiskars rounder decorative
  edging scissors (optional)
* 12" length of ⅛"-wide holographic
  ribbon
* masking tape

a BL-79. To make a stencil, photocopy this image at 53 percent and use a sharp craft knife to cut out the design.

a

1 Stencil with glue

Place a small amount of glue on wax paper. Position stencil on notecard and secure with tape. Stencil notecard using glue instead of paint. Allow to dry thoroughly. A heat gun or hair dryer may be used to speed drying. Carefully remove stencil.

2 Apply foil

Lay foil over glue image, gold side facing up.

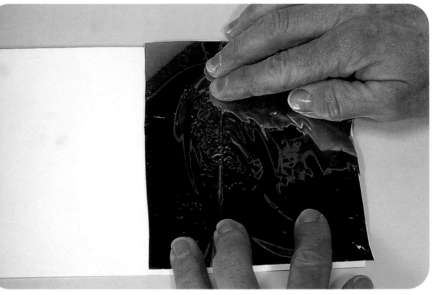

3 Burnish

Thoroughly burnish foil onto card with the flat side of the embossing tool, pressing firmly.

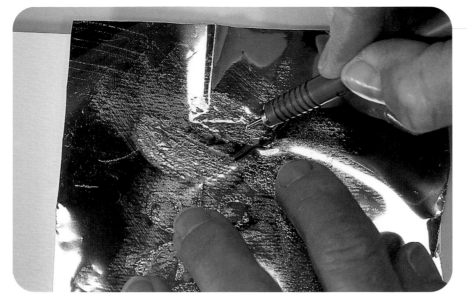

Burnish edges ④

Use the ball point of the embossing tool to press firmly along the edges of the design.

Remove foil ⑤

Gently peel away the foil. Only the foil transferred to the ornaments should remain.

Remove excess foil ⑥

Remove any out-of-place specks of foil with masking tape.

7 Add dots of glue

For extra sparkles, apply dots of glue where desired using the tip of the embossing tool.

8 Add glitter

Sprinkle glitter onto the glue, shaking off the excess.

9 Add ribbon

If you wish, use corner rounders or regular scissors to round the card corners. Wrap holographic ribbon around middle of the card at the fold and tie.

Double-Embossed Glossy Leaves

Double layers of embossing powder can create dramatic effects. Use these leaves to decorate your cards or other craft projects.

Materials

* American Traditional stencil
  GS-136 Falling Leaves
* Paper
  3" x 3" white cardstock
* Shiva Paintstiks
  Azo Yellow
  Naphthol Red
* ³/₁₆" stencil brushes
* Zig 2-Way glue
* Clear embossing powder
* Black embossing powder
* heat gun
* wax paper
* craft knife or scissors

a To make a stencil, photocopy this image at 50 percent and use a sharp craft knife to cut out the design.

a

1 Make leaf base

Start by stenciling a leaf with
mixtures of yellow and red.
Sprinkle with clear embossing
powder, shaking off excess powder.
Heat to melt. Cut out the leaf.
Next, outline veins on the leaf
with glue.

2 Add black embossing powder

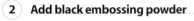

Sprinkle black embossing powder
over the wet glue.

3 Shake off excess

Use the heat gun to melt
the powder.

The finished leaf ✻

Apply the finished leaf to cards or other craft projects.

Clay and Crinkle Sun Card

Here is a truly unique use for your stencils. When a stencil is run through a pasta roller with polymer clay, the stencil embosses the clay. Cut the design from the clay, and you have a work of art!

Materials

* American Traditional stencils
  * FS-918 Sun
  * MS-210 Grapes & Scroll
* Paper
  * 5½" x 8½" beige or tan cardstock folded to 5½" x 4¼"
  * 2"x 8" green paper
  * 2"x 4" beige paper
* Shiva Oilstick in Sap Green
* Premo! polymer clay in Gold
* ³⁄₁₆" stencil brushes
* embossing tool
* pasta roller
* Fiskars paper crimper
* light box
* craft knife
* glue (such as Crafter's Pick, The Ultimate Tacky!)
* gold glitter (optional)
* heat gun or hair dryer (optional)
* wax paper
* masking tape
* scissors

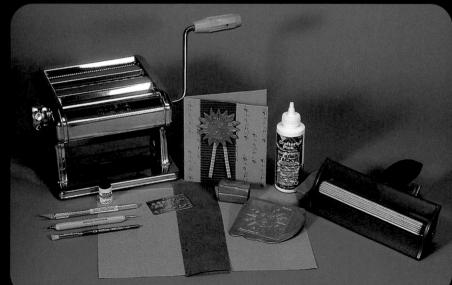

(**a**) FS-918. To make a stencil, photocopy this image at 55 percent and use a sharp craft knife to cut out the design.

(**b**) MS-210. To make a stencil, photocopy this image at 50 percent and use a sharp craft knife to cut out the design.

(a)

(b)

1 Flatten polymer clay

Use your palm to flatten a 1-inch cube of gold clay. Place the clay in the pasta roller and roll it into a ⅛-inch-thick sheet.

2 Roll clay with stencil

Place the sun stencil on the flattened clay and run them both through the pasta roller.

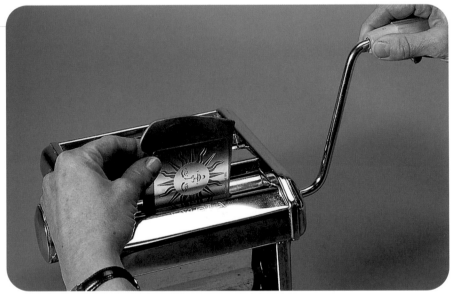

3 Remove stencil

Carefully remove the stencil from the clay to reveal an embossed image of the stencil.

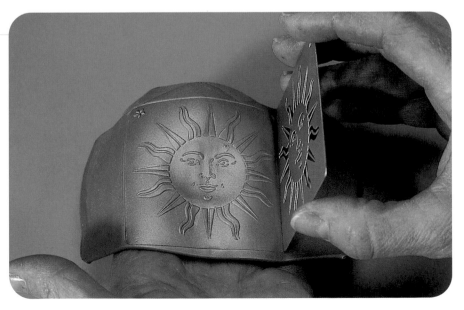

Cut out design ④

Use a craft knife to trim away the excess clay from the design. Bake the clay sun in your oven following the manufacturer's instructions, or use a heat gun or hair dryer to harden the piece. Save the leftover clay in a plastic bag for future projects.

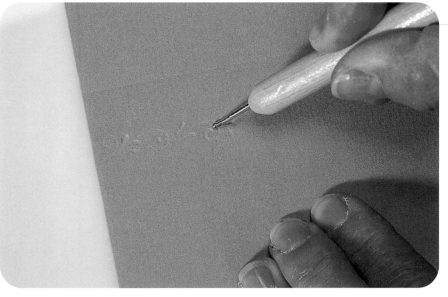

Emboss scroll on card ⑤

Attach the scroll pattern from the border stencil on the front of the card to make a vertical line down the left side. Flip stencil and card over onto light box and emboss.

Stencil scroll ⑥

Flip card to front and stencil the scroll pattern in Sap Green.

7 Finish embossing and stenciling

Repeat steps 5 and 6 until you have two or three vertical lines on both the left and right side of the card.

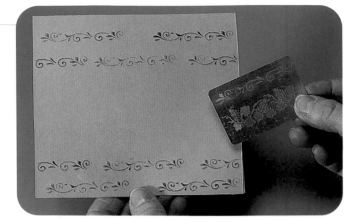

Cut and crimp green paper 8

Measure the unstenciled area down the center of the card. Trim the green paper to a width that will fit the crimper opening and run it through the paper crimper. If you don't have a paper crimper, you can accordion-fold the paper by hand or leave it uncrimped.

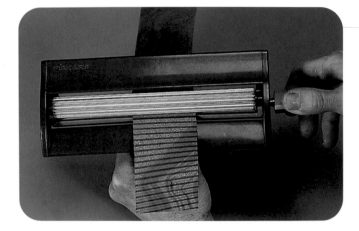

9 Cut and crimp beige accent strips

Run a piece of beige paper through the crimper and cut two ¼-inch-wide strips to approximately 2 inches long. If you don't have a crimper, make tiny accordion folds by hand.

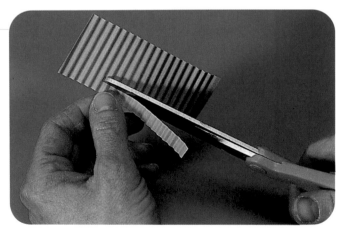

Attach green paper 10

Apply glue to the unstenciled portion of the front of the notecard. Affix the green crimped paper. Trim to fit.

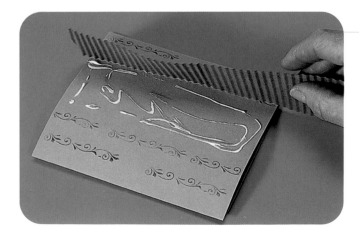

(11) Attach beige accent strips

Apply glue to the two beige strips of paper and affix them to the center of the card in the shape of an upside-down V. Touch on a little glue, then sprinkle glitter if desired.

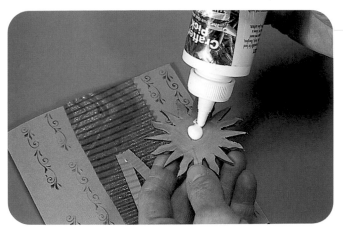

Attach the clay sun (12)

Apply glue to the back of the dry clay sun. Center it on the card front just above where the beige strips are glued.

✳ The finished card

Shrink Plastic Ornament Card

Shrink plastic is back and is being used for many craft projects, including rubber stamping and stenciling! Use shrink plastic in this chapter to make ornaments to hang from stenciled tree branches. If you decorate both sides of each ornament, the recipient can actually use them!

Materials

* American Traditional stencils
    * BL-79 Ornaments
    * BL-300 Ornaments 1
    * BL-301 Ornaments 2
    * BL-124 ⅜" Alphabet
    * FS-898 Merry Christmas (optional)
* Paper
    * 5½" x 4¼" white notecard with
        matching envelope
    * 8½"x 11" white cardstock
* 8" x 10" sheet of Aleene's Shrink-It
    or other shrink plastic
* Shiva Paintstiks
    * Azo Yellow
    * Naphthol Red
    * Ultramarine Blue
* DecoArt Americana acrylic paints
    * Hauser Dark Green
    * Yellow Light
    * Santa Red
* ³⁄₁₆" stencil brushes
* scissors and craft knife
* masking tape
* pencil
* glue
* glitter in copper, green and
    silver or white
* heat gun
* fishing line
* Fiskars Scallop decorative
    edging scissors
* wax paper and foam plate

a BL-300. To make a stencil, photocopy this image at 200 percent and use a sharp craft knife to cut out the design.

b BL-301. To make a stencil, photocopy this image at 200 percent and use a sharp craft knife to cut out the design.

a

b

c   BL-79. To make a stencil, photocopy this image at 118 percent and use a sharp craft knife to cut out the design.

d   BL-124. To make a stencil, photocopy this image at 100 percent and use a sharp craft knife to cut out the design.

e   FS-898. To make a stencil, photocopy this image at 100 percent and use a sharp craft knife to cut out the design.

e

c

Aa Bb Cc Dd Ee
Ff Gg Hh Ii Jj Kk
Ll Mm Nn Oo Pp
Qq Rr Ss Tt Uu
d   Vv Ww Xx Yy Zz

1 Trace tree on cardstock

Position tree from the stencil labeled Ornaments 1 on cardstock and trace with pencil.
Do not trace the vertical cut line.

Cut new tree stencil 2

Cut out the entire tree. You have now
created a new tree stencil. (You can keep
the tree cutout for other projects.)

3 Stencil tree on plastic

Position the paper stencil on the shrink
plastic and stencil it in Hauser Dark
Green acrylic.

Cut out the plastic tree 4

Remove the paper stencil and cut the tree
from the shrink plastic.

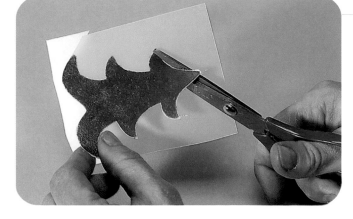

5 Add hole for hanging

Use a craft knife to cut a hole near the top of the tree. Make it large enough to allow for shrinkage.

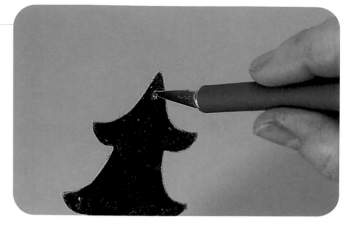

Shrink the plastic 6

Hold the heat gun close to the tree to shrink it. The plastic will curl, but continue applying heat and it will flatten. You can use a chopstick or pencil to hold the piece as you are heating, if necessary.

7 Decorate tree

To decorate the tree, apply lines and dots of glue. Sprinkle glitter over the glue and shake off the excess. Apply the glue and glitter one color at a time.

Make more ornaments 8

Repeat steps 1 through 7 with the ornament shapes of your choice from Ornaments 1 and 2 stencils. Decorate with stenciling and glitter as desired. Thread 6 inches of fishing line through the hole at the top of an ornament and tie the ends in a knot.

9 Stencil lettering

Tape a piece of wax paper as a guide on the
card front, about ½" from bottom. Stencil
your message using green made from blue
and yellow oil sticks. To center your lettering, find the middle letter and write it in the
center of the card on the guide. Then fill in
the rest. Or, center the "Merry Christmas"
stencil on the card.

Stencil branches 10

Stencil the branches from the stencil labeled
Ornaments on the front of the card using
the green oil stick mixture made from blue
and yellow.

✳ Finish card

Trim the edge of the card with the decorative edging scissors. Drybrush a border on the inside card edge in green.
Make small holes on the tree branches with a craft knife

where you would like the ornaments to hang. Attach the ornaments to the tree branches by pushing the knots through
the holes. Decorate your envelope to match the card.

Woodburned Teddy Postcard

Here's a unique project that creates not only a card, but a keepsake. If you back the wood veneer with stiff cardboard, this postcard will be strong enough to mail without an envelope. (Some veneers are strong enough without the backing.) Be sure to affix enough postage!

Materials

* American Traditional stencil BL-148 Floppy Bear
* 3 ½"x 5" piece of thin wood veneer
* 3"x 3" piece of clear Mylar
* craft knife
* scissors
* pencil
* fine-point black permanent marker
* colored pencils
* wood burner
* scrap paper
* stiff cardboard (optional)
* glue (optional)
* masking tape

(a) BL-148. To make a stencil, photocopy this image at 65 percent and use a sharp craft knife to cut out the design.

(You may also use the woodburner to cut the design out of Mylar.)

(a)

1 Cut veneer and trace stencil

Use scissors to cut the veneer to 3½" x 5". Tape stencil to veneer and trace design with a pencil.

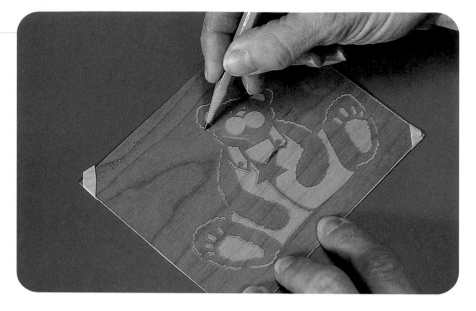

2 Burn design

Remove stencil. Trace over your pencil lines with the wood burner.

3 Add details

Use the tip of the wood burner to add little dots to represent fur and shading.

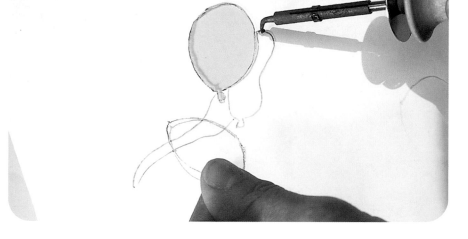

Create balloon stencil ④

Draw balloons on a piece of paper. They should be drawn to fit on the veneer. Place Mylar over the drawing and cut out the stencil with the wood burner.

Trace balloon design ⑤

Place the balloon stencil on the veneer and trace with a pencil. Remove the stencil.

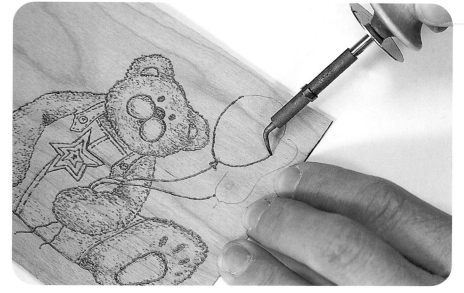

Burn balloon design ⑥

Trace over the pencil lines with the wood burner.

7 **Add message**

Write your message in pencil and then trace with the wood burner.

8 **Singe edges**

Use the inside of the wood burner to singe the outside edges of the postcard.

9 **Add color**

Color the teddy and balloons with colored pencils.

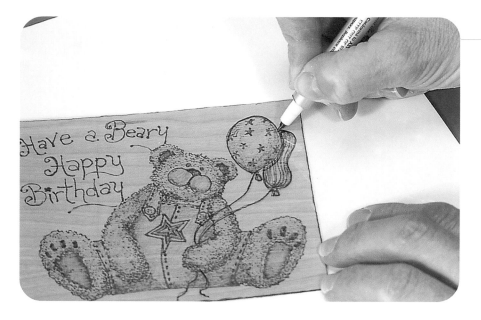

Use a fine-point black permanent marker to add any finishing touches to the colored design.

If the veneer is thick and strong, it can be mailed as is. If not, adhere a piece of stiff cardboard to the back with regular white glue. This will give you more room for a longer message. You can also enclose the postcard in an envelope to protect it.

RESOURCES

Stencils

You can purchase American Traditional stencils in quality art and craft supply stores worldwide. To purchase through mail order, contact:

American Traditional Stencils
442 First New Hampshire Turnpike
Northwood, NH 03261-3401
(603) 942-8100
www.americantraditional.com
or

The Stencil Outlet
P.O. Box 287
Northwood, NH 03261-0287
(603) 942-9957

Organizations

For more information on stenciling, contact:

Stencil Artisans League, Inc.
P.O. Box 3109
Los Lunas, NM
(505) 865-9119
www.sali.org

Tools and Materials

Here's a list to help you find the tools and materials used in the projects in this book. Try your local craft store first; if you can't find it, you can always look here.

Glue and Shrink Plastic

Aleene's/Duncan Crafts
5673 E. Shields Ave.
Fresno, CA 93727
(800) 438-6226
www.aleenes.com
Stencils, Brushes, Oil Sticks, Light Table, Embossing Tool and Cardstock

American Traditional Stencils
442 First NH Turnpike
Northwood, NH 03261-3401
(603) 942-8100
www.americantraditional.com

Mounting Memories Keepsake Glue

Beacon Adhesives Co. Inc.
125 S. MacQuesten Pkwy.
Mt. Vernon, NY 10550
(914) 699-3400
www.beacon1.com

Pigment Inks

ColorBox by Clearsnap, Inc.
P.O. Box 98
Anacortes, WA 98221-0098
(888) 448-4862
www.clearsnap.com

Acrylic Paints

DecoArt
www.decoart.com

Duncan Enterprises
5673 East Shields Ave.
Fresno, CA 93727
(800) 438-6226
www.duncancrafts.com

Zig 2-Way Glue and Markers

EK Success, Ltd.
(800) 524-1349
www.eksuccess.com
Decorative Edge Scissors and Paper Crimper

Fiskars, Inc.
7811 W. Stewart Ave.
Wausau, WI 54401-9328
(800) 500-4849
www.fiskars.com

Paper

Paper Adventures
901 S. 5th St.
Milwaukee, WI 53204
(414) 645-5760
www.paperadventures.com

Premo! Sculpey Polymer Clay

Polyform Products Co.
1901 Estes Ave.
Elk Grove Village, IL 60007-5415
www.sculpey.com

Embossing Powders and Heat Gun

Ranger Crafts, Inc.
15 Park Rd.
Tinton Falls, NJ 07724
(800) 244-2211
www.rangerink.com

Cray-pas Oil Pastels

Sakura of America
30780 San Clemente St.
Hayward, CA 94544-7131
(800) 776-6257
www.gellyroll.com

Pigment Inks

Tsukineko, Inc.
17640 NE 65th St.
Redmond, WA 98052
(800) 769-6633
www.tsukineko.com

Ribbons

Wrights
West Warren, MA 01092
(877) 597-4448
www.wrights.com

Publications

Stencils, rubber stamps and scrapbook memory pages all complement one another. Here is a list of magazines and books that are full of great ideas for cards!

The Rubber Stamper

Hobby Publications, Inc.,
225 Gordons Corner Rd.
Englishtown, NJ 07726
(732) 446-4900

Somerset Studio
22992 Mill Creek, Suite B
Laguna Hills, CA 92653
(714) 380-7318

Making Great Scrapbook Pages
Published by Hot Off the Press

More Than Memories II
by Julie Stephani

Photo Keepsakes
by Suzanne McNeill

Creative Rubber Stamping Techniques
by MaryJo McGraw

Making Greeting Cards With Rubber Stamps
by MaryJo McGraw

page 10

page 24

page 248

page 249

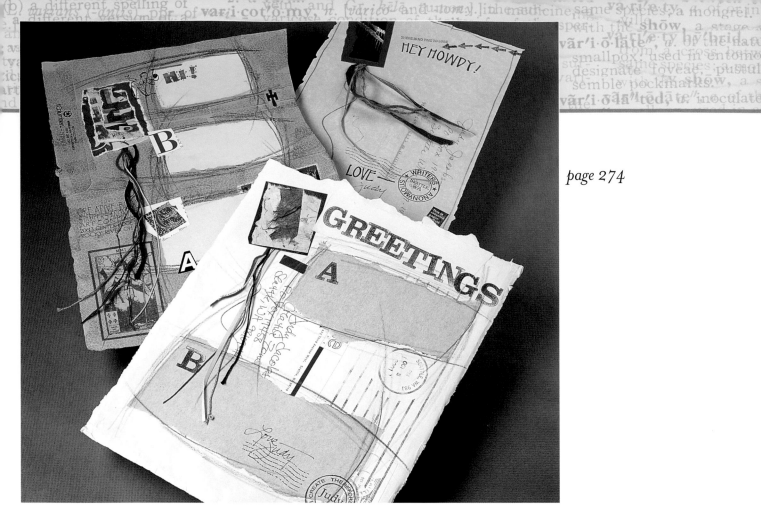

page 274

page 276

page 314

THE CREATIVE ZONE
P.O. BOX 19458
SEATTLE, WASHINGTON
98109-1458

WRITERS
ANONYMOUS
SEATTLE
WA

50th

page 318

Yo BeTSY and Paul,

Greetings from the Pacific Northwest, where it's 25 degrees (quite cold for us) and snow is predicted. Brrrrr! Thanks for your last two cards. It's always a pleasure hearing about your travels. Glad you enjoyed the nature printing conference--the location must have been energizing.

Exciting news on this end. We now have studio space on the second floor of a beautiful turn-of-the-century brick building in Georgetown, a funky industrial neighborhood a few miles south of downtown Seattle. The building was part of a brewery and has massive timbers and floors made from 2 x 6s turned on edge. During the last earth-quake, only one figure fell off a shelf; nothing else moved. We hope we're here working if (when?) the next one hits.

Speaking of work, time to get back to it. We hope this letter finds you both healthy and happy. Keep us posted on your whereabouts. One of these days we'll all be in the same place at the same time and we'll do that dinner we keep talking about.

LOVE-

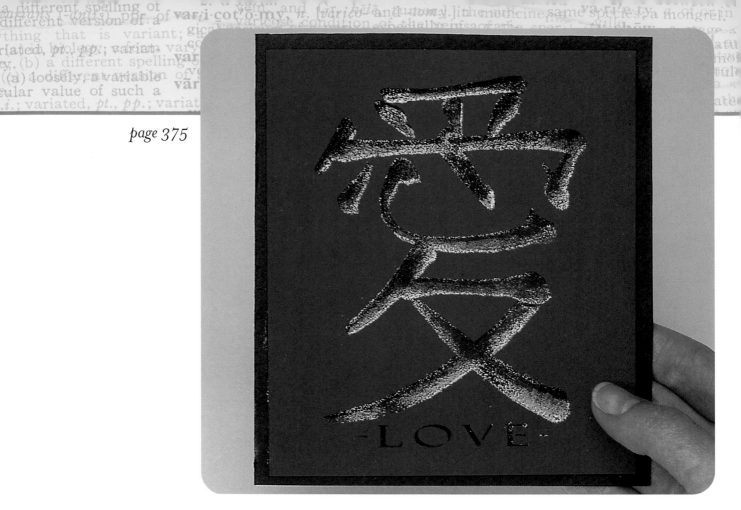

page 375

page 387

page 393

page 411

page 436

Merry Christmas

page 461

478

GET CREATIVE WITH NORTH LIGHT BOOKS

The Essential Guide to Handmade Books

Gabrielle Fox teaches you how to create your own handmade books—one-of-a-kind art pieces that go beyond the standard definition of what a "book" can be. You'll find 11 projects inside. Each one builds upon the next, just as your skills increase. This beginner-friendly progression ensures that you're well prepared to experiment, play and design your own unique handmade books.

ISBN 1-58180-019-3, paperback, 128 pages, #31652-K

The Big Book of Greeting Cards

This book presents a variety of fun, festive and stylish ideas for making cards perfect for any occasion. Discover more than 40 step-by-step projects using a wide range of techniques including rubber stamping, stenciling, quilling and embroidery.

ISBN 1-58180-323-0, paperback, 144 pages, #32287-K

How to Be Creative if You Never Thought You Could

Let Tera Leigh act as your personal craft guide and motivator. She'll help you discover just how creative you really are. You'll explore eight exciting crafts through 16 fun, fabulous projects, including rubber stamping, bookmaking, papermaking, collage, decorative painting and more. Tera prefaces each new activity with insightful essays and encouraging advice.

ISBN 1-58180-293-5, paperback, 128 pages, #32170-K

Greeting Card Magic with Rubber Stamps

Discover great new tricks for creating extra-special greeting cards! Pick up your stamp, follow along with the illustrated, step-by-step instructions inside, and ta da! You'll amaze everyone (including yourself!) with your beautiful and original creations.

ISBN 0-89134-979-0, paperback, 128 pages, #31521-K

These and other fine North Light titles are available from your local art & craft retailer, bookstore, online supplier or by calling 1-800-448-0915.

The material in this compilation appeared in the following previously published North Light Books and appears here by permission of the authors. (The initial page numbers given refer to pages in the original work; page numbers in parentheses refer to pages in this book.)

McGraw, Mary Jo	Greeting Cards For Every Occasion © 2004.	Pages 1, 4-126 (5-127)
McGraw, Mary Jo	Vintage Greeting Cards with Mary Jo McGraw © 2003	Pages 1-3, 6-126 (128-252)
Jacobs, Judy & Michael	Creative Correspondence © 2003.	Pages 1, 4-93, 95 (253-344)
Barker, Judith	Stenciling & Embossing Greeting Cards © 2000.	Pages 1, 4-127 (345-469)

Other fine North Light Books are available from your local bookstore or direct from the publisher.

08 07 06 05   5 4 3 2

Creative Cardmaking: A Complete Guide/ edited by editors of North Light Books-1st ed.

ISBN 1-58180-665-5

Cover Designer: Clare Finney
Production Coordinator: Mark Griffin